CAMBRIDGE LIBRA

Books of enduring s

Travel and Exploration

The history of travel writing dates back to the Bible, Caesar, the Vikings and the Crusaders, and its many themes include war, trade, science and recreation. Explorers from Columbus to Cook charted lands not previously visited by Western travellers, and were followed by merchants, missionaries, and colonists, who wrote accounts of their experiences. The development of steam power in the nineteenth century provided opportunities for increasing numbers of 'ordinary' people to travel further, more economically, and more safely, and resulted in great enthusiasm for travel writing among the reading public. Works included in this series range from first-hand descriptions of previously unrecorded places, to literary accounts of the strange habits of foreigners, to examples of the burgeoning numbers of guidebooks produced to satisfy the needs of a new kind of traveller - the tourist.

William Cotton Oswell, Hunter and Explorer

The life of English explorer William Cotton Oswell (1818–93) was marked by adventures and discoveries. At nineteen, he left Essex for Madras, where he worked for the East India Company and became a renowned elephant catcher. Due to poor health, he was sent to South Africa, the 'empire of wild sport', where he specialised in hunting and exploration. He discovered the River Zouga and Lake Ngami during an expedition across the Kalahari desert, and travelled to the Zambezi River with Scottish missionary David Livingstone. Originally published in 1900, this two-volume biography was written by Oswell's eldest son. Since Oswell kept no diary, his life is here reconstructed through the many letters he sent to his family and friends. Volume 1 focuses on Oswell's youth. It describes the seven years he spent in India, where he trained as a surgeon, and his five African expeditions from 1844 to 1852.

Cambridge University Press has long been a pioneer in the reissuing of out-of-print titles from its own backlist, producing digital reprints of books that are still sought after by scholars and students but could not be reprinted economically using traditional technology. The Cambridge Library Collection extends this activity to a wider range of books which are still of importance to researchers and professionals, either for the source material they contain, or as landmarks in the history of their academic discipline.

Drawing from the world-renowned collections in the Cambridge University Library, and guided by the advice of experts in each subject area, Cambridge University Press is using state-of-the-art scanning machines in its own Printing House to capture the content of each book selected for inclusion. The files are processed to give a consistently clear, crisp image, and the books finished to the high quality standard for which the Press is recognised around the world. The latest print-on-demand technology ensures that the books will remain available indefinitely, and that orders for single or multiple copies can quickly be supplied.

The Cambridge Library Collection will bring back to life books of enduring scholarly value (including out-of-copyright works originally issued by other publishers) across a wide range of disciplines in the humanities and social sciences and in science and technology.

William Cotton Oswell, Hunter and Explorer

The Story of his Life with Extracts from the Private Journal of David Livingstone, Hitherto Unpublished

VOLUME 1

WILLIAM EDWARD OSWELL

CAMBRIDGE UNIVERSITY PRESS

Cambridge, New York, Melbourne, Madrid, Cape Town,
Singapore, São Paolo, Delhi, Tokyo, Mexico City

Published in the United States of America by Cambridge University Press, New York

www.cambridge.org
Information on this title: www.cambridge.org/9781108032117

© in this compilation Cambridge University Press 2011

This edition first published 1900
This digitally printed version 2011

ISBN 978-1-108-03211-7 Paperback

WILLIAM COTTON OSWELL

ÆTAT 32

WILLIAM COTTON OSWELL

Ibunter and Explorer

THE STORY OF HIS LIFE

WITH CERTAIN CORRESPONDENCE AND EXTRACTS FROM THE PRIVATE
JOURNAL OF DAVID LIVINGSTONE, HITHERTO UNPUBLISHED

BY HIS ELDEST SON

W. EDWARD OSWELL

OF THE MIDDLE TEMPLE, BARRISTER-AT-LAW

With an Introduction

BY

FRANCIS GALTON

D.C.L., F.R.S., F.R.G.S., ETC.

PORTRAITS, MAPS, AND ILLUSTRATIONS

IN TWO VOLUMES

VOL. I

LONDON

WILLIAM HEINEMANN

1900

PREFACE

IMMEDIATELY after my father's death I resolved to publish a memoir of him, and with this object collected information from numerous sources, and collated letters, including many hundreds written to myself—a large proportion of them during nine or ten years of my life in London. These alone would have made a volume of deep interest to anyone who knew and loved him, containing as they did his matured views, very freely expressed, of men and things, and touching on an extraordinary variety of subjects. The manuscript was well advanced when it, and the materials upon which it was founded, were totally destroyed by fire.

At first it appeared impossible to recommence the task, but the unexpected discovery a year later of some thousands of old letters and papers—the fruits mainly of the executorships of Mrs. Oswell and her brother, Benjamin Cotton—and the kind interest and encouragement of friends, induced me to make a fresh attempt. More especially I was influenced by one for whose opinion, character, and judgment, my father, in common with everyone who knows him, had the highest respect and admiration—I refer to General Fred Cotton.

'The life-history,' he wrote, 'of my noble friend—one of the most really noble of men—ought to be recorded from first to last. No better man could have been found to treat of his characteristics as a sportsman and explorer

than Sir Samuel Baker; but there is a younger life and
an older life, both full of fine qualities, that ought to be dealt
with, and I hope with all my heart it may; for I cannot
fancy any volume that would contain better instruction as
to what a man should be than a biography in detail of
him.'

As to the general plan and contents of this book, the
early pages sketch the family and surroundings into which
William Cotton Oswell was born—the foundation of ' the
brave and blameless life,' as Sir Henry Acland calls it.

The Rugby days under Arnold, in the Augustan age of
Stanley, Vaughan and Clough, are described by the boy
himself : while his schoolfellow, Tom Hughes, supple-
ments the description with reminiscences in his own
inimitable style, and tells of his hero-worship for him.

Of the seven years spent in India in the Company's
service, after he had passed out of Haileybury with the
highest distinction, the lifelong friendships formed, the
hard work, the sport, the study of the peoples among
whom his lot was cast, their religions and languages, his
letters to his mother speak.

And then came, by accident, as it seemed, the most
stirring period, the most abiding interest, of his life. In
1844 a succession of terrible attacks of fever had brought
him to death's door, and he was ordered to the Cape as a
last chance. He remained in Africa two years, and with
Mr. Murray of Lintrose as the companion of one, and
Captain Frank Vardon of the other, penetrated far beyond
the utmost limits of previous geographical knowledge,
exploring, hunting, revelling with them in shooting such
as no men ever had before or will ever have again, the
first Europeans and the first guns among the myriads of
animals—a very empire of wild sport.

Meanwhile, a friendship sprang up between him and
Dr. Livingstone which thenceforward until the death of
the great missionary, in 1873, never for a moment wavered
or faltered. The correspondence that resulted has been

freely drawn on, and will no doubt be read with the attention which anything concerning that remarkable man
deserves.

In 1847 he returned to India, and accepted the charge
of the *coopum* organized by the Government. Of this
he wrote a graphic account, which is here included.
Towards the end of the year he revisited England, arriving
just in time to bid a last farewell to his gentle mother.

The concluding months of 1848 found him again at the
Cape, preparing for the most notable and arduous of all his
journeys, the first of which exploration was the sole object.
Starting from Graham's Town on March 10, 1849, he was
joined by Murray on April 23, and by Livingstone at the
beginning of June; and by the end of July he had led an
expedition across the Kalahari, and discovered the River
Zouga and Lake Ngami. The story of the journey, sent at
the time to his family and Captain Vardon, is full of interest.

The next season he devoted entirely to hunting over the
ground traversed in the previous year. Making his way
to the Lake first, he shot down both banks of the river
with extraordinary and unvarying success.

In 1851 he enabled Livingstone and his family again
to join him by giving them a wagon and supplies; and
pushing northwards to the country of Sebitoané, they met
with the heartiest welcome and most courteous consideration from that famous chief.

Having obtained permission for a further advance, they
shared the important discovery of the Zambesi in those
regions. The exploration of the course of that river to
the coast, and the establishment of a new missionary
station at a convenient spot on its banks, were the next
objects to which they proposed devoting themselves; but
his fellow-traveller's advice, and the experience of the
three preceding years, had determined Livingstone never
again to expose his wife and young children to the perils
and hardships necessarily incident on boring into a new
country; and as it was too late in the season for useful

work, and Oswell was anxious to keep a promise he had
given to visit his family by the end of the year, it was
decided that the whole party should at once start for the
Cape. How this and the subsequent voyage was made
possible for the Livingstones by their devoted friend, the
Doctor himself explains.

When Oswell went on board the first homeward-bound
ship, it was with the full intention of returning in the
course of a few months. But his brother's state of health
detained him indefinitely, and thus, to his never-ending
regret, his African career came to an end. The short
history of it is collected from his own writings and
Dr. Livingstone's private journal, which his daughter,
Mrs. Bruce, with rare kindness and generosity, placed
unreservedly at my disposal; while Sir Samuel Baker
with unimpeachable authority confirms the story of the
vast numbers in which the game was found in those days
and speaks of my father's methods of hunting, and of the
estimation in which he was held as a man and sportsman
by white and black alike.

After his brother's death he went to Paris, and was
summoned thence to Constantinople by his friend Major
Steele.

In 1854 and 1855 he was at the front in the Crimea,
volunteering to carry secret service money and despatches
for Lord Raglan, and assisting the overworked surgeons
on the field and in the hospitals.

On the fall of Sebastopol he left for a long tour in
North and South America and the West Indies, meeting
his future wife on the voyage out.

In 1860 he married, and the remaining thirty-three
years of his life were passed quietly in a country village.
He was much occupied in 1865 in revising the MS. and
proofs of Livingstone's work, ' The Zambesi and its
Tributaries.' In 1892 he wrote an article for the ' Bad-
minton' Series on the ' Big Game of South Africa,' to which
I would acknowledge my obligations, and in 1893 he died.

With the fullest recognition of the numberless defects
and most unskilful workmanship of this book, on which I
humbly deprecate the strictures of critics, I nevertheless
confidently assert that no one could have laboured more
abundantly, more anxiously or more lovingly to tell the
true, unvarnished tale of a life—for me the life of the
noblest gentleman I shall ever know. I have resisted the
temptation of putting a construction upon facts or at-
tributing motives. Letters have been allowed to speak
for themselves, and comment has been made only where
it seemed necessary as a link or explanation. My father
kept no diaries, and made a practice of destroying all his
papers. Save with his wife and children, he had no
regular correspondence; he rarely talked of what he had
seen and done. Even in competent hands, therefore, his
biography would have been a difficult undertaking.

As my apology, if one is needed, for a somewhat unusual
amount of purely personal detail, I would cite and adopt
an extract from an admirable review in the *Daily Chronicle*:
'There is not a page which does not bear witness to his
unwearying and unforgetting kindness to mother, wife,
children, and household pets—a tenderness expressed with
manly and unaffected simplicity. We are not of those
who hold that the world should not thus be admitted into
the privacy of domestic life. The world can only gain,
and he certainly cannot lose, by this intimate and un-
studied self-portrayal.'

I do not expect, I scarcely venture to hope, that the
public will care to read about a man who for the last
thirty years of his life dwelt so entirely among the un-
trodden ways that his very name must be unknown,
except to the few who have heard of him as a mighty
hunter and a pioneer of African exploration half a century
ago. But the story will give pleasure to his nearest and
dearest, and to the wide circle of relations and friends who
respected, admired, and loved him.

In conclusion, I would tender my thanks to my father's

old friend Mr. Francis Galton, for his interesting and graceful Introduction ; to Dr. Scott Keltie, of the Royal Geographical Society, and the Rev. Wardlaw Thompson, of the London Missionary Society, who have kindly allowed me access to their records ; and to all who have aided me with information and material.

To Messrs. Longman, too, I am particularly indebted for their readily-accorded permission to make use of the illustrations to my father's article on ' Big Game.' ' They are,' he writes, ' by the best artist of wild animal life I have ever known, Joseph Wolf. After describing the scene, I stood by him as he drew, occasionally offering a suggestion or venturing on two or three scrawling lines of my own ; and the wonderful talent of the man produced pictures so like the reality in all essential points that I marvel still at his power.'

I should perhaps add that I have not attempted to correct or render uniform the spelling of African and Indian words, but have purposely left them as originally written.

W. EDWARD OSWELL.

HILLSIDE,
GROOMBRIDGE, KENT,
May 1, 1897.

INTRODUCTION

By FRANCIS GALTON, D.C.L., F.R.S.

Sixty years ago the interior of South Africa was a blank on our maps, the modern knowledge of its geography being based for the most part on numerous explorations made since that date. One of the most epoch-making of them was that which, by traversing wastes previously impassable to Europeans, succeeded in connecting the pastoral uplands over which great game had been hunted by many travellers, with the lakes and rivers of the equatorial part of the continent.

This notable Expedition was made by a party of three— Oswell, Murray, and Livingstone. Its furtherance required wagons, oxen, stores, and a capable leader, and these desiderata were mainly supplied by Oswell. Livingstone was at that time comparatively inexperienced, while Oswell had spent years in persistent travel, and had become the most dashing hunter and successful explorer of his time in South Africa. Murray was also a hunter, but by no means of equal experience. The idea of the desirability of such an Expedition was not due to any one of the three alone: it was in the air, and shared by many others, but its achievement was due, first and foremost, to

Oswell. Murray joined Oswell with his wagon. Livingstone accompanied them as a guest, most welcome on
many accounts, and not least for his familiar knowledge
of the language of the native races, and for the personal
love and respect with which he was regarded by many of
them. Still, the Expedition would have gone all the same
without Livingstone, while Livingstone could not have
moved without the assistance of Oswell and Murray,
especially of the former. Yet, notwithstanding Oswell's
eminent services to geography, notwithstanding the loyal
attitude of Livingstone towards him, and, again, notwithstanding the attempts of many of his friends in England
to induce the public to appreciate him as he deserved, his
work soon began to pass into oblivion. The chief cause
of this lay in his invincible laziness as a writer, which
rendered him a deplorably bad correspondent, even to
his nearest relations, who craved for tidings, and whom
he dearly loved. His dilatoriness in these respects was
enforced by a strange shrinking from publicity, and from
even the most legitimate forms of self-assertion ; and,
again, he honestly took greater pleasure in ministering to
the reputation of Livingstone than to his own. It followed
that the story of the Expedition was first learnt through
the letters of Livingstone, which were published and
widely discussed weeks before a scrap of information
reached England from Oswell's own pen. He was the
despair of the Geographical Society, whose authorities, as
I well know, did what they could to induce him to com-
municate a substantial memoir worthy of himself, but in
vain. He was then placed on their Council, but he did
not seem to appreciate the honour, and rarely cared to
attend it. So, owing to his persistent abnegation, it

naturally followed that his achievements should gradually pass out of mind, but I think it not unlikely that in later years he may have felt some regret at his neglected opportunities. Murray, the third member of the travelling party, of whom little is known except his love of hunting, was also a man who never cared to write ; he was hardly seen by geographers, and fell quite out of touch with them. I never to my knowledge had the pleasure of meeting him. Now the usual desire of a hero-worshipper is to worship a single hero at a time, and not to divide his homage in perplexing proportions among those who shared in the same great action. Consequently, as the years went by, when the frequent and elaborate descriptions written by Livingstone of what he saw from time to time, together with the grave missionary purpose of the man, and his unresting progress, monopolized public attention, a retrospective credit became popularly given to him (which he himself never claimed) for the paramount conduct of the first great journey across the sandy wastes to Lake Ngami, which was the beginning of his heroic career.

It is gratifying to read the few letters and memoranda of Oswell, and the other contents of this book. They confirm what many as well as myself well knew at the time, and they extend that knowledge. Let it not be supposed for a moment that the slightest rivalry existed between Livingstone and Oswell; on the contrary, they were the warmest friends, though, the one being a missionary with a keenly observant eye and a strong scientific bent, and the other a roving hunter, their ideals of life must have differed in many ways. Touching evidences of their mutual esteem are to be found in many pages of these volumes.

It was my good fortune to gain the friendship of Oswell after his final return from Africa, when I quickly appreciated the remarkable nobleness of his character. I was at that time closely and eagerly connected with the Geographical Society, so that I was brought into frequent contact with every contemporary traveller of note. Among these Oswell, with his clear-cut, aquiline features, keen glance, and lithe frame, suggested perhaps the most typical specimen of a man born to adventure. His striking physical gifts, combined with his aristocratic bearing and winning but modest address, seemed a living realization of the perfect and gentle knight of whom we read in old romances.

As my name occurs two or three times in the letters in connection with Lake Ngami, I may mention that I never went there, because on arrival at the Cape I was assured by the Governor, Sir Harry Smith, that the Boers had barred the passage to travellers. I therefore changed my destination and went to Damara Land instead.

CONTENTS OF VOL. I.

CHAPTER I.

PARENTAGE AND BIRTH.

1745—1832. AGE 1—14.

CHAPTER II.

EDUCATION : RUGBY AND HAILEYBURY.

1832—1837. AGE 14—19.

b

CHAPTER III.

INDIA.

1837—1844. AGE 19—26.

CHAPTER IV.

AFRICA.

1844—1846. AGE 26—28.

FIRST EXPEDITION (WITH MURRAY) TO BA-KAA HILLS— RETURN BY LIMPOPO.

CHAPTER V.

AFRICA.

1846—1847.   AGE 28—29.

SECOND EXPEDITION (WITH CAPTAIN FRANK VARDON)—
EXPLORATION OF COURSE OF LIMPOPO, AND
DISCOVERY OF RIVER MOKOLWÉ.

CHAPTER VI.

INDIA AND ENGLAND.

1847—1848.   AGE 29—30.

CHAPTER VII.

AFRICA.

1848—1849. AGE 30—31.

THIRD EXPEDITION (WITH LIVINGSTONE AND MURRAY)—
PASSAGE OF KALAHARI DESERT, AND DISCOVERY
OF RIVER ZOUGA AND LAKE NGAMI.

CHAPTER VIII.

AFRICA.

1850.   AGE 31—32.

FOURTH EXPEDITION (UNACCOMPANIED)—EXPLORATION OF RIVER ZOUGA—SECOND VISIT TO LAKE NGAMI.

CHAPTER IX.

AFRICA.

1851—1852.   AGE 32—34.

FIFTH EXPEDITION (WITH LIVINGSTONE)—VISIT TO SEBITOANÉ—DISCOVERY OF RIVERS MABABÉ, SOUTA, CHOBÉ, AND ZAMBESI.

LIST OF ILLUSTRATIONS IN VOL. I.

SKETCH-MAPS

MAPS

WILLIAM COTTON OSWELL

CHAPTER I.

PARENTAGE AND BIRTH.

1745–1832. AGE 1–14.

Captain Joseph Cotton, his wife and family—A first ball and
a proposal—Miss Amelia Cotton and William Oswell—A
husband's love-letters to his wife ninety years ago—
'The Gentleman in the black Gown'—Birth of William
Cotton Oswell—Funeral of Queen Caroline—A last Will
and Testament—*L'art d'être beau-père*—A son of consolation—Death of William Oswell—His widow's diary and
correspondence—Sir Charles Grandison—A profession of
faith—A 'Dutiful and Affectionate' child—The Rev.
Thomas Bowdler's opinion of Mrs. Oswell—Death of her
four little daughters—She sets up house with her brother
Benjamin—A goodly heritage.

JOSEPH COTTON, the maternal grandfather of William
Cotton Oswell, was the son of Nathaniel Cotton, M.D.
(to whose charge the poet Cowper was confided during his
insanity), and of his wife Anne Pembroke. He was born
March 7, 1745, entered the navy in 1760, quitted it after
passing his lieutenant's examination, and, beginning as
fourth mate in the Mercantile Marine of the Honourable
East India Company, worked his way up, and was
appointed Captain of the *Royal Charlotte*. A man of distinguished ability and probity, and possessing extraordinary
commercial acumen, on retiring from his profession and

settling at Leytonstone, in Essex, his services were eagerly sought by many of the famous companies of the day. He became a director of the London Assurance Company, chairman of the Copper Company, and of the East India Dock Company, and Deputy Master of the Trinity House, of which he wrote an interesting and complete memoir. On January 28, 1779, he married Sarah, daughter

CAPTAIN COTTON.

From a Portrait by Sir Thomas Lawrence, P.R.A.

of his neighbour and friend, John Harrison, by his wife Charlotte Branfill. Mr. Harrison was a director of the Bank of England, and later associated with him on the Board of the East India Dock Company. Of Captain and Mrs. Cotton's family of ten children, six only appear in these pages : John, born October 10, 1783, who, after long residence in China and India, was appointed a member of the Court of Directors of the East India Company ; William, born September 12, 1786, who was elected Governor of the Bank of England ; Phebe, born October 22, 1787, who married the Rev. Thomas Bowdler ; Amelia, born January 13, 1789, the mother of William Cotton Oswell ; Benjamin, born February 10, 1794 ; and Louisa Decima, born September 6, 1795.

On January 22, 1807, Amelia went to her first ball. Next morning, when she came down to breakfast, she found a letter awaiting her :

'It is with an anxious, trembling eagerness that I take up my pen, but oh! with what language shall I address my dear Miss Cotton to acquaint her with the sentiments of a heart which is entirely at her disposal. . . . My dear Miss Cotton will not be alarmed, and I hope not much surprized at the receipt of such a letter as this, though from one to whom she is not immediately known. She need not be surprized when I tell her that from the first moment I had the happiness to see her, which was in September last, when I was not even acquainted with her name, she made an impression which I fondly hope to cherish and cultivate as long as life shall last. It was at Church, and I am not ashamed to confess that the dignified and reverential deportment of Mr. Cotton, and the unaffected piety, sweetness, and good-humour which seemed to pervade the whole family, at once interested my attention

MRS. COTTON.

From a Portrait by Sir Thomas Lawrence P.R.A.

and excited my curiosity. I followed therefore the natural dictates of my feelings when all I heard and all I saw only tended to strengthen and improve the opinion I had formed for myself. Can you wonder then that I should catch the general contagion and so much revere a family which the more it is known, the more must it be admired. And can my dear Miss Cotton be angry if I felt an inclination to be allied to such a family, when I am not only charmed by your person, but convinced by your conduct that you are one of the most amiable of women ? . . . After my self-introduction to Miss Cotton in the Ballroom last night, you will perhaps think my conduct there with regard to yourself rather at variance with my professions. I hope however it will admit of a very different construction. I had no one to introduce me, and I could not for the world have obtruded myself on your notice without an introduction. Had I had the pleasure of dancing with you it might certainly have given *you* a fairer opportunity of deciding, but for *myself* I confess my sentiments I am sure will never alter. It is not merely that countenance whereon are so charmingly painted complacency, good sense, Innocence, honour and truth, that I admire ; but it is that retired delicacy, that unobtrusive modesty and sweetness of behaviour which captivate my heart, and which can never fail of commanding respect even from the most abandoned. But you may naturally be allowed to ask what are my claims, what my pretensions, to so great a treasure. Alas ! I feel my deficiencies and my un-worthiness, and thus conscious of them, it is some comfort to consider that the natural effects of Love is to create in the admirer some similitude of the object admired. As to my fortune and prospects, the enclosed letter to Mr. Cotton (which I must leave to your decision to deliver or not) will explain them. I wish to do nothing without your privity and approbation, nor do I wish my Dear Miss Cotton to determine without reposing upon the judgment of an affectionate Father, or till Mr. Cotton is perfectly satisfied and informed of everything relating to me. . . . Oh ! could I but flatter myself that I should have the honour and happiness of passing the remainder of my life in a uniform and constant endeavour to promote your happiness, and evince my gratitude ! But after all Miss Cotton is the mistress of her own affections, nor would I pretend to controul them. Should this application (which Heaven avert!) meet with a rejection, it would become me to be resigned, in the hope that Miss Cotton may hereafter meet with some more deserving object of her regard than him who, notwithstanding, will never cease to pray for her happiness, and would deem it the sweetest distinction of his life to be allowed to subscribe himself as he is in truth

  'Her most affectionate friend
   'And most obliged and obedient Servant
       'Wm. Oswell.'

William Oswell was the son of William Oswell of Shrewsbury, who traced his descent in a direct line from

St. Oswel, Oswal, or Oswald, King of Northumbria, and pointed to an ancestor on the roll of knights who fought round Harold at the Battle of Hastings. He had towards the end of 1806 taken a house at Leytonstone as being conveniently distant from London, whither his business, that of a Russian merchant, called him daily. A reply to his letters was despatched by Captain Cotton without an hour's delay:

WILLIAM OSWELL
(FATHER OF W. C. OSWELL).
From a Miniature.

 'Dear Sir,
  'Your letter addressed to my Daughter and its Enclosure, she put into her Mother's hands observing that you was so totally unknown to her, it was impossible to commit herself to pay attention to what it contain which could only be sanctiond by previous acquaintance. The respectful Tendency of both Communications and the Candour you have manifested in respect to your Situation in Life, I cannot but be sensible of, but at the same Time concur in my Daughter's Sentiment

that untill a better acquaintance Existed, the proposition
to her should have been withheld.   The Subject is to both
of the first Importance and should be founded on mutual
Regard and Esteem, the Result of frequent Intercourse.
A precipitate Engagement on your part, or Encouragement on hers, might otherwise prove a Source of Em-
barrassment and Unhappiness.   I regret therefore this
premature proposition to her, which cannot be decided
as you wish ; and her age is also a bar to any early
Engagement.   Tho' I feel persuaded of your honourable
Motives and of the Compliment to my Family, I feel also
the Justness of her Conclusions too forcibly to encourage
any Expectation of a speedy Decision when so much is
at stake.   Your better judgment must approve of this
Reserve, nor can the Respectability of your Character be
in any way affected by my Daughter's present Determination.   ' I am, Dear Sir
                ' Your very Sincere, Hble. Servt.
                        ' JOSEPH COTTON.'

In spite of the father's cautious periods, and the praiseworthy sentiments he reports his daughter to have expressed, we cannot but read between the lines that ' my
dear Miss Cotton ' was certainly not ' alarmed ' or even
' much surprized ' at the receipt of such a letter.   That
self-introduction in the ball-room had evidently prepared
her for some further development.

The enclosure had given ' all references and particulars
I can with respect to my property and prospects.   My
fortune amounts to £1,400 a year,' and William Oswell
did not long remain ' so totally unknown ' to his lady-love.
Early in February they became engaged, and from then
until the marriage there were frequent meetings, and daily
letters from him, quaintly formal, indeed, but instinct one
and all with the deep, *grateful* devotion which thenceforward continued, without one break or one cloud, to the
day of his death :

'*March* 23, 1807.

'Since I had the happiness of my dear Miss Cotton's acquaintance I cannot call to mind a single circumstance in her conduct which has not directly tended to increase my admiration and regard. I feel her sentiments with respect to myself must on many occasions have been of a very different description. But I am content to be on the *obliged* side, and shall ever deem it my greatest happiness to feel myself her Debtor till the last day of my existence. . . . I assure her that I am, with the most delicate attachment that ever entered the heart of man,

'Her affectionate admirer
and
'Sincere Friend and Servant
'WM. OSWELL.'

A month or two later matters had advanced so far that the lover allowed himself to call his mistress by her Christian name :

'*May*, 1807.

'I have nothing new to tell my Dearest Emily and yet I cannot refrain from scribbling these few lines. I am just setting off for town and fear there is a probability of my not being able to see you to-day. . . . Believe me Emily I love and esteem you if possible more than ever. I will not say that at Vauxhall the other evening I made it my business inquisitively to observe the multitude round me in order to be *dissatisfied* with Emily, but I must say that after the most particular observation, I did not see a single individual that looked so *good* or so *handsome*. This is no flattery my love and you know I am not much addicted to compliments. *Indeed, Indeed* I every day see more occasion to be thankful to that Providence which has in a wonderful manner conducted me to so

great a Treasure and as often before observed I hope
to make it the business of my life to express my gratitude
to my dearest Emily by that tenderness and attention
which she so eminently deserves. I only hope it will not
now be long before Emily condescends to make me the
guardian of her happiness and comfort. The first or
second week in August will not surely be too soon?
Bless me if you think I deserve it with a gracious answer,
and through all the changes and chances of life believe
that I shall ever remain my Emily's most affectionate and
obliged Friend

'WM. OSWELL.'

The wedding took place on August 20, 1807. The
bride was only eighteen years old. She was tall and
slight; her complexion was clear and glowing; her hair
curly and brown; her eyes and eyebrows dark; her nose
a delicate aquiline, which in later years became somewhat
pronounced, without, however, detracting from the extreme
gentleness of her expression. She is described by all who
knew her as a beautiful and radiant young creature, but
there is unfortunately no satisfactory likeness of her extant.
The bridegroom inherited the good looks of a handsome
family. Clean-shaven and black-haired, his eyebrows
were strongly marked; his eyes large and blue; his
features regular; his face pale and refined.

The honeymoon over, they had no difficulty in deciding
to remain at Leytonstone. Her affectionate disposition
naturally inclined her to dwell among her own people;
and to him, after the somewhat lonely life he had passed
(he had only one near relation, his brother, the Rev.
Thomas Oswell, of Shrewsbury) the constant intercourse
with her large family, who accepted and welcomed him as
one of themselves, was an unfailing source of happiness.
On the other hand, she and her brother-in-law became
fast friends, and he made her house his home whenever
he journeyed South. In April, 1809, he had a sudden

attack of illness, and William Oswell posted* across England to see him. During his absence he wrote daily to his wife:

'*April* 20, 1809.

'MY DEAREST LOVE,

'. . . My principal object in writing is to convey to you several kisses which I received on your account this morning. Their being presented through my medium will not I hope render them the less acceptable, and if I venture to enclose for you a few *hundreds of my own,* pray do not frown and send them back, Ems, for you are very welcome to them all. Indeed, my dear Wife, raillery apart, I begin to think it a very long and tedious time since we parted. My sleeping and my waking thoughts are full of the dear image I so much admire and so deservedly esteem. . . . A separation from the object of my fondest affection is what I can no longer bear; it is like the dividing asunder of soul and body, or the amputation of a favourite member. I am absolutely lost, and seem a Wanderer without your fostering care and kind attentions, though at the same time I feel I very little deserve them. . . . To-day I determined on a journey

---

* Amongst his papers there is the following note :

LONDON TO SHREWSBURY, APRIL, 1809.

Horses and driver to		Uxbridge	...	£1	14	0
,,	,,	High Wycombe		1	1	6
,,	,,	Oxford ...	...	...	0	17	6
,,	,,	Woodstock	...	...	0	12	0
,,	,,	Chapelhouse	..	...	0	16	0
,,	,,	Shipston	...	...	0	15	0
,,	,,	Stratford	...	...	0	16	0
,,	,,	Hockley...	...	...	0	17	6
,,	,,	Birmingham	...	...	0	14	6
,,	,,	Hampton	...	...	1	0	0
,,	,,	Shifnal ...	...	...	0	17	6
,,	,,	Heygate...	...	...	0	12	0
,,	,,	Shrewsbury	...	...	0	15	0
Turnpikes...	...	...	...	...	0	16	8

£13 3 2

It is a remarkable fact that the third-class fare to-day from London to Shrewsbury is thirteen *shillings.*

to Westbury, so mounting my Brother's horse at about
10 o/c, I accomplished the undertaking. . . . I could
not help remarking with some degree of emphasis and
feeling, that my steed was rather *rough* or that I was not
very *tough*. . . . Westbury looked very well, much improved by the gravel, painting and planting, and most of
all adorned by the presence of the dear little happy
inmates. Maryanne is really grown to a very interesting
and *Elegant* little girl. Her complexion, shape and eyes
beautiful. As for little William he is twice the size he
was at the Sea, very healthy and stout, the characteristic
roughness of the boy tempered with a very soft and affectionate disposition. It is quite delightful to see them
clasp and hug each other with all the innocent playfulness
of infancy and love. Pretty little dears, they are to come
to town on Thursday to spend the day with us. Maryanne
was very gracious with me, and gave me many a kiss for
dear Aunt. William was rather shy but still vouchsafed
me several kisses to dispose of as I think fit ; and depend
upon it dear Ems shall come in for her share. . . . Heaven
bless you my dearest wife. It is the constant prayer of
your most affectionate.

'WM. OSWELL.'

'*April* 21, 1809.

'I fear my dear Emily will be almost tired of seeing my
handwriting, and begin to think me extravagant in the
matter of postage. It is therefore a happy circumstance
that having heard from you on Monday does in some sort
furnish me with an apology. . . . Accept my best thanks
for your very kind and interesting letter which I have
feasted upon over and over again, and blessed a hundred
times the hand that penned and the heart that dictated
its contents. Indeed Emily, I love you so well and at
the same time am so selfish, that I cannot allow you to
receive half the pleasure from my letters which I do from
yours, especially when they talk *a great deal about your-*

self, which is to me the most interesting of all subjects.
I take therefore a wonderful concern in all your movements be they never so minute, in all your little rambles
and stories and intentions. To others who possess not
the same feelings they may be insignificant, but they are
all the World to me. You complain of my omitting to
say how I felt after my journey. . . . That I was a little
tired I will not be stoical enough to deny . . . but the
next morning saw me all fresh and vigorous again, and
I have no doubt when I make my appearance amongst
you, you will pay me the Compliment to say that I am
very *handsome*. . . . I hope it will be in my power comfortably to leave my Brother on Saturday. . . . I really
shall scold if the Greenhouse is not tolerably filled. What
else have you had to do, you idle *baggage ?* . . . I hope
my dearest Wife is as well as I could wish her. Good-
night dear Ems; may Heaven watch around your bed.

'I am, believe me,

'Your affect. Husbd. and sincere friend,

'WM. OSWELL.'

It was not until March 12, 1810—two years and a half
after the marriage—that the first child, Amelia, was
born. Three daughters followed: Mary on November 15,
1811 ; Louisa on March 13, 1813 ; Eliza on December 29,
1814. They were an hourly delight to their father, who
was never too tired or too busy to play with them, plan
for them, or write to them.

'*July* 1814.

'MY DEAR LITTLE M*A*,

'You are the funniest little girl I ever knew. *Me*
has a good deal of Tongue and plenty of Teeth, and yet
me cannot speak plain. *Me* goes to Church and falls
asleep there I am afraid. But still Papa loves *me*, little
me, very much, and therefore he writes her a letter He
hopes she will very soon begin to learn her A.B.C. which
will enable her to read and to talk very prettily, and that

she will go to Church without falling asleep, because little
girls are supposed to go to Church to learn to be *good*,
and if they fall asleep they cannot hear what the *Gentleman
in the black Gown* may say to them to teach them to be
good. . . . Papa is very sorry indeed to hear that Dear
Mamma has not been quite so well for the last two or
three days, and he is sure little *Ma* will not make a noise
or be naughty, because that would hurt poor Mamma and
make her worse, and he knows very well little *Ma* loves
her Mamma too much to make her ill.   Papa is going
again this morning to the new nursery at Wanstead, and
then he thinks he shall have done everything to make it
comfortable for his little Girls.   Aunt Berthon asked after
little Mary very particularly.   She seems a great favorite
there.   And as long as she is a good little girl everybody
will love her, and nobody can love her more or better
than her Dear old Papa, William Oswell, who begs her
to give Mamma and Sisters plenty of love and kisses for
him.'

A few months later they moved to a larger house at
Wanstead, and the next two years were the brightest and
happiest of their lives.   Entirely wrapped up in each other,
and their healthy, beautiful children, with ample means
and many friends, their only trouble was occasional brief
separation.   And this was a pain that was almost a pleasure,
giving excuse as it did for such correspondence as this :

                              ' SHREWSBURY,
                                  ' *October* 9, 1815.
' MY DEAREST LOVE,
        ' I am anxiously longing for a letter from Wanstead,
and must still live upon mere expectation till tomorrow
evening.   And expectation to a hungry soul is very meagre
fare.   It seems really a tremendous length of time since
these eyes beheld my dear Wife and little ones.   These
eyes, I say, for in imagination they are ever present and

with me, an impression strengthened perhaps by the
distance which now unfortunately separates us. . . . How
long I may be detained here must in some degree depend
on causes beyond my control; but were I to consult inclination alone, depend upon it, my dear Emily, I should
fly back to Wanstead on the Wings of the Wind. How
are our dear little babies? do they often talk of Papa?
do they love him dearly? do they long for his return,
and treasure up pretty little Stories in their Memories to
relate to him on his return? Oh, the sweet interchange
of Parental and of Filial love is not to be foregone for all
the jewels upon Earth! I hope my little lambs are good,
and behave properly and kindly and obediently to all. . . .
    ' With love and affection,
       ' I remain ever, my dear Wife, and entirely yours,
                        ' WILLIAM OSWELL.'

In 1816, by a misplaced and, it must be added, in-
excusable confidence in a friend, he lost half his fortune.
An immediate removal to a smaller house became necessary.
Hardly had this been effected when, in June, 1817, the
four children caught small-pox from one of the servants.
Happily, the disease did not assume a severe form, except
in the case of Amelia. Their mother nursed them devotedly
and unremittingly, and in August was able to take them
to Worthing, where her husband had secured rooms.
He had hoped to be with them during the first week of
their sojourn, but yielded to her wish that he should take
the opportunity of paying a long-deferred visit to his
Shrewsbury relations. His letters to her thence are even
more affectionate than usual:

                          ' *August* 15, 1817.

' I cannot be thankful enough for the enduring activity
and kindness and resignation you have displayed; though
at the same time it hurts me the more that they should
have been put to so severe a trial. . . . If there is one
truth more certain than another, it is that I love my Wife,

who will I hope ever continue to love me and pray for her unworthy but most affectionate Husband.'

'*August* 16, 1817.

'My dear, dear Wife,

'. . . All desire their most affectionate remembrances to the best of Wives, my dearest Ems. . . . Excuse for this time so short a scrawl, my dear Love, you shall hear from me every day without fail. . . .

'Believe me, my dearest Wife,

'Your most faithful and affectionate husband.'

'*August* 17, 1817.

'Pray kiss for me all my little darlings, and tell them Papa loves them most affectionately . . . and accept yourself, my ever dear and affectionate Wife, the assurance of my never-ending friendship, Love and regard.'

'London,

'*August* 19, 1817.

'To-morrow, my Love, is our Wedding-day, a day to which I am much indebted, and therefore a day on which I will put up a special prayer for your happiness here and hereafter. And, if it please God, may the years that are to come shine with brighter and warmer beams upon my indulgent and affectionate Wife, and may I strive and be enabled to add in every way that I can to her comfort and happiness. . . . We had a grand party yesterday. . . . I certainly was not smitten by either of the Brides. *As yet*, therefore, my heart is all my Wife's! . . .'

'Oh, my dearest Wife! I wish we had but a Cottage in some rural spot where we might live in peace and join in prayer and praise to Him, Who is always more ready to hear than we to ask. I have much reason I know to be thankful . . . but I know not how it is, or why, my heart often sinks within me. The repeated parting from all I

love is almost more than a counterpoise for the pleasure
of meeting. Let me hear however that you are well and
that my dear little Emily continues to improve, and I
shall be thankful. Kiss my pretty little ones for papa,
and

' Believe me for Ever and Ever, My dear Wife,
' Your most affectionate friend.'

On April 27, 1818, to the great delight of parents and
sisters, a son, William Cotton, was born.

Meanwhile, Mr. Oswell was steadily retrieving his losses,
so that in 1820 he was in a position to discuss with his
wife the possibility of returning to the house at Wanstead.
With his increasing family, he did not think he would be
justified in trenching at all on his capital for the expenses
of moving, the purchase of the lease, and the many other
outgoings attendant on the change from a small house to
a larger one. After careful consideration, therefore, the
idea was abandoned. This decision reached the ears of a
cousin of Mrs. Oswell's—Miss Catherine Clarke—and she
immediately forwarded a draft on her bankers sufficient
for every purpose, begging the Oswells to regard it as a
loan, and to pay it back with interest, if they insisted
upon it, when it suited them to do so. No sooner had
they gratefully availed themselves of her kindness, and
established themselves in the house, than she wrote to
Mrs. Oswell :

' 1821.

' My dear Emily,

' You must not deny me this request I have to
make, which is that you and Mr. Oswell will from this
moment consider yourselves entirely out of my debt. The
pleasure I have experienced in assisting you with a Sum
of Money upon your retaking possession of this house will
be increased by your considering yourselves perfectly free
from the debt, both principal and interest. Do not, my
dear Friends, put me to the pain of even listening to a

refusal which I cannot take, but receive this from one who
sincerely wishes by every means in her power to contribute
to your happiness and Comfort, and who is ever
'Your very affectionate
'CATHERINE E. CLARKE.'

MRS. OSWELL AND W. COTTON OSWELL AT THE
AGE OF THREE.

From a Sketch by Delacour.

Mr. Oswell signalized this happy return by commission-
ing Delacour in the early days of 1821 to execute a sketch
of his wife and little boy. On March 14 another son,
Edward Waring, was born. The parents at once begged
their generous cousin to be his godmother, and she gladly

consented. This year the little daughters constantly sent notes to their father when he was away, and he made a point of replying promptly. On the day of the funeral of Queen Caroline he writes to eleven-year old Emily:

'MY DEAR GIRL,— *August* 14, 1821.

'That I should so long have suffered a Lady's letter to remain unanswered, or at least without a specific reply, betrays, I fear, a want of *Gallantry* on my part and is a proof that the age of *Chivalry* is past. . . . We have had a sad squabble to-day about the poor Queen. The Ministers said the Funeral should not come through the City. The *Mob* said it should, and I am very sorry to say the *Mob* succeeded at last, for they completely stopped up the other roads by pieces of timber, carts, coaches, stones, etc., etc., so that the procession could not pass, and they were obliged to halt for fresh orders from Lord Liverpool, and the result was that it came through the City about 4 o'clock, when I saw the whole of it passing the Exchange. It was nothing very splendid and the people were there very orderly, but report says they were very much the reverse in the morning and that several persons were killed in the bustle. I hope this is not true. . . .'

A year passed away. At the beginning of 1822 he had a very severe illness, from which, however, he appeared to rally completely. But there were two relapses, and regarding his condition as precarious, he writes on June 7, 1822:

'Having this day received a second warning it seems high time that I should make this simple declaration of my last Will and Testament while the ability is yet spared me.

* * * * *

'All the residue of my little property of every sort and description. . . . I give and bequeath, without any reserve, to my ever dear and most affectionate Wife, who has been

to me the kindest, tenderest and best of friends, whose
love has Solaced my happier days, and supported me in
affliction and distress; ever Smiling, Cheerful and Resigned, notwithstanding the fretfulness and impatience
which I have too often exhibited, and for which, as well
as for numberless other iniquities, I would humbly and
earnestly and anxiously implore the forgiveness of
Almighty God for the alone merits of Jesus Christ our
Lord and Saviour. I commend her to the care of many
kind friends, and above all I commend her to a Gracious
God, the Father of the Fatherless and the Husband of the
Widow. I have the fullest Confidence in her judgment
and discretion with respect to the management of my
dear Children, and I ardently and anxiously pray that
she may be supported in the arduous task, and that it
may finally please Almighty God of his goodness, to
reunite us all in his appointed time, a family in Heaven.
Amen, for Jesus Christ's sake, Amen.'

When he was sufficiently recovered, it was decided that
he should spend a month at Hastings with his wife, and
the winter abroad. His father-in-law sent a letter to
his house on the day of his departure:

'Layton,
'*August* 10, 1822.

'My dear Friend Oswell—
'I cannot allow you to go from my Neighbourhood
without some token of my great and sincere Regard and
Affection, altho' I have not been permitted personally to
assure you of the Esteem and Solicitude I entertain for
your future welfare, and that of all belonging to you, and
the unremitting Desire I have to be instrumental to all
your Comforts and the restoration to health and the
Embraces of all that are dear to You, and to assure you
of my fervent prayers to that Effect, and for a sincere
blessing on the Endeavours to promote them. May the
Providence of God support you and Sanctify the Means
about to be adopted for your Recovery. I have it full in

contemplation as soon as you are comfortably settled, to come down for a month, and will bring any of your Children with me; therefore look out for a House within that distance of your own that may enable us to keep up the Intercourse, and pray spare no Expence that may conduce to your Ease and Satisfaction. My purse is open for your leaving England, and as it is our Duty to submit to dispensations we are sure must be founded in Mercy and Goodness, so let this chear you; and bound as we all are to Endeavour at the preservation of Life and all its benefits for both ourselves and families, leave no opportunity to improve such as may offer, being assured I will be attentive to all your dear Family to the Utmost of my power. And as the Health of your excellent Wife is one of the first considerations, so do not let her omit to use Exercise and Air as she has been accustomed, nor let her fatigue herself by undertaking more than her Strength and delicate Constitution will allow of. And may the blessing of Almighty God be with You and Her and again permit me to see you both in Health and the enjoyment of every blessing which any reasonable Being has Hope of, thro' the kind and merciful Dispensations we have all so long experienced, and myself beyond the Term of Life, the most unworthy of them. My affectionate good wishes and Regards are Yours and Hers. A single Line to express your Welfare will be most acceptable at all Times and the Greatest Comfort and Cordial to us all.

'And having only to commend you to the providential charge of that Being who sees even the Sparrow fall,

'Believe me most truly your affectionate

'Friend and Father

'JOSEPH COTTON.'

'I thank God I feel well in health. May my Daughters be careful of theirs for that is my next apprehension.'

The visit to Hastings was a terrible strain on poor Mrs. Oswell. She was torn asunder by the conflicting claims of husband and children. She could not, dared not, leave him alone for an hour. She had never before been parted from them for a single day.

Mrs. Oswell to her Children.

'THE BATTERY HOUSE,
'HASTINGS,
'*Aug.* 14, 1822.

' MY DEAREST CHILDREN,

' I fear you have been expecting a letter from me some days. I certainly should have written but dear Papa has occupied all my time. He has, I am sorry to say, been very languid all day, but I hope, now we are comfortably settled, he will, with the blessing of our Heavenly Father, improve in strength. We were quite glad to get from the Inn. Our Sitting-room was over the Kitchen, and, as you may suppose, very hot, and dear Papa was obliged to be carried up fifty stairs to bed. The going up and down has made my legs stiff, and poor Nurse walks quite lame. We have a comfortable small house by the Sea, it is called the Battery House. It is very cheerful and I only hope we shall not find it too noisy. There is to be a grand sailing match on Friday which I hope will amuse dear Papa as we shall see it from our Drawing-room Window. There are a great many children here and I look at them as they pass, but cannot find *one* like my Willy and Teddy. What would I give for a kiss from you all! But I must not think of it, as if the change of air be of service to dear Papa, I shall be fully rewarded for all the pain I now feel at being separated from you. I thought it best to write to all of you first, but tell William the next letter shall be to him *by the post*. . . . I fear I left all my things in great confusion, but really I could not think of anything but dear Papa. When he gets a little better I hope to have you down, but till then you must all try to make one another happy. . . . I am very thankful we have got to our

journey's end, and we must think ourselves very well off
to get a house so soon. . . . I send you a sad scrawl
and almost fear you will hardly be able to read it, but
you must put all your *wise heads* together and try to make
it out. You must ask Uncle William to get you a frank
some day that you may all send me a short letter. It
must not weigh more than an ounce. . . . It is now
quite teatime, therefore I must wish you all Good-bye.

   ' Believe me ever your affectionate Mother.

 ' A great many kisses to dear Teddy, Willy, and all
from Papa and Mamma.'

Days and weeks passed, but there was no improvement.
On the contrary he grew steadily worse, and his wife,
recognising that the end could not be far off, wrote to her
sister Louisa, who during her absence from home had
taken her place at Wanstead, to bring the four elder
children down to see their father once more. Early in
October, worn out with grief, watching and nursing, she
thankfully accepted the offer of her brother-in-law to join
her, and remain as long as he could be of any assistance.

Meanwhile her brothers William and Benjamin came
whenever they could, and her father drove over from
London or Tunbridge Wells frequently, never failing to
bring strength and consolation with him. On the 19th
he saw his well-loved son-in-law for the last time; the
conviction that it was so was strong upon him, and the
noble-hearted old gentleman determined that so far as lay
in his power the end should be faced by husband and
wife free from anxiety for the future. If anything could
comfort their sad hearts, it would surely be such a letter
as this :

       ' TUNBRIDGE WELLS,
        ' *October* 20, 1822.
 ' MY VERY DEAR AMELIA,

  ' As I returned hither yesterday it occurred to me
to write to You in your affliction, thinking that a letter

might be acceptable and help to compose and comfort you. I have undertaken it to-day, and although I can add little to the suggestions of your own Mind and of those who are with you, to fortify you against the event which I perceive is fast approaching, yet I cannot but assure You how deeply and sincerely I have felt for you in your affliction. And heavy as it is and will be, Still my dear Child we must consider it as the Visitation of a merciful God who does not wantonly, or without some good intended, send such heavy dispensations upon us: and to His Mandate all must bow and it is the part both of Religion and philosophy so to do. That your excellent Husband and Man has been so early called upon to pay the Debt incumbent on us all, is to be deplored, but neither repined at or murmured at, seeing it is of the Lord who will I trust receive him into the arms of His Mercy and Love and blessedness. This Earth and all its enjoyments are insufficiently bestowed for the attainment of unmixt happiness. It has pleased God to allow me the comfort of seeing most of my children grown up and deriving from their Connexions and Intercourse with Society all the kindly felicity and Respect with which we can ever flatter ourselves. But these Gifts are occasionally interspersed with Visitations that manifest the uncertainty of all sublunary Consolations, and it comes home in succession to each and every one of us. You have shared an affliction and Sorrow and Anxiety beyond the Common Tenor from its Continuance as well as from its Termination. But where are those who can plead an Exemption? or who have the hardihood when such calamity comes, not to feel its dire Effects and Consequences? Believe me, none are proof against the poignancy of such Sufferings or their Results. And I bless God you have had Strength and Fortitude to fullfill your severe Duty with the resignation that behoves us fallible Creatures to entertain. My heart has most truly felt for You under the afflicting Rod. But my dear

Child do not be discouraged or shaken in your Faith or your Hope. That the Widow and fatherless Children are the peculiar Charge of providence we learn in all the Sacred Scriptures, and that will be your portion. Should your dear Man be yet Sensible, it may be some Consolation to assure him I have not failed of the promise I made him when he left Wanstead, of my Continued Supplications to the Throne of Grace on his behalf; and there is nothing within the whole Compass of my Life that I can do for You and his Children that shall not be done, and for a provision for them when it shall please God to move me hence, which cannot in the Course of things be far off as my advanced age and manifold Infirmities suggest day by day. I trust you will have no hesitation in your Removal to my House at Leyton, where your Children will find Room, a good Garden for Exercise, and an affectionate Welcome. There will be no difficulty in accommodating You all, and I shall be happy in affording You this asylum, and housing You. But should you prefer a Lighting-place here, as being nearer to remove to, I will find you a Comfortable House where you may pass a few Months prior to your coming into Essex. As this Event must be looked to, so I would not have you at a loss when the period comes, and from the Conduct of your Children here I am sure they can be no annoyance to me, either here or at Leyton. Let your heart therefore be Comforted and Consoled under the Distress we anticipate, by knowing that if you lose one protector you have others; and the Beneficent Being, whose Mercy, forbearance, and Goodness I have experienced in most trying Situations and for so many Years, will not fail to give you his Blessing be you where you may. It is impossible that any Reasonable Being should expect his Family to be exempt from this usual fate of others, or that he is to share protection beyond the general Lot of Mankind. The Loss of your dear and ever lamented Mother, of poor Sarah and Mrs. John, have been such Inroads into my Comforts as to Exhibit the fallacy of any such Impressions, did I entertain them. My Grief has been and is a constant Repetition, but I hope so chastened and corrected as to place me in that state of Resignation that will be acceptable to my Maker and obtain his gracious Favour and Consideration, which I earnestly pray may be extended to my Children and Grandchildren who have been augmented a Day or two ago by Mrs. Joseph's delivery of another Son. May God Almighty, my Dearest Daughter, take you and yours under his protection, support You under this Heavy Trial and give You Strength and Ability to fullfill the more extensive Duty that now devolves on You. And under all Events only rely on my assistance and affection which never will desert you. Give your Children a Kiss for me. I shall delight to see them under my Roof, and with my sincere and affectionate Regards to Yourself, Louisa and the Young folks,

'Believe me, your very affectionate

'Parent and Friend.

'Make my Respects acceptable to Mr. T. Oswell, with thanks for his attentions and comfort to your dear Husband, Yourself and Family. The lasses desire their duty and Love, and all beside join in affectionate Regards and good wishes for everything that can chear You under the present Calamity.'

In a corner of the paper there is a postscript from Benjamin Cotton:

'I can add nothing to my Father's letter save that I participate in all his feelings towards you. . . . I will come to you immediately I hear that my presence will be acceptable or useful to you.'

On the 22nd the end came very quietly. William Cotton had driven down for the day, and remained to see carried out Mr. Oswell's wish to be buried in the church-yard of All Saints, Old Hastings.

Thus at the early age of thirty-three Mrs. Oswell was left a widow with a family of six children, the eldest only twelve years old, the youngest nineteen months.

Some time later she writes in her journal:

'In October 1822 it pleased the Almighty to visit me with my *severest* affliction. My beloved Husband was taken from me. He was of a most affectionate disposition and to me the best of husbands. We were more tenderly attached than I can describe. We had known prosperity and adversity together (so far as regards worldly enjoyments) and I own I felt at times that I could not continue here without him; but it was ordered otherwise for me. May our union, begun in this world, be continued through all eternity! How thankful should I be that I was permitted to attend him so constantly, though he would not allow me to sit up with him till quite the close of his illness, which though not painful was particularly trying to one of such sensitive and affectionate feelings. His dear brother came to him a fortnight before his death, and was a sincere comfort. This time of severe trial is not to be expressed by writing. My dearest Husband's illness was for several months, and I saw him gradually ripening for eternity; and at the last, by God's grace, I was enabled to say, "Thy will be done." O, my God Thou alone knowest what I then went through!'

It is pleasant in the midst of her trouble to read this entry:

'On November 2nd, 1822, My four elder children and I, joined my other two who were with my dear Father at Tunbridge, and we all spent the winter at Leyton with him; his delightful reception of me and mine was more than I can express.'

In the following February five of the children had measles, and their mother found a sad comfort in nursing

again. Grandpapa's and Uncle Ben's kindness was un-
bounded. They vied with one another in amusing the
little invalids, and giving them presents, the delight in
which was greatly enhanced by the letters which always
accompanied them :

'Noah's Ark with Noah, Shem, Ham, and Japhet, and
their Wives to stand in front and behind, and the animals
to fill the doors or the Inside as may suit. Grandpapa's
Love to William Oswell.'

(*With a copy of the Rev. T. Bowdler's expurgated Shake-
speare.*)

'*March* 13, 1823.

'A Gentleman and Poet of some reputation desires to
congratulate Miss Oswell upon her birthday. Being a
native of Stratford-on-Avon he could not possibly pay
his respects earlier. He now desires to be admitted into
Miss Oswell's Library and to have the happiness of her
acquaintance, and of occasionally endeavouring to entertain her. He trusts that his manners are such as will
not give offence to any of her friends. He has been re-
educated on purpose to fit him for the Society of Ladies
and will be happy to be re-dressed in any fashion that
may be most approved, if his present appearance is too
homely.

'Introduced to Miss Louisa Oswell by her affectionate
Uncle Benjamin Cotton.'

The next two or three years may be dismissed with a
few extracts from Mrs. Oswell's diary :

'*November* 1st, 1823.—We returned home from our
lodgings. My sister Louisa having most kindly arranged
my furniture in a house I had taken at Woodford, was
ready with my three other children to welcome us *home*
and a happy meeting we had. To feel once more surrounded by my Treasures, *at home* was a delight though

deprived of my greatest earthly comfort (he may have been permitted to witness).'

'*February*, 1825.—My most dear, honoured and beloved Father passed peacefully away. This short extract from his last Will I have taken down with the earnest hope that it may be a further inducement to me to continue in a stedfast and sincere faith and in the practice of every Christian virtue:

' " I profess to have lived as I hope to die in the faith of a Crucified Redeemer, relying solely on his Atonement and Mediation for Mercy and Salvation, earnestly entreating, nay enjoining my Children to continue stedfast therein, and in the Practice as well as Profession of a Christian, it being the only certain means of attaining Comfort here and Happiness hereafter; which Injunction I have every reason to believe is and will be their Chief Consideration. I desire to be buried in a decent manner, without Parade, in the Vault that contains the Remains of my most excellent Wife, whose soul I believe to be amongst the Blessed." '

'*September*, 1825.—I have been indeed a Source of anxiety and trouble to my family, though they, most kindly, never shew it. Sister Louisa is a second mother to my sweet Eliza. Dear Girl she engages everyone to love her.'

Six months later pretty little Eliza was dead. Her mother thus describes her illness:

'*April*, 1826.—My little Eliza had a severe attack of jaundice in January, and for days was in danger. She however rallied and was able, dear girl, to leave her room. The sweet little dear was constantly employed; her behaviour and countenance were Angelic. Then came a relapse and for six weeks previous to her departure she kept her bed; I only occasionally lifted her out while it was made, and she sat on my lap in my arms. Her delight was in showing kindness to others. The last night I took her up, she kissed me very often.

It was a sweet sight to see her of a night before going to sleep, with her lamp on her bed, saying her prayers. She had requested I would write them out. Many days before she died we thought her spirit departing; and as early as Ash Wednesday I had been watching some time by her bed, she had been dozing, and she seemed by her countenance at Heaven's Gate. Her dear sisters, just returned from Church, were anxiously looking at her, when, all of a sudden, she revived, seemed to awake, and asked for something to eat. I was not allowed to sit up with her not being strong in health; it was a trial to me. Her spirit left her without a groan at 9 o'clock on Easter Sunday, March 26th 1826. She had laid her head upon her hand and fell asleep. Miss McDiarmid and I were with her. When it was over I felt as if I were a block of marble; it was most distressing. I do not think the dear Child was aware of her danger, but we were so urged by her medical man not to name it to her. I do not know if we were right. She was the most affectionate of children. I cannot say how much I loved her. I only hope I did not love her too much.'

Miss McDiarmid was Mrs. Oswell's governess and friend. She taught little William as well as his sisters, and, young as he was, her great intelligence and strong original mind left their impress on him. In an age of conventional expression, it is refreshing to read such a letter as this:

Miss McDiarmid to Miss Louisa Oswell.

'TOTTERIDGE.

'I have heard Dr. Gordon spoken of as a very clever and a very *kind* man. The latter qualification is I think a great recommendation in a physician; I never could go to a Bear however skilful he might be. I cannot agree with you, dear, in liking Sir C. Grandison. I believe I differ from most people in my opinion of that book. It is generally among the first novels that are put in a young person's hands. But I consider it *prosy*, very *stupid*, and in many parts *far-fetched*. The hero and the incomparable Miss B. are characters much too perfect to be natural; not that I should like any hero to be a *bad* man—but to err is human. Sir C. G. never even *thinks* amiss, and seven volumes of it !'

At this date it was only in her journal that Mrs. Oswell allowed her grief and anxiety to appear. To her children she was always bright and cheerful, and home the happiest, merriest place imaginable. They idolized her, and their love for her and hers for them was the comfort and joy of her life.

Amelia Oswell to her Mother.

'*June* 19, 1826.

' My very dearest Mamma,

'My dear Aunt* and Cousins are so kind as to wish me to prolong my visit beyond Wednesday, and as Aunt has written to you about it I need say nothing more; only pray let me have what you really and truly wish. You my dearest Mamma know my feelings. At home I feel that I enjoy the height of human happiness, far, far, more than I deserve. Away from you I experience a sort of resigned pleasure which looks forward with hope to the time when I shall again be united to you. I think I shall like to be with you by next Sunday, but your letter shall decide me. Dear Phebe enters into my feelings ; it is my greatest pleasure to talk to her of you and home. I hope you will not over-fatigue yourself this very hot day. . . . With the kindest love to my dear Sisters and darling Teddy and Willy if with you,

' Believe me, Dearest Mamma,

' Your ever Dutiful and Affectionate Daughter.'

Towards the latter end of 1827 Mary became seriously

* Mrs. Bowdler.

ill, and Mrs. Oswell for the first time since her husband's death sought to relieve her aching heart by confiding its sorrows and troubles to sympathetic ears—those of her favourite sister, Mrs. Bowdler.

Many years later—in 1855—just after the death of his wife, whose executor he was, the Rev. Thomas Bowdler wrote to William Cotton Oswell:

' MY DEAR WILLIAM,

' Upon opening a little box the contents of which are directed to be burned, which is the case of all papers, (only that they may be read by me) I find this little packet of letters written by your dear Mother to the friend of her heart during one portion of her heavy trials, and possessing the great charm of shewing her feelings and her character in all the genuine simplicity and strength which she possessed in so remarkable a degree. It seemed to be no common gift of grace and power which was vouchsafed to her, if indeed it be lawful to speak of anything as extraordinary in the dealings of Our Heavenly Father with his Children. The packet should now be in your hands, so I commend it to your care. The contents are very interesting and touching to me.

' Ever very much yours,
' T. BOWDLER.'

Mrs. Oswell to Mrs. Bowdler.

' WOODFORD,
' *Oct.* 31, 1827.

' . . . I try all I can to comfort and support Mary. My earnest prayers are to be enabled to do my duty, but I feel in such a responsible situation, and the irreparable loss of the greatest of earthly blessings, my dear, dear Husband—but I must not repine. The Almighty who has promised to be a Father to the fatherless, has likewise promised to be Husband to the Widow.'

'*Journal, December,* 1827.—On her dear Father's birthday, November 27th, 1827, I was called on to resign my Mary into the hands of a Merciful Father. Just before the end as she lay on the sofa taking her supper she said, " In all probability this will be my last birthday in this world." It had been her dear Sisters' custom to make little presents to each other on the return of their birthdays. They asked what they should do. I advised them to omit their usual trifles but I made her a present of a Sovereign knowing the pleasure she always felt in being able to help the poor. She immediately appropriated part of that sum to a very worthy but distressed family and requested I would send for a leg of mutton, which she had brought up to her to look at, and which with a proportionate quantity of potatoes she begged might be sent. She was a sweet girl and a most pleasing Companion. She was not generally known as she was shy, and so sensitive that anything not perfectly correct gave her a disgust. At home she was the most cheerful of the party. She was fond of reading, and read with great spirit aloud. The last day she was downstairs she would read me those sweet lines in Lalla Rookh on the repentant Tear. Her likeness to her dear father was very great. Beautifully neat and delicate in her figure, and of a sweet and affectionate disposition, her loss was the entire breaking up of our circle. She was always ready to do any kindness for her sisters, and to promote their pleasure gave her *sincere* delight.'

To Mrs. Bowdler.

'*December* 22, 1827.

' . . . I cannot tell you, my dearest Phebe, what I have suffered. My mind is so distracted that I can, at times, hardly think, for the extreme exhaustion I felt when all was over, seems to have weakened both mind and body. The great desire I had for perfect rest and quiet was not

granted, for my good no doubt.   I trust I shall be enabled
to wait patiently till the Lord sees fit to lighten my affliction.'

Mary's death was so great a shock to her sister Amelia,
who was tenderly attached to her, that she never held up
her head again.   Broken-hearted and spiritless she lingered
on for a year, growing gradually weaker.

Mrs. Oswell to Mrs. Bowdler.

' WOODFORD,
 ' *February* 16, 1828.

'. . . My dear Emsie is certainly much improved, but
my anxious mind will not be quite at rest.   I look at all
my dear Children very differently to what I did.   It is
perhaps as well to consider them as lent me by the Lord.
May I be enabled to do my duty towards them while they
are with me !'

' BRIGHTON,
 ' *February* 3, 1829.

' Do not, my dear Phebe, think too highly of my bearing
up against these heavy trials.   The support that has been
given me is more than I can describe.   That my most
precious darling may possibly soon be taken from me is
what I can hardly dare to think of.   But I must bow
down, *I* shall be the sufferer.   I am thankful to say I am
able to do all for her at present, and she is so grateful and
so pleased with my endeavours that it is quite overcoming
at times.   If you have made any plans for coming at any
time, pray come.   Your prayers dear, dear Phe.'

' BRIGHTON,
 ' *February* 18, 1829.

'. . . Because I have given you a rather more cheering
account you must not think I flatter myself with hopes of
amendment.   I wish to feel that these little comforts are

only helps and refreshments, and to leave all in the hands
of a Merciful Father.   I own it is sometimes very difficult.'

She had lost her husband and her father, but to the end
of her life she was never without the strength, wisdom and
ever-ready help of such brothers as few sisters possess.
Their visits and letters were at this time a wonderful solace
to her.

Benjamin Cotton to Mrs. Oswell.

' Light Office,
'Trinity House,
' 26 *Feby.*, 1829.

' I thank you for your kind letter received this morning.
It is a great gratification to me to hear of your comfort
under this severe affliction.   I shall feel the bereavement
as of a Child of my own, and must learn with you the
great lesson of Resignation, and trust in an allwise and
gracious Father.   Assure the dear Girl of my love and
affection and of my remembrance of all her goodness.   I
am glad Louisa will stay with you.   Do not hesitate to
make me useful in any way to your relief and comfort.   I
am ready to supply all your pecuniary wants, and will
either send by Mr. Williams or pay into your Bankers as
you like best. . . . You do not mention the Boys so I
trust they are well.   Young John from Newick I expect
to meet to morrow at Walwood. . . . I hope he will like
his habitation and business. . . . I will send the Boys
some treacle, the first opportunity.   It is pleasant to me
to be able to' report well of yourself.   I have many
enquiries about you all. . . . It makes me sad to see Mary
and Kate Clarke both shut up, solitary, and both appearing
to want a Companion more than Physic. . . . I was at
Hackney two days ago.   My Aunt Charlotte was well, but
not yet free from great terror about this Catholic business.
So that those who have no particular cares and troubles
make unto themselves spears and arrows out of public

affairs. I will not longer detain you, but commend you earnestly to the loving kindness of our Heavenly Father, assuring you that you have no friend on earth more willing to bear your burdens and assist and sympathize with you in all your troubles than your most affectionate Brother.

Mrs. Oswell to Mrs. Bowdler.

‘ BRIGHTON,
‘February 26, 1829.

‘. . . I have felt much more comforted and trust these heavy dispensations may be sanctified to me, and a time may come when I shall bless God for them ; though so contrary now to flesh and blood I would not have anything contrary to His Will.’

Next day Emily died.

‘ In January, 1829,’ writes Mrs. Oswell, in her journal, ‘ my sweet girl took to her room and never came out of it. She made no complaint but seemed to fade away. It is too trying to give a particular description. She had a constant smile particularly the last week whenever I looked at her.’

Then the poor mother, utterly broken down in mind and body with incessant, hopeless attendance on her favourite daughter, became seriously ill. As soon as she was well enough to be moved, her sister Louisa took her and her three children to Brighton, but she failed during a long stay to regain her lost strength, though her mind became more composed.

To Mrs. Bowdler.

‘ BRIGHTON,
‘March 13, 1829.

‘. . . I am not at present called upon to feel any particular anxiety about any of my dear Children. My mind now goes from one to the other of those dear departed; and it has been quite a refreshment to lay me down and think of them, and of her who was the Comfort and friend of my heart. She is at times greatly present with me. . . . I cannot express my thoughts as I should wish ; my head from frequent nervous headaches will not permit me.'

Louisa returned to her brother Benjamin at Leyton-stone, but when two or three weeks passed with no improvement in the accounts of their sister, they both wrote urging her to come to them and try what home life would do for her. She acquiesced, and they welcomed her and her children most affectionately. They were greatly concerned at her appearance, and extreme physical weakness and nervous prostration. Gradually, however, in the congenial atmosphere of love and sympathy, she began to improve.

To Mrs. Bowdler.

'LEYTON, 1829.

' MY DEAREST PHEBE,

'. . . Some comfortable sleep the last two nights, with the assistance of a composing medicine has made my head rather stronger, and my hand a little steadier. The day I wrote to you I could hardly hold my pen. A little bodily strength would contribute I make no doubt to my comfort. The small interest (Do not my dear Phebe wonder that I can use such an expression) that I feel in things around me makes it quite painful.

' (*Sunday Night*).—I have had more comfort to-day than I have experienced for some time. The great depression I have felt lately was removed for a short time and the thoughts of my dear departed Children were sweet. I was able to go to evening service but I felt very much tired and not able to attend so much as I could wish. . . . The want of a Dear Husband to assist me is—but I must not say so; the Almighty will direct and assist me if I trust sufficiently in him. No one knows the sorrows of my heart. My friends are all ready I know to assist me, and most thankful should I be to them. What I did at Brighton without them now distresses me a good deal. I fancy I may have acted too much on my own judgment at times. . . .'

Early in June, detecting symptoms of delicacy in her only remaining daughter Louisa, she hastened to consult Sir Astley Cooper, who, however, assured her that there were no grounds for alarm.

To Mrs. Bowdler.

'LEYTON,
'*June* 6, 1829.

'. . . To feel comfort or free from great anxiety after seeing a Doctor is something so new to me, that I hardly know what to think. My severe bereavements lie so heavy on me that I fear I am not thankful enough. You may be able to feel in some measure for me, and you do, I know. . . .'

Night after night, when she had gone to bed, the brother and sister discussed what was best for her in the future. Their brother John was on his way from India to take possession of the old home, and it had long been determined in this event that Benjamin should settle in London for the convenience of his business, and find a house near his for Mrs. Oswell. But as the time approached he fancied, though she spoke no word of demur, that she dreaded the change of place and mode of life. A conversation with Louisa settled the question. If the facts were as he suspected, he would give up all idea of London, she would cede the headship of his house to her sister, and they would all live together. Next morning as he mounted his horse, he asked Mrs. Oswell to do him the favour of going over and letting him have her opinion of a large vacant house in the neighbourhood which he had some thoughts of taking. Her look and exclamation of astonishment and delight were ample amends to him and Louisa for the sacrifice they were about to make; but he said no more at the moment, merely calling out as he rode away that he should sleep in town, and would write thence; thus with graceful tact avoiding making his proposition to her face to face, and giving her time to think it over. In a few hours the letter was in her hands:

'Light Office,
'Trinity House,
'Novr., 1829.

'My dear Sister,

'I hope you have been to see the house to-day, and write a few lines to assure you it will contribute greatly to my happiness if I can by any means make a comfortable home for you and your Children. I have considered over and over again where to fix my residence, when John and his family come to Leyton, and unfit as I am from my want of hearing for general society, or to form new acquaintances, I cannot do better than remain in the neighbourhood, and your being with me would make me a home and I should take an interest in it; and you know me well enough to be assured that it would be a source of happiness to me to support you in every way. I would take the house and keep it up, and pay taxes, etc., and the gardener, and you should either keep house on my account and pay a certain sum towards it, or on your account and let me pay for my board. Wine, tea and sugar I would provide in either case. We should have very good rooms to receive any visitor, and you may rely on my being perfectly at ease, and I trust you would be the same on that head. However if you think that in my absence from home, for days or a week or two together you would find so large a house dreary, I would by no means persuade you to the undertaking. My principal object is that you should not give the house up on the score of expence. You shall be rent and tax free, giving me a room upstairs and one down, and the house-keeping shall be arranged in any way you please. I have written in haste, just going to dinner, but not the less sincerely, and I will see you to-morrow afternoon when we will talk the matter over.'

She thankfully and joyfully hailed the proposition, and it is a high tribute to the whole-hearted generosity of her sister and brother that they succeeded in entirely evading the vigilance of her sensitive unselfishness, and making her believe they were grateful to her for falling in with an arrangement which had originated in their own desire. For the next fifteen years Benjamin Cotton devoted himself body and soul to the service of his sisters, and became a father in the best and truest sense to his young nephews.

Mrs. Oswell to Mrs. Bowdler.

'*Nov.* 3, 1829.

'. . . I have much to praise the Lord for, for though Nature must have her part at times to mourn for such sweet Companions as I have been deprived of, yet, I trust, in spirit we are more than ever united. I may not be able to-day to say all I wish. My heart is full, *very* full. Another happy spirit has, I trust, been united to those that are gone, and I must mourn the loss of an affectionate Brother, and my Children a dear Uncle. Our accounts from Shrewsbury had of late been very comfortable. Mr. Oswell had spent the summer at Westbury with great satisfaction to himself and his poor neighbours. Last week he was with his family at his Wife's Father's, and on his return was quite as well as usual. On Saturday, whilst dressing, he was a little faint, and whilst sitting with his family at dinner he fell back in his chair, and his spirit returned to God who gave it.* . . .

---

* It is a curious and noteworthy fact that one of his sons, the Rev. Henry LLoyd Oswell, died sixty-five years later under

Dear Phebe, this awful event has been a great shock to me. I had looked forward to sending my dear William shortly to be under his Uncle's care and attend Dr. Butler's School. I felt that it would be such a relief to me to think that my dear boy would be not only improving in worldly knowledge, but his higher interests would be attended to, and that daily, both by precept and example; But man proposes, God disposes. *I* have lost a kind and affectionate friend, one that I felt perfectly at my ease with; but his *family*, a parent, a father, a friend. I know how to feel for them, and their poor Mother. . . . Dear Benjamin would not tell me this sad news till after breakfast. I am thankful he did not. Yesterday I felt very poorly. A good night's sleep and some comfortable thoughts on the unity of spirits, which arose in my mind, prepared me to hear what has greatly distressed me. I often wish I could set down many pleasing thoughts which arise within me. They seem sent to cheer and refresh, but whether my mind has been weakened by affliction, or these remaining long would exalt me, they are not permitted to continue. However I should be most truly thankful for them and the calm they leave behind.'

At the beginning of the following term little William, who had been at Dr. Oke's school at Walthamstow for two years, became one of the fifty pupils of Mr. Delafosse of Hackney.

'*Journal, April* 7, 1830.—My dear girls had been particularly brought before me by looking over some of their memorandums, and I spent a very quiet evening with dear William, and with great pleasure perceived his improvement in many important things. I went to bed with a thankful heart, and whether asleep or awake, I had the

---

almost identical circumstances. He had just finished dinner and was sitting in his armchair taking a nap, when he passed away in the presence of his wife and children, without a sigh or a struggle.

most delightful ideas of being united to my dear departed
ones to be ever with God. I cannot describe them, but
every time I awoke I felt so happy, which is not generally
the case, for it is then mostly that I feel much depressed ;
the troubles and anxieties of this life appeared less than a
vapour, the greatest trials I thought were as nothing; it
was a night of great delight.'

But the poor gentle lady's cup was not full. She was
to lose her last surviving daughter. On April 22nd of this
year Louisa, who had been ailing for many months, took
a chill, and at once becoming seriously ill, died a week
later.

'*Journal.*—I have frequently made notes of my many
severe trials and the many Mercies I have experienced. I
will endeavour to collect them, they may remind me should
it ever be necessary, how the Almighty supports the
weakest of his creatures. Those who know me, know how
little able (humanly speaking) I was to bear up against
affliction and endure fatigue, but the same Almighty power
that chastened me, in mercy upheld me that it might be
to my profit. The awful question presents itself to me,
"Have my trials worked in me the good my Heavenly
Father designed, or have I resisted and not endeavoured
by His Grace to become His obedient servant and follow
my Blessed Saviour in all things?" It is our belief as
Christians that no affliction happens to us but by the Will
of God. . . . If it should ever happen to any of us that
God should seem to have gone out of His way to visit us,
because the blow may have fallen upon us not once but
again and oftener, stripping us, it may be, successively of
the treasures and supports of our existence, and our hearts
should sink and our faith be confounded at the extent of
our calamity, let us turn awhile in thought to Abraham
and consider his trials. . . .

' For four succeeding years to watch the deathbeds and
close the eyes of four beloved children ! What can I have
done to have received such chastisement ? I am humbled

indeed. They have at times been brought before me as punishment. I would not dismiss the thought but have made it a time of repentance. " How have I done my duty towards them ?" has been another searching consideration. When first I became a Widow my thought when on my knees was " My duty as a Wife is finished, how have I fulfilled it ?" These are awful considerations, and we are too apt to neglect calling ourselves to account before the scene is closed. When I look back and think what I have gone through, I would first acknowledge with gratitude and praise the mighty Power who has supported me. I feel almost singled out. What manner of person ought I to be ?'

'Journal, April 22, 1832 (Easter-Sunday). — On this day 1826 I was called on to resign my dearest Eliza, my youngest girl, a most heavenly-tempered child, and one I can say that never gave me any anxiety or trouble, except as to her illness. Oh my God I beseech thee for thy support during this day. It was on this day in 1830 that my dear, dear, Lou attended at the Altar for the last time. Grant that I may not be too much overcome, but that my thoughts may be so directed that I may forget those things that are past, and behold my dear children purified by that Blood which was shed, and which with that Body broken I am about to partake. May my sinful, sinful body be made clean by His Body and my Soul washed with His most precious Blood.

' (Five o'clock).—I thank thee O Heavenly Father that Thou hast enabled me to go through this day with composure of spirit. Though now my heart is ready to burst, I will rejoice in my dear Sister's happiness.'

An endeavour has been made in the preceding pages to give a slight sketch of those members of William Cotton Oswell's family whose characteristics he inherited in the most remarkable degree. The noble generosity, manliness and deep religious conviction of his grandfather; the tender, almost womanly devotion of his father to wife, children and home; the selfless, loving, simple nature of his mother, whose strong faith was proof against eight consecutive years of the cruellest tragedy, and whose gentleness, decision, and dearly bought experience made her an ideal nurse; the affectionate very present help in trouble of his uncles—these were the influences that surrounded him and moulded his early life. Truly the lot fell unto him in a fair ground. Yea, he had a goodly heritage!

CHAPTER II.

1832–1837. AGE 14–19.

Rugby in 1833—Dr. Arnold a great reformer: 'Lord Paramount
of the whole concern'—William Cotton Oswell entered
on the boards—Half-holidays and 'wiskers'—Aptitude for
classical versification—'Monstrous cute' Vaughan—Pride
in Dr. Arnold—'Signs and symbols'—Escapes expulsion;
Boughton Leigh dispute—Judge Hughes' reminiscences
—Leaves Rugby—Discussion as to profession—Tour
through England—Acceptance of writership, H.E.I.C.S.
—Dr. Arnold's testimonials—Haileybury—Passes out
brilliantly—An unselfish mother.

IN September, 1832, William Oswell, then aged fourteen, had passed over the heads of boys of fifteen, sixteen,
even seventeen, and was at the top of Mr. Delafosse's
school. His mother fully recognised the danger of the
position for him, and after consultation with her two
brothers, resolved to move him as soon as he could be
received elsewhere.

Four years before this—in August, 1828—Dr. Arnold
had become Headmaster of Rugby, and already he had
revolutionized public school life. To manly, honourable
men such as William and Benjamin Cotton, and to a
woman accustomed from her infancy to manly, honourable
men, there was a peculiar attractiveness in the thought
that it was possible for the boy they all loved so dearly
and understood so well, to continue his education under a

man whose system was founded on honour and manliness. Accordingly they made numerous inquiries, and a letter from her husband's closest friend finally decided Mrs. Oswell on sending her son to Rugby :

Mr. Richard Corfield to Mrs. Oswell.

'*January* 14, 1833.

' . . . With respect to Rugby I had two sons there in 1825, and though the school was then in its decline, yet I was very partial to it, and my sons will not be happier than they were there.

DR. ARNOLD.

' Under the present *régime* the School has considerably increased in numbers, and the present Head Master, Dr. Arnold (whom I do not at all know) being a great reformer in Church, as well as that, has placed the whole of the old system in Schedule A. Being therefore one of the *old School*, and seeing with suspicion, perhaps with prejudice, modern changes as well as those who are given to change, I am not one of the admirers of modern Rugby, though very likely it may prove a very good school—indeed in fairness I shall give you the opinion of an intimate and clever friend of Dr. Arnold's. Speaking of him to me he said, " He is a highly talented scholar, but I doubt whether he understands training *winning horses* for the University prizes ; he will however turn out many good ones." Rugby

has certainly every advantage of situation for a Public
School, being not only central but sufficiently retired; dry
and healthy, I should say particularly so ; the school
buildings are very handsome and admirably arranged for
the convenience and comfort of the boys ; a delightful
playground of ten acres, quite like a park to the mansion ;
the town small, and over which as to Public Houses, etc.,
the Head Master has a sort of Casting-net Control, so that
he is Lord Paramount of the whole concern. It is also a
cheap school—about £120 per annum—and therefore when
elder sons have gone to Eton or Harrow, younger ones
have generally been found at Rugby. Many sons of Merchants, Clergymen, and occasionally a sprinkling of Aristo-
cracy are to be met with. As to the habits of the School I
have no doubt they are what you would approve, for though
Dr. Arnold is not very popular with some of the boys, he
has produced in many instances within my observance
honourable and gentlemanly feelings.'

Mrs. Oswell at once entered into correspondence with
Dr. Arnold, and on February 10th, 1833, her brother
Benjamin took William to Rugby for his entrance examin-
ation.

Benjamin Cotton to his Sister, Mrs. Oswell.

'*Tuesday, February* 12, 1833.

' Although I desired William to write to you to-day, and
expect the pleasure of seeing you on Thursday, I will, for
fear of his omission, send a few lines to announce the
success of my mission. We had a fine day after we passed
St. Albans, and neither of us suffered from the exposure.
Nath. had been over and after seeing Dr. Arnold and Mr.
Anstey, left a letter for me which damped all my prospects. However, nothing attempted nothing done. I
went to the Doctor's house, and after being much pleased
with Mrs. Arnold and interesting her on your behalf, we
were shown into the awful study and entered William on

the Boards.   The Doctor confirmed all I had heard of his
house, Mr. Grenfell's and Mr. Anstey's being perfectly full,
and told me the only Master's house in which he knew of
a vacancy, was that of a foreigner, M. Pons, of whom he
spoke well.   Having ascertained that it was not necessary
to determine for a few days, I went next morning to see
M. Pons', Mr. Grenfell's, and two other Masters' houses,
and could only obtain a conditional promise from Mr.

DR. ARNOLD'S HOUSE, RUGBY.

Grenfell that if he was disappointed of an expected Boarder,
he would receive William.   On Sunday a letter came to
the Doctor saying that the pupil would not come till the
20th of April, quarter day, and by liberal use of Mr. Charles
Lane's name, which is all powerful with Mr. Grenfell, I
persuaded him to receive William and to make accommodation for another by April ; and very much pleased I am
at my success.   There are but ten boys at Mr. Grenfell's
house, about a quarter of a mile from the school, quite in

the country, and everything new and in good style. I
dined with Mr. and Miss Grenfell and the nine boys at
one o'clock, and a better dinner and better served, I never
wish to see. I found Mr. Grenfell, a nephew of Mr. Pascoe
Grenfell, the copper Merchant. He has a sister who would
please you greatly ; and you may be perfectly satisfied that
William will be well taken care of, and happy with them.
I staid at Rugby till he came out of school at a quarter
before five, having passed his examination, but he did not
know where he was placed. More particulars you shall
have when we meet. . . . If not otherwise employed in
your service let Fordham bring my Gig and be at the Light
office at four or a quarter past, on Thursday. . . . I trust
you have gained strength and have not suffered by your
exertion in fitting out your boy. . . . Mr. Grenfell is quite
a young man, mild and gentlemanly, and I heard a very
good report of the only Sixth Form boy in this house. I
have stolen a list of the School in which you will see
many names you know. . . . Dr. Arnold does not in
any case determine for the parents, further than recom-
mending a Master's rather than another Boarding House.
I trust to see a good account of William when I reach
Leytonstone.' . . .

When William Oswell entered Rugby he was within ten
weeks of his fifteenth year—a boy of whom any mother
might well be proud. Tall, lithe and active, his great
strength soon earned him the nickname of ' Muscleman ' ;
and his singular beauty that of ' Handsome Oswell.'

To his Mother.

' RUGBY,
' *February* 23, 1833.

' . . . I am much obliged to you for your offer of milk
for my dogs, but do not let them have it without barley-
meal or some other substance as it makes them thin. . . .
I hope you will have got me another horse by Midsummer.

Do not get one too small. I should like one about fifteen hands high. . . . You say I am much remembered by my friends, for which I thank them. This certainly proves the song of Lord Byron, *Absence makes the heart grow fonder*, for whilst I was at home I am afraid not one even knew that such a being existed as W. Oswell, and I am now afraid they only remember me as a plague of which they are glad to get rid. Nevertheless you can give my love to all of them. . . . Mind you get me a horse if you can. . . .'

Dogs, horses, and Lord Byron were interesting to him to the end of his life.

To his Brother Edward.

' RUGBY,
' *March* 4, 1833.

'. . . I am particularly comfortable here at Rugby sitting in a little study of my own with a capital good fire. In this study I have breakfast and tea. . . . There is not half so much fagging as I thought there would be. I believe I can lick all the house I am at.' . . . Our regular number of half holidays are three in a week. We usually have four, and often five. We have 330 boys here—a pretty tolerable number I consider. We ought to have a good XI at cricket and we have got a very good one indeed by all accounts. There are about thirty fellows with thick wiskers, obliged to shave every morning, which according to my calculation must be a great bore ; they are much older than I have been accustomed to. . . .

Modern Rugby, with larger numbers, would seem to be less favoured in the matter of half holidays and 'thick wiskers.'

To his Mother.

' RUGBY,
' *March* 22, 1833.

'. . . Concerning the Tutor regulation, there is to be no extra charge, and the only thing the Tutors do is to

look over the exercises we do in School and at the same
time to explain our mistakes more minutely to us than
has hitherto been done, as we have had our exercises
merely superficially looked over and the faults marked.   I
on my part think this a good regulation. . . . Tell Uncle
Ben that though I never did Greek Iambics before I came
here, I can do them nearly as well as, and in two exercises
more I shall beat, most of the class.   I believe I am
(without *much* flattery) the best at Latin verses in the
class, and hope soon to be so in Greek.   We either have
Milton or Shakspere to translate into Greek Iambics.   I
am afraid they have made a new rule that every boy must
stay in the class he is placed in a year.   If so I shall not
be put out sooner, but if not I think I stand a fair chance
of being put out at Midsummer. . . .'

The aptitude for Greek and Latin versification rapidly
developed, and before he left Rugby he had attained to
such facility that his assistance was in continual demand,
and he gladly gave it in exchange for a stipulated period
of tickling on the face with a feather.   In later years
nothing soothed him more than this when he was worried
or in pain.

To his Mother.

‘ RUGBY,
‘ *April* 10, 1833.

‘ We had our Speeches to-day, *i.e.*, they were recited
before a congregation formed out of the lower orders of
Rugby society.   I enclose you a card of the Speeches,
thinking you may like to see it. You will notice Vaughan’s*
name twice on it ; he is monstrous cute, and besides the
prizes marked for him in the list, has obtained another
which being a minor prize he did not recite publicly.
Those on the list are two of the highest he could possibly

* The late Rev. C. J. Vaughan, D.D., Master of the Temple
and Dean of Llandaff.

obtain. He is only sixteen ! ! . . . Much heavier men ride across country in this part of the world than Uncle Ben ; why, I see farmers out hunting weighing upwards of 16 or 17 stone ! You ask whether Hackney would be a good school for Teddy, or not. I think *not,* for though it is excellent perhaps in some points, yet in others it is to be condemned. One of the bad points is that it is next to an impossibility for a boy who wants to study to do it, for there is a continual hum of voices which although I could learn in, being accustomed to it, Teddy, being used to the quiet of a small private school, I do not think would be able. That is the advantage of Rugby, each form has a different school and a separate master, who devotes his entire time to the good of the boys in his form. . . .'

Hunting had been the boy's chief delight since he was old enough to sit a pony. When at home he rode regularly to hounds with his Uncle Ben, whose pride in the pluck and daring of his gallant young nephew knew no bounds.

It will be noticed that Mrs. Oswell asks the advice of her son, not yet fifteen years old, on so important a matter as the sending of his brother to school ; and in this instance she acted on it. This was in keeping with her invariable attitude to him. In those days of rigid parental control and consequent filial reserve, she treated her boys as reasonable responsible beings, and without losing her authority over them, gave them the freest rein, and was repaid by their obedience, chivalrous devotion, and entire confidence, even as to their most serious love affairs !

To his Mother.

' Rugby,
' *September* 4, 1833.

'. . . . If not too much trouble would you be kind enough to send me a workbox for our housekeeper as a little present. She will not accept money. Let it be a

good one and rather a handsome one, as she is a great deal
above the common level of housekeepers. . . . In your
next letter will you look at my bills and see whether there
was any money for " Glazier," as they have called upon
me for 4s. 6d. for breaking windows. . . . Rugby is not
so wanting of boys as it was supposed it would have been
after Midsummer; we have 50 new ones and are only
minus 20.   We number at this present time 310-315.
Pretty tolerable! considering that when Arnold took the
school there were only 135. . . '

It is characteristic of him that the workbox was to be
'a good one and rather a handsome one.' The glazier
item is certainly equally so ; and one recognises with pleasure the pride of the boy in his Master.

In after years he used often to say that many of his
schoolfellows had never spoken to Arnold, and that to
many more he was not personally attractive, but that there
was not a boy in the school in whom he failed to inspire
confidence and an aggressive pride as regarded outsiders,
a quality far more remarkable and far more to be desired
than mere popularity.

Mrs. Oswell to her Son William.

                                     ' LEYTONSTONE,
                                       ' *March* 7, 1834.
' MY DEAREST WILLIAM,
         ' As you say I cannot write too often, I sit down.
Your last was *particularly* welcome to me as I began to
feel very anxious for a letter, but I promise you I will not
be very exorbitant or expect mine punctually replied to
by you.   Be assured however yours are always acceptable,
the oftener the better and the more they tell me of yourself the better. . .   The agreement about your allowance
I do not forget, but you must promise me to keep an
account book ; I do not mean for my inspection, but you
are now growing *an old gentleman* and it is of great use to

                                          4—2

know the value of money and articles. This you, I dare
say, think is very *prosy* of me, but sometimes I must put
in a little *good advice*, though I do not mean to say you
are extravagant, particularly in clothes ! . . .

'Accept my best love, my dearest boy, and
'Believe me,
'Your ever affectionate Mother and Friend.'

That he gave the required promise and punctiliously
kept the account-book, his invariable deference to his
mother's wishes leaves no room for doubt; but it may
be safely asserted he never kept another; and it is to be
feared that the only value he ever learnt that money
possessed was to buy 'articles' for someone else, to lend,
and to give away.

Mrs. Oswell to her Son William (just before his Confirmation).

'MY DEAREST WILLIAM,   '*May* 26, 1834.
'. . . That the Almighty may bless, direct and
guide you is my constant prayer. I shall be very glad to
hear from you, but will not press it if you are engaged.
There is one thing I should particularly recommend you
to read, which is the Baptismal Service. I remember
Uncle William recommended dear Emily to do so, as
one of the best preparations for Confirmation; and she
you know was a sweet pattern for us all. I cannot help
hoping sometimes she may be permitted to look down
upon us; and if her happiness can be added to by any
earthly circumstance, it will rejoice her to witness your
taking on yourself what was promised for you at your
Baptism; for she so tenderly loved you that your eternal
welfare was her affectionate desire even at the last. . . .
A letter from Teddy tells me of your having gained a
French Class. It always cheers me to hear good tidings,
and particularly of you my dearest boy. . . I wish this
was better worth your reading, but such as it is accept it
with much love from   'Your affectionate Mother.'

W. Cotton Oswell to his Mother.

' RUGBY,
' *June* 6, 1834.

' . . . The Rugby XI play the Arden on Friday week, and a tolerable good dinner is given after as a kind of solace to the beaten party and as a rejoicing to the victors. Arnold has made a new plan about going home ; all of us are to post, but very luckily I have taken my place by the *Independent* and won't be hoaxed into changing it. . . One of my study companions leaves me next half which is rather a good thing in some respects, but bad in others as I shall have to teach the other all the signs and symbols, which this one, although his head is none of the most retentive, has learnt to such perfection that it is hardly necessary to speak one word, for any ordinary purpose, during a day. On the other hand he understands no more Greek than a donkey, not having yet mounted the *Arduous steep* of the second form. Of this language he is so totally ignorant, that he is incapable even of acting as my *under* Lexicon researcher, which is most grievous, as that office necessarily devolves in nearly all its weight on me, and although I do not admire the plan of fagging, yet nevertheless two or three words are usually obliged to be searched for in each lesson if I deign to look at it. But really I sometimes take the trouble, remember for *your* sake, to answer a question now and then, or rather to make a tolerable guess at it, and have so far worked up that I believe I am pretty well sure of raising myself a couple of forms. If you remember I have already been put up in French, so that of course I shall not be put up again, as that only belongs to those who superabound in wisdom—pshaw !—*fagging* I mean. There are not above four *clever* fellows in the School. That one who got the Merton Scholarship is only tolerable.

One wonders what were 'all the signs and symbols which this one has learnt to such perfection,' and what was the advantage to a bright and talkative boy in finding it 'hardly necessary to speak one word for any ordinary purpose during a day.'

A few weeks later he narrowly escaped expulsion. Judge Hughes thus describes the incident:

'We all knew that the school paid a good rent for the fields on the Rugby side of the Avon, where were the bathing places, and assumed that this included the right of netting the river. This was disputed by the owner of the Brownsover bank, and many squabbles and collisions arose between the boys and Mr. Boughton Leigh's watchers and keepers. At last the crisis came when a keeper tried one day to seize the nets and the boys ducked him in the river. Complaint was at once made to Arnold, who appealed to the Sixth to find and give up the names of those concerned, but nothing came of it. So at the next calling over the Doctor appeared with the Squire and the keeper to identify the boys who had ducked the latter. Probably Arnold's power of ruling was never put to so severe a test, for the whole school was against him, and the præpostors of the week—the four Sixth Form boys—instead of stilling the tumult, walked up and down the big school calling out, " S-s-s-ilensce." However, he prevailed, the names were at last called, and as the boys passed out the keeper identified five, who were then and there expelled. After fifty years the names may be safely given—Cox, Price, Torkington, Wynniatt, Peters, cock of the school, and another I have forgotten, unless it was Gaisford, son of the Dean of Christchurch—names treasured as those of heroes for following generations! A tremor ran through the school as Oswell, handsomest and most renowned of athletes, passed out; but he was not recognised.'

We are indebted, too, to Judge Hughes for the following charming description of his school-fellow hero:

' Though we small boys were proud in a way of Stanley
and Vaughan, of Clough and Burbidge, and other scholars
and poets, we looked on them more as providential pro-
viders of extra half holidays than with the enthusiasm of
hero-worship. This we reserved for the Kings of the
Close, round whom clustered legends of personal en-
counters with drovers at the monthly cattle fairs (which
were held in High Street and came right up to the school
gates, tempting curious yokels to trespass on the sacred
precincts), or the navvies who were laying down the first
line of the London and North Western Railway, or the
gamekeepers of a neighbouring squire with whom the
school was in a state of open war, over the right of fishing
in the Avon. I did not myself share in this rather in-
discriminate enthusiasm, for the Kings of the Close were
as a rule a rough and hard set of taskmasters, who fagged
us for whole afternoons and were much too ready with
the cane.

' But for this very reason I had all the more to bestow
on the one who, to my boyish imagination, stood out from
the rest as Hector from the rest of the Trojan Princes :
and this hero was William Oswell. It was not from any
personal knowledge of, or contact with him, for we were
at different boarding-houses, and at opposite ends of the
school ; and I doubt whether he ever spoke to me in his
life, though I often shared his kindly nod and smile when
we met in the close or quadrangle. It was the rare mixture
of kindliness and gentleness with marvellous strength,
activity and fearlessness which made him *facile princeps*
among his contemporaries. I don't believe he ever struck
a small boy or even spoke to one in anger. And so there
was no drawback to the enthusiasm with which one
watched him leading a charge at football, or bowling in a
big side match, or jumping two or three pegs higher on
the gallows than any other boy. He *cleared* eighteen feet
nine inches in Clifton brook, which means, as you know,
twenty feet from take-off to landing. No doubt his good

looks added to the fascination ; he stood six feet high in his stockings when he left school, at eighteen, but did not look his height from the perfection of his figure—broad in shoulders, thin in flank, and so well developed that he was called " The Muscleman."

' I will give one instance of his early prowess in athletics. I do not know what the record has been in late years, but in my time Parr was the only man who was ever known to have thrown a cricket-ball a hundred yards both ways.

THE PLAYING FIELDS, RUGBY.

No record was kept here, but this I saw Oswell do : From a group of boys at a wicket on Little Side ground as it then was, he threw a cricket ball *over*, as I believe, or at any rate *through*, the great elms (which were then standing in a close row at right angles to the school buildings) into the Doctor's garden, for there it was picked up. Measure it how you will, that throw must have been considerably over a hundred yards. He left a great blank in the school life when he left.

W. Cotton Oswell to his Aunt Louisa Cotton.
' RUGBY,
' *April* 20, 1835.

' . . . . You had a great share of my late thoughts. I have sat nearly half an hour since writing the last half-sheet. For I being, like a fool as I am, rather dull, was thinking of those pleasant days which by your kindness we spent at Southend, and was wondering whether such days would ever return, not at Southend in particular, but any-where. I decided not. . . . . They were the most happy days I remember, though perhaps you consider I am gay enough in general. . . . . My only object in writing this was to ask you how my mother is, for she does not write as if in good spirits.' . . .

This letter was written at the beginning of a curious restlessness and depression which took possession of the boy at this time. Not much more than two years had passed since he wrote to his mother that one of the boys was ' much older than I have been accustomed to,' and now he felt older than the oldest. He was eager to leave school and begin the career to which his inclination strongly disposed him—that of a soldier.

As a child he had as eagerly desired to be a sailor, but the mother's heart was still bleeding from the loss of four children, and she could not make up her mind to part with either of the two left, least of all with ' her dearest boy '; and he was obliged to solace himself with Marryat's or Fenimore Cooper's novels, which he read till he knew them almost by heart. Now, however, she considered it would be selfish to thwart his wish, and long and anxious were the conversations she had with her brothers, on the receipt of each fresh letter from him.

To her Son William.

' MY DEAREST BOY,   ' *June* 4, 1835.

' Our letters crossed on the road. I wish mine may have been as welcome to you, as yours was to me. . . . .

You say you should like not to remain another half at Rugby. I cannot tell you how anxiously I am looking forward to the prospect of some plan being settled that will please you, my dear boy, and be likely to be eligible. I think of you night and day. I know uncle William's wish was that there should be some prospect of employment before you left, and that you should have some time between leaving and entering upon it, that you might enjoy yourself either by Land or Water, but remember dear William you have too affectionate a mother to keep you on even a *quarter*, unless it was agreeable to you, or you could reconcile yourself to it. I sincerely hope some plan will be thought of before we meet. Uncle William is much interested about you and is much pleased at the standing you have gained. He does not object to the Army, but then it must be the Indian, and how far you would like that, my dear boy, will require your consideration. It shall be my constant desire to promote every wish of yours that lies in my power.

' Many things shortly may turn up that you may prefer ; I own I am disappointed that they have not done so already, but I will hope it is for the best. Do not be discouraged, you have many kind friends, together with health, strength and good abilities for anything you can undertake. . . . .

   ' With my very best wishes,
     ' Believe me, my dear boy,
    ' Your ever affectionate Mother and Friend.'

In quite a different strain is the following letter. The postscript happily illustrates her confidence in her son and the serenity of her mind in trouble :

           ' *July* 11, 1835.
' MY DEAR WILLIAM,
   ' Perhaps I ought to have had a blackedged sheet of paper as you have lost an old, faithful friend. On

Saturday night the 6th inst — Dash Esq departed this life without, we hope, much suffering. Thomas found him on the mat at the back door in the morning; he lay in state on Sunday, and on Monday a decent funeral was bestowed on him. Fordham preceded, and dug his grave under the willow; Thomas bore his remains, and young Frank acted as Chief Mourner; Aunt Louisa and I followed at a respectful distance. Poor fellow, this hot weather would have tried him very much. He had not been up-stairs for three days, though the evening before he appeared much as usual. . . . I have not erected any monument over him. A few Latin or English verses must be composed. . . .

'Believe me, my dearest William,
'Your affectionate Mother.

' P.S.—I do not like you should not know that Brassey and Lier have failed. Happily I have not lost much. It has vexed me a little, but will not be of much consequence. I will tell you more another time. I thought you might see it in the paper. My dividends will soon be due again, and it will make but little difference to us.'

He left Rugby at the end of the Summer Term 1835, and after a few days at home, joined his uncle William at Tunbridge Wells.

William Cotton to his Sister Mrs. Oswell.

'TUNBRIDGE WELLS,
'*July* 27, 1835.

' We were very glad to see William on Saturday who arrived in good time for our early dinner and took a ride with us in the evening. I have this morning had an hour's conversation with him on his future arrangements. Setting aside the ordinary occupation of young men in business in copying letters and sitting at a desk, which I should not think desirable for him, I have endeavoured to explain the course which I should think it sensible of him to take, to acquire commercial knowledge, first at a foreign University, and then in a foreign Counting House. He did not appear inclined to Commercial occupation, and said he should much prefer going into the Indian Army. I put it to him that if not disposed to Commercial engagements, he might direct his attention to a manufacturing or mechanical business or that of a Civil Engineer. To this he objected his want of mathematical knowledge and his disinclination to the study. We talked over the English Army—the difficulty and expense of obtaining promotion, and the want of intellectual occupation for those who have not interest or money to obtain high stations. I offered to make some enquiry about the Artillery at Woolwich, but he said he should prefer a cavalry appointment in India. We had some talk about the Sea Service, and should any serious obstacle occur to his going to India or to his occupation here, I think it might be deserving of consideration if he had not better make a few voyages to India, and then pursue the sailor's life if any opening occurred ; or settle in England in some occupation connected with shipping, as by that time they may have again become profitable. There are one or two objections to this arrangement : that the Sea Service is not, and will not be, what it has hitherto been—a respectable and Gentlemanly profession ; and we may entertain some doubt if the Continuation of sea voyages and sea provisions, would ultimately suit him. There are, I think many things to reconcile us to his going to India : the probability that the occupation, the climate and the liberal provision for his comfort will suit him, and that his attachment to horses and active exertions and pursuits will be supplied, with rational occupation. In the Indian Army he will have inducements to improve his mind and to qualify himself for situations of honour and usefulness. And on the whole, without being very decided in my opinion, I think the bearing of my mind is in favour of

the course his own inclination points to. All this however requires more consideration; the choice between a
commercial life and a profession should not be hastily
made. The selection of either one or the other of the
different professional and commercial occupations is a
great difficulty. Nine times out of ten the selection is
made from peculiar opportunities which do not at present
guide us. Under all the circumstances of health and
inclination, should India be the scene of his occupation
the difference between a civil appointment and a military
and if the former is obtainable should be well considered.
My wife desires her love and a kiss to little A. B. C. . .'*

A month later he fulfilled a promise made long before.
Starting from his house at Leytonstone in his own carriage,
and travelling slowly, he took his nephew to all the principal ports and manufacturing centres of England. They
remained at each town until they had seen and digested
everything it had to show. William Cotton's position
gave him the *entrée* everywhere, and his commercial and
mechanical genius made him a most admirable guide;
so that his nephew laid in a solid stock of information
during this expedition which lasted him his life.

William Cotton to Mrs. Oswell.   ' 1835.

'. . . William will give you an account of our journey,
of that therefore I shall say nothing. We have been perfectly happy and comfortable together, and there has been
every inclination on the part of your boy to make himself
useful and agreeable to the old fellow. We have seen
much, as I was anxious not to miss any opportunity to lay
in a store for pleasant and useful reflection. We have
returned rarely burnt but better in health and substance.
The air and exertion have agreed with William, and I
hope you will think him looking well. We had not much

---

* His youngest son.

conversation on his future plans, except that from his observations he does not like the idea of any business or manufacture, and he told me to-day that his opinion was the same as when at Tonbridge. I am confirmed in my opinion that a sedentary life will not suit him. I should have preferred the civil to the military service in India, but if a son of my own had taken a fancy to a military life, I should say the military service in India is the best. With every disposition to assist you, I feel a hesitation and difficulty in advising, but considering all the circumstances, if William was my son, I should follow up the bent of his inclination and accept a cavalry cadetship for him in India.'

Finding the boy's heart was set upon the Indian Army, and that their brother William, on whose judgment they placed great reliance, was disposed to favour the idea, Mrs. Oswell and Benjamin Cotton offered no further opposition, though they both hoped and believed circumstances might arise that would induce him to remain in England. It was therefore a surprise, and not altogether a pleasant one, when their brother John, who was a director of the East India Company, without previously consulting them, obtained and placed at his disposal the offer of a writership:

John Cotton to W. Cotton Oswell.

'ORIENTAL CLUB,
'*Nov.* 23, 1835.

'I am very anxious, and so I may say are all your friends, that you should well consider the option you now have of going out to India in the Civil Service rather than in the Military, and not injure or defeat your future prospects in Life by a hasty decision. I have therefore not had any communication with Mr. Ellice on the subject of his kind offer, but will let the matter remain over till I return to Town in next week. There is not, I am sure, anyone at all acquainted with the two Services in India, who would not at once give you all, and everyone, the same advice, and say that you would not be in India a week before you would deeply regret the choice you made of the Military in preference to the Civil.   Do let me therefore strongly recommend you to submit to the judgment and experience of others in this instance.   The discipline of the College at Haylebury is nothing to what you are to expect in the Military line of the Service, and really my opinion is that if you were to go there you would easily get out in two terms, that is one year.   But I wish you now very seriously to weigh this Matter in your Mind and then to give me your determination in writing that there may be no mistake ; and be assured that I will then do all I can to further your views and wishes.   If you go to Haylebury your Mother will have you so much longer near her, and you will then, I trust, before you leave, have the happiness of seeing her in much stronger health than she is at present.'

The following day brought him a letter on the same subject from Benjamin Cotton's colleague at the Trinity House :

'Light Office,
'*Nov.* 24, 1835.

' . . . The intelligence I heard yesterday concerning the offered appointment for India, has brought to my mind a short conversation we had a little time since in which you expressed a strong objection to the Civil Service.   However, as there had not been a Writership then placed at your disposal, you could not so deeply have considered the subject as is now required for you to do, both in duty to yourself and relatives ; if that can be said to require deep consideration, the advantages of which are notorious.   Perhaps my dear friend you will say, "What the Deuce is it to *you* where or how I go ?" But surely we are all bound to assist each other with any advice or suggestion which either the circumstance of more general experience has given, or where we have particular information. To your family I have considerable obligations, and it is in few cases only that the opportunity offers of shewing in what estimation such kindness is felt. These are my excuses for venturing to say a few words. I will not fancy to myself that I can say anything that others have not said before and better, altho' I much fear, at present, with little success. My dear William Oswell, this must be because you, having set your mind on one object, will not allow it so to expand as to admit even the consideration of any other. But do so my dear Friend, and it cannot lead you to any decision but the one which will give such deep satisfaction to your beloved and excellent Mother, and your very numerous friends. A steady residence of one year at College, and your work is over. You arrive in India with an appointment which in a very short time gives a competent income, and in result a handsome independence; your hours of business and recreation being almost at your own disposal. In the Army how different! Income small in comparison, and progressing with tardy steps; the hours of drill occupy the best part of the day for out of door exercise, and the controul under which juniors are placed, and the submission required, are very irksome and burdensome to most young men. Look also at the difference should ill health require you to retire early, or even to visit Europe. All this you must surely know, and have but to admit into your consideration that you may be led to the better choice. Pray consider this note as one of friendship, and do not look upon it as or impute it to uncalled for interference. Offer my bounden respects to Mrs. Oswell, whose journey I hope has not been one of much fatigue, and

    ' Ever believe me to be,

       ' Your sincere friend and earnest well-wisher,

          ' PHILIP SMITH DUVAL.'

At first William Oswell was inclined to resent what he not unnaturally regarded as a species of coercion, but ultimately, after careful and intelligent consideration, he yielded to the arguments advanced in these two letters, and announced his readiness to forego his cherished project of the Indian Army in favour of the Civil Service. It was arranged he should go to Haileybury, then the Training College for the Company's Service, in the following January. Meanwhile, as the authorities required references from his last school, he wrote to Dr. Arnold, who forwarded them without delay :

'Fox How,
'*December* 21, 1835.

'Mr. Oswell was for some time at Rugby School under my care, and his general conduct was regular and gentlemanly. 'T. ARNOLD,
'*Headmaster of Rugby School.*

'Mr. W. Oswell was with me at Rugby from February 1833 to July 1835, in the course of the time he passed through the Shell, the Lower Fifth, the Middle Fifth and Upper Fifth, Forms of the School. From the masters of these forms I constantly received creditable reports of his progress in the Greek and Latin Classics, and Modern History. Previous to his leaving the School he had read Thucydides, Demosthenes, Sophocles and Æschylus, Livy and Horace and Cicero's Orations. He was a very fair French Scholar and had made some progress in Euclid and Algebra. His compositions were spirited and indicated a good deal of general knowledge. Of his conduct and character I have already expressed my opinion. *He is capable of much.*'

His house-master, Mr. Grenfell, appended a few lines :

'To the above testimonials I am happy to add that Mr. W. C. Oswell boarded in my house during his stay at

Rugby, and that I have every reason to speak highly of his general conduct, and of his attention to the work of the school.'

In January, 1836, he passed into Haileybury, and thus modestly acknowledges his mother's congratulations :

'HAILEYBURY COLLEGE,
'*Jan.* 27, 1836.

' There was not one single man plucked passing inwards, so that it would have been a terrible thing to have been the *only* one.   But I am much afraid (and in saying this I really mean it) that I shall find it a very different thing passing out again.   If I am plucked I suppose I may still have a chance of going out in the Military.   But I am croaking before my time, so I am, we will therefore drop that subject and hope for the best.'

To his Mother.

'HAILEYBURY COLLEGE,
'*Feb.* 9, 1836.

' I have had a most terrible pain in my face. . . . It quite paralysed my jaw for the time it lasted.   It came on about four and lasted till seven. . . . .   I find Sanscrit pretty tough ; it has eight declensions, and seventy-two cases in each—rather pleasant ! and besides this a very hard character, the vowels mostly being put before the consonants and sounded after.   Persian is easy enough.'

He was all his life subject to this curious pain in the face, or rather jaw, when fever was on him, and relief could only be obtained by the inhalation of chloroform.

It certainly indicates a remarkable force of character and strength of will in the boy, who, having set his heart on one profession, was able not only to turn his attention to another, but by concentrating all his energies and ability

upon it to obtain in eleven months such a report and testimonial as follows :—

November, 1836.

Classics	Great Progress.	Prize.
Mathematics ...	Some Progress.	
Political Economy ...	Good Progress.	
Law...	Good Progress.	
Sanscrit	Great Progress.	Third in year.
Persian	Great Progress.	Fourth in year.

' HAILEYBURY,
'*Dec.* 6, 1836.

' We, the Principal and Professors of the East India
College, do hereby testify that William Cotton Oswell
entered College, January, 1836, . . . has resided therein
two terms . . . and has also attended the Public Ex-
aminations of May, 1836, and of December, 1836, when he
obtained a Prize in Classics, and was highly distinguished
in other Departments.   The College Council, in consideration of his Industry, Proficiency and Conduct, place him
in the First Class of merit, and assign him the rank of
Second on the List of Students now leaving College for
the Presidency of Fort St. George. . . . .

' (Signed) J. H. BATTEN,
'*Principal.*'

The next five months he spent in visiting all his friends
and relations.   His approaching departure accentuated his
extreme popularity ; and the consciousness that his future
was settled to the general satisfaction, increased his natural
flow of high spirits.   His mother was not behindhand in
speeding his parting, and up to the very day of his leaving
home, September 14th, 1837, assumed a cheerfulness and
contentment she was very far from feeling.   Her great
unselfishness, however, enabled her to deceive completely
even those who knew her best.   Her sister Louisa wrote

5—2

strongly on the subject, pointing out that she might justifiably have placed her influence in the scale against William's going out of England, having regard to her loneliness and delicate health.

She took the interference meekly and replied with wonderful gentleness:

' You said in your letter, my dear Louisa, you wondered how I could have made up my mind to William's going, and that you did not think I was justified in so doing. I have by many heavy afflictions been so called upon to sacrifice selfish feeling, that though I may bitterly feel *afterwards*, yet my *present* feelings are completely set aside, when my dear Children's interest is in the case, or duty calls on me to resign what I consider most to my happiness. I do not say this to boast of my own resignation, but I have been brought to it by heavy dispensations. Listen to me and see how matters have now brought me to this painful thought that a few months must soon separate me from my dearest boy. I could almost say my best-beloved. When he came from Rugby, and the Indian Army was thought of, he having expressed an inclination for a military life, Benjamin's remark was that *if* he did not like it after a year or two, he could but come back again, and as a young man could not in these times get employment in the Country till one or two and twenty, he might, he thought, be more inclined to settle on his return. Our brother William likewise advised me to rest and consider the thing settled for a few months. The first time I heard of any civil appointment being thought of was when calling on Mrs. Dickenson, at Brighton, and Mrs. D. said John was negociating for one for me. I must say I was a little surprised as he never said a word to me. I felt in a grea hurry to get home. When I did, I found W. had had two letters on the subject. Brother W. advised the plan of his going to Haileybury as a manner of passing two years to advantage. I trust an overruling Providence has ordered all for his good, but my hopes were certainly kept up that other employment might be found without his going so far away.   I do not even recollect either of my brothers ever proposing *anything* to me, except Benjamin's thinking of a Solicitor's office.   But when I named the Law to brother W. his remark was, " I would not confine William to the desk : and what hopes have you afterwards of his being taken into partnership ?   It would be different if he had a Father or relative in the Law.   And as to a Barrister, it requires great interest and talent (the latter *I* am sure dear William has).   I intend to bring Harry* up to it."   But he seemed not to think of it for my William. I particularly wish this burned directly you have read it, and that my expressions of disappointment may not be repeated.   I am fully satisfied that my family have been extremely kind and affectionate towards me, and that I have, at times, given them great uneasiness and anxiety. I am sure my trials are sent me for my good, and my greatest wish is to bear them as a Christian ought, know-ing that there is a *rest* in store, *already purchased* by Him who laid down His life for us.'

* The late Lord Justice of Appeal.

CHAPTER III.

INDIA.

1837–1844. AGE 19–26.

Intelligent interest in new surroundings—Medical studies—
Brahman village—Granite carvings—A moonlight festival—South Arcot; Mr. and Mrs. Ashton and Brooke
Cunliffe—'The *beau-idéal* of a civilian'—Two feats of
arms—A typical Indian day—Pig-sticking—The straits
of £650 income—A bachelor's den—Bison-stalking at
Cuddalore—A cousin's testimonial—Assessment of Shevaroy Hills—'Doing Adam'—The Gates of Somnauth—
A bear-hunt—'The workings of an anxious old mother'
—Hill and low-country tigers—The Todas—The Purdey
gun—Fever—Ordered to Cape—'I love a hill'—Picturesque sport—Indian gipsies—Lord Ellenborough as
Governor-General.

THE next seven years William Oswell passed in India,
working hard and heartily enjoying his life and surround-
ings.   He found ample scope for his athletic and sporting
proclivities in hunting, cricket, racquets, boxing, pig-
sticking and shooting, while his natural aptitude for language enabled him to acquire so complete a mastery of
Tamil that he discharged his public business without the
aid of an interpreter—a very rare accomplishment in those
days.   This, and the possession of a vigorous intelligence,
led him to converse with the natives, who, attracted by
his courtesy and the evidently sincere interest he displayed, talked freely of their manners, customs, history and

religions. He supplemented the knowledge thus gained
by reading all the books he could obtain dealing with the
country and people, and to this source may probably be
traced the fascination ethnology had for him throughout
his life.

In another direction, also, his active mind found employment. When his work first took him up-country he
was forcibly struck by the great mortality among the
natives from trivial diseases, and the amount of unneces-
sary suffering they endured. There were, of course, no
doctors away from the towns, and it occurred to him that
a very moderate acquaintance with medicine and surgery
would enable him to be of incalculable service. Accordingly he bought the leading works in every branch of
the subject, and by close and constant application made
their contents his own. The study, begun from motives
of humanity, became a source of profound interest and
delight to him, and throughout his stay in India and his
subsequent wanderings in Europe, Africa and South
America, he had hundreds of opportunities of turning it
to practical account. He never lost a chance of profiting
by the experience of the medical men with whom he was
brought into contact, and he met the kindest readiness to
assist him on all hands.

His letters at this time were almost exclusively to his
own family. They are uniformly cheerful in tone, and·if
they contain any allusion at all to his troubles, misfortunes
and illnesses, it is of the slightest nature, and generally
after they are over. When at home, within easy reach of
his mother, he had been accustomed to open his inner-
most soul to her, and to her alone ; but now that he was
separated from her by many thousands of miles, he deliberately denied himself the comfort of her sympathy. He
knew that her outward brightness covered a broken heart,
and, unselfish as herself, he would not add to her anxieties
by describing his ; he had pity on her, for the hand of the
Lord had touched her.

' MADRAS,
  ' *September* 14, 1837.

' DEAREST MOTHER,

'. . . Here I am in this land of India. . . . We started on the 10th June and anchored in the Madras Roads on the 13th of September, thus making our voyage in three months and three days, not a bad one under any circumstances, but a most excellent one under ours. . . . The *Seringapatam* is a beautiful ship to look at, a fast sailer, and a capital sea-boat. She behaved right well in a very heavy gale which we had off the Cape. One night I think I shall never forget. It had been blowing very hard and the sea was running high, when all of a sudden the wind lulled, and it became blacker and darker than ever, while at each masthead and at the main yardarm a small blue phosphorescent light was burning. As suddenly as it had lulled, the wind again rose, and during that night it blew tremendously. . . . Write me a particular account of *everyone*.'

To Miss Louisa Cotton.

' MADRAS,
  ' *Feb.* 18, 1838.

' I have explored some very pretty villages, and old out of the way places, that not half a dozen people in Madras know of. About a week ago I went to a village inhabited solely by Brahmans. It is situated in a very uncultivated-looking plain, and is in truth a perfect oasis in a desert. I had passed it many times before, and never thought of its existence, it lies so far back, completely hidden by high avenues of cocoa-nut trees and thick underwood. It is built as nearly all the villages in India are, in a square, that is the houses are all erected round a large tank. There are some very odd pagodas and shrines belonging to it, supposed to be many hundreds of years old, and the most extraordinary part of it is that all the temple work is

A MOST COMPLETE INDIAN SCENE.

of solid granite. Now there is no granite in India within
four or five hundred miles of this, and even that, I believe,
in no great quantities, and did you but know the difficulty
of carriage all over India, you would indeed wonder at the
arduousness of the undertaking. The supporting pillars
are one solid mass of this stone, and, in common with the
rest of the building, beautifully carved with all kinds of
images and devices. The art of carving on granite is, I
understand, now totally lost. The other night, as I was
riding out, I by chance came upon a large body of natives
celebrating one of their feasts. The spot fixed upon was
a vast tank in the neighbourhood of Madras, surrounded
by tall rows of cocoanut-trees. The moon was just up,
and was throwing a most beautiful mellowed light over
the whole scene. Different kinds of native fireworks would
occasionally light up some dark nook or corner into which
the light of the moon did not penetrate. A barge was
being towed round the tank to the music of gongs and
colorie horns. Discordant as it generally is, in this
instance it sounded well enough. On it were all the
dancing girls of the neighbouring pagoda, forming altogether a most complete Indian scene. . . . To my Mother
of course all my letters belong, she will see them all and
know that the matter contained is hers more than anybody else's, although not directed to her. . . . If she does
not fully understand this, and I did not feel that all letters
I send home are *hers*, I should be very unhappy. Uncle
Ben is the next whom I shall write to and then again to
my *dear* Mother. God bless her! I am sure my letters
can be coveted by none, so that it matters but little to
whom I address them. Tell the dear Lady that I am going
to send her home some moon-creeper seeds for her garden.
Give my very best love to her, Teddy and Uncle Ben.'

Read in the light of his later life, this letter is singularly
suggestive. The exploring instinct, the geological knowledge, the quick appreciation of the picturesque, and,

lastly, the loyal devotion to his mother, characteristics of the boy of nineteen, were equally the characteristics of the man of seventy-five.

'I am appointed,' he writes on January 10, 1839, 'to do duty with the principal collector of the Southern Division of Arcot—William Ashton.'

WILLIAM ASHTON.

Mr. Ashton already had one assistant—Brooke Cunliffe—an ardent sportsman, and a first-rate cricketer and racquet-player. Similarity of tastes first united the young men, and very early in the three years they were together a warm affection sprang up between them. Fifty-six years later Mr. Cunliffe writes:

'My dear friend was then a well-grown, powerful young man, six feet in height with an unusually handsome, intelligent face. He was an excellent horseman but knew little about shooting, and was by myself introduced to that sport in which he was afterwards to be so famous, and in which he had so often to trust his life to his own ready eye and hand and indomitable courage. . . . Coursing the Indian fox with Affghan greyhounds was one of our favourite amusements, and this entailed some fast work and often over bad ground. He was always quite to the front. . . . He was the *beau-idéal* of what an Indian Civilian should be—a gentleman born, a public school-boy, of fine physique, of generous feelings, kind and considerate, gifted with good sense and intelligence and bearing himself like an English gentleman. These are the qualities which, in greater degree than talents, or genius, attract the natives of India and secure their goodwill and co-operation. . . . He became endeared to many by his generous disposition, tenderness for others, and his modesty and self effacement.'

Another old friend of these early days, General E. O. Leggatt, writes of him:

'He was a very powerful and active man and could jump over a high-backed chair with only a quick step or

THREW HIM DOWN INTO THE PADDY-FIELD WITH A
TREMENDOUS SPLASH.

two before jumping. He once placed himself on his back on the floor with his arms stretched out beyond his head, made me stand on his open hands and lifted me straight up without bending his arms at all, to the surprise of all in the room. Of course I was not a heavy weight! One day when we were out snipe-shooting he happened to be walking along a ridge in the paddy-fields, and a big

Mahomedan was coming towards him on the same ridge. The Mahomedan had no idea of yielding one inch to allow him to pass, but evidently expected him to step off into the paddy-field. However, as soon as he was near enough Oswell, who would have made room for anybody, but was not the man to allow himself to be pushed into the mud, passed his gun to the shikarry behind him and getting the Mahomedan by his waist-cloth lifted him up in the air, and threw him down into the paddy-field with a tremendous splash. He was naturally hot-tempered . . . but at the same time one of the kindest-hearted men I ever came across. He was also remarkably handsome. . . .'

Mr. Ashton was as fond and proud of ' my two handsome boys' as if they were his own sons, and they most cordially reciprocated his affection, undeterred by the somewhat bluff overbearing manner which he assumed as a sort of protest and quite vain protection against the possession of the kindest, tenderest heart. His charming wife, highly educated, a capital rider and a graceful, gracious hostess, helped to make his house very attractive to the young assistants. When she returned to England, Oswell writes of her to his mother:

'You will see her I have very little doubt; if you do, love her for my sake, *remember*.' And later: ' God bless her! She has written me a delightful account of the visit you paid her. I hope she gave a good account of your far awa' son—I am sure she would, I only fear it would be *too* good. But you must not believe everything she says; we always speak of the absent in extremes.'

To his Mother.
                                              ' *March* 20, 1840.

'In Ned's last he asks me how I spend an Indian day. Up at half past five—never later than six, or the sun

shines straight upon me, immediately proceed to the
racquet-court and play till half past seven; getting warm,
go home, lie on a sofa and read till nine; bathe in a large
tub for half an hour, delicious! dress; breakfast at about
ten; then to cutcherry, in which I am detained in proportion of course to the work. Some men eat tiffin; I do
not for fear of growing as fat as —— ! I hear by the way
that there is a capital caricature on this subject; make
Teddy send it out. He will perchance pretend he knows
nothing about it. Don't believe him. I'll answer for it
he knows all the picture-shops between Whitechapel and
Hyde Park. I think I did myself. Why shouldn't *he* ?
Want of proper education if he doesn't! Well to return:
Suppose I leave cutcherry at three; read till five; racquets
or riding till half past six, dress again, dinner at half past
seven or eight; bed at ten in a meat safe to defend my
flesh from mosquitoes. So the days roll on with, of course,
occasional interruptions, *e.g.*, I may be in the district,
and then nothing but hunting and shooting (no sport
close to Cuddalore) and instead of racquets, about twice
a week my HOUNDS throw off—two terriers, two curs, two
pugs and a poodle. I have rather exaggerated their breed
I think. Sometimes, however, we get a most excellent
run. I have seen out of a field of eleven, only three or
four anywhere near them. . . .'

To his Brother.

' CUDDALORE,
' *June* 21, 1840.

' . . . What would you give for a good galop with me
after a pig on Friday next ? Read all the descriptions
of the ancient hunts, witness the whole of the runs in
England with the hounds for the next ten years: the
imagination and reality alike fall immeasurably short. A
wild-looking country, a burning scorching sun, three to
four hundred beaters, instead of the sixteen couple of

hounds, a patch of high elephant grass some mile or two
in extent, so high and dense that you can neither see
over it nor into it. "All's ready Sir"—you leave your
tent, mount your nag, and ride forward towards the
ground. The beaters advance in a thickly serried line,
every moving object being carefully removed in the
direction in which you wish the pig to break. You hide
yourself and then *listen*, and that same *listening*, how
exciting! At last, after about an hour's discordant yell-
ing, beating of bush, blowing of horns, etc., you hear the
welcome sound "*Thuray, Thuray, otho punne*" (Sir, Sir,
there are pig) you're in your saddle in a moment and
then hurrah! for the best rider and the fastest horse. . . .
How is the dear old Lady? Give her plenty of kisses
for me.'

When Mrs. Oswell read Uncle Ben and Teddy the
following lively picture of poverty and discomfort on
£650 a year, they must all have laughed to find Willy
the assistant-collector so very like Willy the schoolboy:

'CUDDALORE,
'*Septr.* 18, 1840.

' . . . My pay is now £650 a year. Why it really
looks a tolerable sum . . . but whether it is that I want
the bump of domestic economy, or from some other cause
unknown, it has been, up to this time, living as I do more
uncomfortably than many upon half the sum, barely sufficient. . . . Talk of Indian luxury, what a mistake!
Could you but see my room now you would say, " My dear
boy, I must set things to rights a little." In size it is about
14 × 12. Can I describe the would-be furniture? I'll
try. Lying as I am now on a sofa, at this moment the first
thing that meets my eye is my old ship chest of drawers,
with a small bookcase on the top of them; further to the
right hang some ten or twelve different kinds of coats on a
string. . . . Immediately below them, on the ground, is a

box used for carrying clothes when travelling, two gun
cases, a clothes bag, an empty bottle, and a worn out pair
of racquet shoes.   A little further to the right on the wall
are the symbols of my magisterial authority in the shape
of two cat-o'-nine-tails; a pair of braces, a belt, all on one
nail; a little on, a pair of spurs and two whips ; beyond that
again a rack on which hangs a moor cap and divers kinds
of straw and Manila hats, under which are placed the
washing stand and your little worsted-worked stool.   I
have at last come to my own corner, and am obliged to turn
up my head to see its adornments which consist of two
hairless fox brushes and two pads of the same animal.
Immediately behind my head hangs a favourite racquet.
I would tell you what is on the table if I could, but it is
impossible, three bats and the beautiful slippers you sent
me are the only things distinctly visible.   The rest of the
articles are in admired confusion.   Books, papers, bottles,
blistering ointment, brushes, form part of a very variegated
whole.   *Now* talk of comfort !   I wish Master Teddy
could have been out with me a fortnight ago.   I could have
shewn him a sight worth all the lions of Oxford—five or
six bison, within thirty yards of me snuffing up the air at
my intrusion upon their native haunts, and gazing foolishly
in my face, giving me a famous shot, but unluckily as
they faced me the balls did not strike a mortal part, and
although badly wounded they escaped.   But it was worth
the day's toil to hear them tear through the jungle making
everything yield to their headlong course.   Had I not
heard and seen them I could not have believed them capable of breaking through, in one moment, jungle that had
taken me, crawling on my hands and knees, full two long
hours to overcome. . . .   So poor C. C. is dead ; well,
the divines say we are all to appear in our bodies, but I
hope hers may be changed, for really she would not be
considered a good-looking angel. . . .'

The true sportsman speaks in this account of the bison-hunt. None are killed, but it is ' worth the day's toil to hear them tear through the jungle, making everything yield to their headlong course.' This, as will be noticed, was always his feeling: the habits of the animal, the excitement and incidents of the chase, and the features of the country in which it took place, were the principal attractions, the actual killing the secondary object.

To his Mother.

' IRAWADDY,
'SOUTH ARCOT,
' *Mch.* 17, 1841.

' I am most terribly annoyed just at present in consequence of being ordered to Cuddapah to act as Registrar to my Junior. . . . When I went to Salem the Governor gave me to understand that should the exigencies of the service admit of it, he would bear in mind my wish to remain in the Revenue line; I dislike the Judicial business excessively. But its no use kicking against the pricks, so go I must. . . . Never mind, I shall see more of this world of India. It is a long march in this roadless country—three hundred miles. . . . I do not think you are careful enough of yourself. I hear of your running all over the country visiting the sick. I would not try to prevent you in any of your charitable deeds, and if I would, I could not, but remember that you must take great care of yourself—"special edict"—as John Chinaman would say. We have not gained much in our negociations with the said inhabitants of China. The Barbarians, as they style us, can fight, but can't make treaties. It is not the first time that England has lost herself with pen and paper. . . .

' 19*th March*. Arrived here (Cuddalore) yesterday morning. To prepare for my start for Cuddapah I play a match at cricket this evening. Does Uncle Ben still keep up his name at that game? Really after all, this is not a bad country. Why, the Gentlemen of England don't know what sport is. The knocking over a brace or two of partridges, and a hare or two in a little bit of a plantation, or an unromantic grain field, called by them *sport*, is not to be compared with Indian shooting. The one is confined in extent, the other boundless; the one dull and tame, the other exciting to a degree. You do not know what kind of game you may stumble upon. The other night I was out, it was most splendid moonlight, and the scene was wild enough to please the most ardent lover of Nature in her most rugged state. Everything was so still that to disturb the repose by the crack of my rifle seemed a crying sin, but crack it did, and to some purpose—a fine spotted deer was the victim. . . . Moonlight is the time at which India appears to most advantage . . . .'

Towards the end of July, 1841, Mrs. Oswell had the great pleasure of receiving from the son of her brother John a generous appreciation of her 'best-beloved boy.' The tribute is the more remarkable that Major Cotton was only eight years his cousin's senior. There must surely have been something very unusual in the latter that the smart, quick-tempered soldier not only listened without resentment to the 'long lecture,' but acted on it. At the same time, one cannot help feeling that honours were divided in 'sense, penetration and candour.'

Major John Stedman Cotton to Mrs. Oswell.

'7TH MADRAS CAVALRY,
'ARCOT,
'*April* 20, 1841.

' MY DEAR AUNT,
' Having had the pleasure during the last month of seeing a good deal of William . . . I can honestly say that there are few men's company I would sooner enjoy than his, and, what I certainly did not expect from my previous idea of him, he, without the smallest effort, gained

6—2

golden opinions from every man in the Regiment. He
was very anxious that I should take his portrait for you,
. . . but independently of his face being a very difficult
one naturally to give at all correctly, at present the difficulty is greatly increased by his hair—whiskers, beard and
moustache entirely concealing the outline. . . . He is
very like you. There are certain tones of his voice which
remind me of you inevitably. The eyes, forehead, brow
and junction of the nose, are *your own,* and when he laugh-
ingly tells a joke which he is enjoying, I can fancy you
masquerading in a beard, telling some funny story to or of
Uncle Ben at breakfast. I dare say you have heard he is
considered the best-looking man in the Presidency, but
this would certainly give you a very wrong idea of him
unless it was also added, and the least vain. Never did I
see anyone pay less attention to external adornments, and
he gave me one day a long lecture on *my* vanity or rather
self-sufficiency of manner, and having really a high opinion
of his sense, penetration and candour, it was not without
its effect tho' I was entirely unconscious of possessing in
any offensive degree so common a weakness. . . . Give
my love to *the* uncle. Don't trouble yourself to answer
this if it is the least irksome. At the same time I know
no one from whom a letter could afford me more pleasure
or with whom I should better like to open an occasional
correspondence. God bless you my dear Aunt.'

W. Cotton Oswell to his Brother.

' MUDDANAPULLY (78 miles from Cuddapah),
'CUDDAPAH DISTRICT,
'*September* 19, 1841.

' . . . I am now staying with Ashton at a place mis-
called, I think, the Sanatorium of Cuddapah. . . . It
does not seem to agree with the natives . . . as you will
allow when I tell you that out of eight or nine servants
five are at present laid up with fever. By the way talking

of fever I have been doing a little in that line myself down at Cuddapah some months ago. Horribly knocked up, I was, I can assure you, for about a fortnight! This was the reason that I did not write by the last overland. I'm all right again now. The attack was brought on entirely by my own foolish boyishness. We had three holidays in Court together and I thought so good an opportunity for seeing something of the district and enjoying a little shooting was not to be overlooked. . . . So off I was sharp, twenty miles into the country, with gun, tents and other appurtenances, and after being chained to a desk, nearly without exercise, for four months, was fool enough to be out on foot for the three days from half past four or five in the morning till the same hour in the evening, and this without any thing to eat. Very boyish, you will say, but what length will not the excitement of shooting carry one, or even *hoping* to shoot, for in this case I saw nothing. The *kindness* which I have always received from Ashton has been very great, but his *attention* and *tenderness* to me during the time I was laid up with fever, exceeded anything I could have imagined, and could *not* have been greater. I have received my Mother's picture at last. . . . You may imagine my joy at the arrival of my long-expected treasure. I am getting to like it more and more every day. At first . . . I was disappointed . . . but now it recalls my dearest Mother most forcibly to my external eye. The first march I made was about fifty miles to a place called Gooroocondah in which I was told there was an old palace belonging in former times to one of Tippoo's employés. A palace it was called, but I should much doubt whether you would have used it for a pigsty. I wandered through the zenanah or apartments of the ladies, and was saluted at every step by—don't let your morality blush, restrain your virtuous indignation, my dear Mother—by crowds and swarms of *beetles* and *bats*!! *not* fairy-formed damsels with tinkling anklets, bearing garlands of flowers to enchain my body, as of course they would at sight have done my mind, with their dark glances. . . .'

The 'little in that line' was a terrible struggle between life and death. For eleven days he lay in agonies of pain, burnt up with fever. Nothing passed his lips all the time save occasional sips of tea. Day and night Mr. Ashton nursed him devotedly, unremittingly, until the fever broke.

To his Mother.

'*Nov.* 18, 1841.

. . . I am on my way to one of the *talooks*, or divisions under my supervision, to be on the spot for the better preservation of the peace during a large annual feast which is on the eve of taking place. From the vast concourse of people who assemble at it, and from the supposed difficulty of detection, thefts, etc., etc. are rife. To deter the mass from sinning, summary punishments of convicted persons with the cat-o'-nine-tails are more common and more expedient than in the general administration of our police duties; and as the said corporal punishment cannot be decreed or inflicted except by, and in the presence of, a European Officer, your worthy son is necessarily present. It is my second trip to the same place for the same purpose (my first was two years ago) and it will, I have every reason to believe, be my last, as I am daily expecting to see my name in orders for the Head Assistantship of Salem, which has been promised me; chiefly, I believe, through the kind interference of Mr. Bird. I hope Uncle Ben does not forget me; I can assure him I remember him and all his kindness more and more every day as I get older and see so little of it with others. . . . If he should at any time think of paying me a visit in a balloon, and only want an impetus to set him going, you may tell him that my *talooks* are the best shooting-ground perhaps in the district, and that I can give him licence ! ! to shoot over seventy miles of jungle in which he may find every kind of game from a tomtit to an elephant. Good-bye, God bless you, my dearest Mother.'

To the Same.

'SHEVAROY HILLS,
'*Oct.* 22, 1842.

'. . . I have been up here nearly three weeks having been deputed by the Collector, in consequence of this hilly range being now for the first time brought under Government management, to fix an assessment, and report generally on the produce and inhabitants. Pleasant work enough so far as the climate goes, but, for fear of falling short of what may be expected of me, not, perhaps, so desirable as it otherwise might be. It is my *début* in this particular line and rather an uncommon duty for a Head Assistant to perform, and although not wont to be nervous, I should not like to make a bungle of it. . . . Matters are wearing a more cheerful aspect in all quarters; an honourable and advantageous peace concluded with China, and complete success in the North-West. I say complete, for although the fact of the prisoners being made over to us is not as yet fully substantiated, yet there appears no reason to attach doubt to the reports which state that they are, or are to be, at least, without delay. So you may now sleep in less dread of your son waking one fine morning to find his throat cut. I'll answer for it that your mind has been not altogether free from such thoughts during the late disturbances. Now confess that you believed me at times to be in imminent danger— Afghan horsemen dashing up to my door, and ravaging my peaceful *talooks!* You people at home have no idea of distance. I'm sadly in want of a good ball gun so don't let Mr. Purdey make more delay than may be necessary with the one I asked Uncle Ben to procure me. . . . I brought a most magnificent bison to his knees the other day, and although he escaped with two ounces of lead in him it was worth all the partridge murdering in the world, to see an enormous brute of eighteen hands charging down within five yards of one. . . . I wish you could have seen my attempt at gardening at Dharmapoory this year. You remember my dislike to doing Adam formerly. Well, having nothing else to amuse myself with at my lively quarters, I was obliged to try my hand at it. . . . I have really a good garden, figs, guavas, grapes, etc., etc., in abundance; but my forte lay in the lettuces and other vegetables, of which I intended to plant only a small supply for my own use and was rather astonished, when they came up, to find that there were about enough for a moderate army. . . .'

It will be difficult for his friends of later years to believe that there was ever a time when he disliked ' doing Adam.'

'Dec. 25, 1842.

'MY DEAREST MOTHER,

'Xmas Day—not much like what I remember of Xmas Days at home. My last was spent counting the Treasury of the Chingleput District. This, as it has fallen on a Sunday, is of course exempt from work. . . . I have just had a concourse of natives visiting me as is their custom on this day, and have attempted an explanation of the reason of our keeping it as a great festival; and in consequence of one of their own Gods— Vishnoo—having, according to their belief, become several times incarnate and visited the Earth, have succeeded, I fancy, better in making them have some distant idea of my meaning, than I otherwise should have done. I excited their astonishment not a little by the proposed new Aerial Steam Carriage, a sketch of which I gave them. One old Brahmin declared that in case of our effecting anything of the kind he should take us for *demons,* a doubtful compliment! as that was the *very* method in which their Rakshutahs or Genii were formerly supposed to travel. Steam Carriages however, in addition to my

knowing but little about them, are difficult subjects for
Tamil, and I much fear that my audience were not very
highly edified. . . . The wars are brought to an end as
you will see by the papers. Lord Ellenborough has, by
the common consent, made a goose of himself. He is so
uncommonly fond of proclamations, and his proclamations
are so *uncommonly* foolish, and show so little knowledge
of the people he has to rule over, that I am not surprised
he should be laughed at. His last proclamation is really
ludicrous. In an address to the Princes and Chiefs of
India, the impression forced on your mind is that his
Lordship (though doubtless he never meant anything of
the kind) wishes to make the said Princes, etc., believe
that the expedition and war in Afghanistan was undertaken solely for the recovery of the gates of the temple of
Somnauth, taken away some thousand years ago by one
Mahmood of Ghuznee, and now being brought back as a
trophy and sop to the Hindus, by our troops. He seems
entirely to have forgotten in congratulating the Rulers,
Princes and Potentates of India upon the restoration of
these gates and the defilement of the tomb of Mahmood,
that a great portion of them (the Mussulmans) are de-
scendants and countrymen of that very Mahmood, and
that although the recovery of the gates may be honey to
the Hindus, it must be gall to them. . . . God bless you
all. A merry Xmas and a happy new year.'

'DHARMAPOORY,
'*Feb.* 23, 1843.

'MY DEAREST MOTHER,
'. . . Last Overland I was down in the very heart
of the jungles on the banks of the river Cauvery, trying
for some fishing!—rather an un-Indian-like sport and one
I should never have thought of myself, but a friend who
had come out for a month's *shikar* to my tents, persuaded
me that was excellent diversion, and we accordingly tried
it, but with very little success. The scenery however was

beautiful. . . . The fish which abounds in this river is the *mahseer*, something like the salmon, growing to an enormous size. Lord Ellenborough has, I am happy to say, after proclamationizing without end, seen fit to stop those precious Somnauth Gates short of their intended destination. Someone has, I suppose, at last given him a hint that their restoration would be likely to cause a disturbance. . . . Somewhere about the same time that Master Ned and Edward Oswell were shooting their one hare and one partridge, I was knocking over a bear and a most magnificent Elk. The former gentleman gave me some little fun . . . I wounded him as he was going up a rocky hill and followed him to his den, in which although I could see him by lying, I could not get a vital shot at him, and it would not have done to move much, as bears are skeary animals, as the Pathfinder says, and I was not above two yards from him, and in the mouth of his den.

STIRRED UP WITH A STICK THROUGH THE CHINKS OF THE STONES.

I was obliged actually to have him stirred up with a stick through the chinks of the stones, and the amusing part of the affair was to see the brute trying to decline the compliment, parrying the stick with his paws, until we sharpened the point, when he took courage and made

a decent roar and charge, ending his life very satisfactorily with a ball through his head. By the by are
bear, tiger or cheetah skins any use to you ? If they are,
pray let me know, they are to be had for the taking
here. . . .'

In one of his letters he mentions that when out in tents
in his district, he keeps Sunday as a rest, but finds the
time hang heavy on his hands. His mother, always on
the watch to do anything she could to cheer or help him,
wrote off at once to her son Edward :

' I want to make a small selection of books for Willy ;
my mind is set on sending him a few to take up on
Sundays if not on other days. Do help me. I have seen
him enjoy a Latin hymn, and in your room I saw some
time ago a small book which called him to my mind. I
think if I could send him something of the sort it would
please him. There is a small "Thomas à Kempis" in Latin
that I should like. What do you think of " Palmer's History
of the Church " for one ? There is a small book called " The
Nestorian Christians " we are going to read, (they were
found in Kurdistan). If it is interesting I shall send it. . . .
It makes me a little nervous when I think of dear William,
quite alone, out in tents, though he writes as if he was
quite well : but he must get so unused to Society. If you
have any books you think of that you could send me for
Willy, will you do so ? He wanted to see your examination papers. I do think he must want something to occupy
his mind when quite alone, and if he could revert at
times to what he used to take a pleasure in—his Classics—
and they could be of that sort to raise the mind to substantial things, I should have much satisfaction. A Greek
Testament might, if small, not be amiss. I feel perhaps
you read this and think it all only the workings of an
anxious old mother, but I am not satisfied without endeavouring to do some good.

' When convenient send me Willy's letter. I do not

wish it sent to Uncle, as dear William charged me never to shew his letters. . . .'

With Edward's assistance a number of books were chosen and despatched, and William, to his mother's great delight, read and enjoyed them all, and made a point of referring to or quoting from them in his letters home.

W. Cotton Oswell to his Brother.

'OOTACAMUND,
'NEILGHERRY HILLS,
'*May* 10, 1843.

'. . . Give me the low country for game. One very odd circumstance is worth remarking with regard to the tigers, etc., up here. Although, without any doubt they wander up from the low country, where they are as wicked as you please, immediately upon snuffing the air of the hills, whether it is the cold or not I cannot say, they lose all their ferocity and would allow themselves to be kicked. It would be labour lost to give you any account of these hills and their inhabitants, as you would find them so much better described in any work on India. If you should have spare time for such reading, I think it might interest you, particularly with respect to the aborigines or Todas as they are called, who are a people entirely distinct and separated from the other inhabitants of India, both in language and appearance. They are supposed, and I think with some show of likelihood, to be part of the lost Ten Tribes ; others again, principally, I imagine, from the similarity of feature, suppose them to be the remains of an old Roman colony, and this is in a way supported by ancient Roman coins having been found in the neighbourhood of these Hills, *i.e.* in my district, Coimbatoor, and so far as I am able to say, in no other part of India.'

At first when the long-looked-for ball-gun arrived it proved a disappointment in some respects ; but it was destined in the next eight years to afford him the keenest pleasure he ever knew, to establish him as one of the greatest shots, sportsmen and hunters of the world; and provide him with an inexhaustible fund of stories and reminiscences for the rest of his life.

'COLLEGAL (36 miles E.S.E. of Mysore, on
the banks of the Cauvery),

'MY DEAR NED,   '*Aug.* 4, 1843.

    ' I had intended writing to Uncle Ben on the receipt of my gun, to thank him for the trouble he had been so kind as to take about it, but as I have some faults to find with it, and as I know he is rather sensitive, and apt, in the goodness of his heart, to be annoyed when anything he has interested himself in does not happen to please exactly, I have thought it better to blow up *you* and Mr. Purdey for what after all is merely all my own fault, inasmuch as I should have sent fuller directions in the first instance . . . Well, the gun is very, very heavy . . . Even supposing so much metal was required at the breach and lower part, nothing on earth will persuade me that half an inch of metal was requisite at the muzzle. This is its chief fault. . . . The rifle-sight is not the thing, but this, my dear lad, was, I believe, an invention of yours. A smooth bore is only used for snap or short shots. . . . Although the gun is not all I could wish it will do excellently well, and shoots sharp and strong. I have, however, a crow to pick with Mr. P. as regards the packing. . . . From his neglect to rub a small quantity of mercurial ointment over the barrels and fittings, the whole reached me in a most disgracefully rusty state. The *look* of the barrels is lost for ever, as the rust has eaten into them and *pock-marked* them all over . . . What are you all about at home that you don't hang Mr. O'Connell ? He'll gain his point (although I can't see exactly what benefit he'll get if he does) if you let him go on much longer. . . . Six years of my banishment passed. Hurrah ! I begin to think of warm firesides and warmer hearts, parsonages and retirement from the onerous duties of office ! Uncle Ben's morning

trumpet, and the dear Mother's "Why, boys, not up yet?"
seem again to sound in my ears. God bless you all; I
never knew what it was to have a Mother, a brother, or
a friend, till I had neither one nor the other. I don't
exactly mean to hint that I'm absolutely friendless in this
country, but India is a wide paddock, and I don't meet all
my chums every day at dinner. . . . I've a heavier charge
in my present appointment than I have ever had before, as
you will believe when I tell you that I have to superintend
the police and magistrates' business of seven *talooks*, each
about the size of an English county, besides the sole
superintendence of the revenue affairs of three more.
These, with occasional cases handed over to me by my
collector for investigation, fully employ my hours of sun-
shine. All my amusements take place between three and
eight a.m. . . . but John Company pay well, better by
far than such grumbling, useless lads as I deserve. . . . I've
read the account of the *lost* Tribes in " The Nestorians,"
and agree with the author that they no longer deserve that
title. The work has interested me considerably. I'm of
a horrid prying disposition, seeking to know the mys-
terious and obscure, and overlooking everything before my
nose. . . . I found some notes of yours in the book, on
Indian mythology. Did you ever compare the grand
features and recorded wonders of our religion with those
of the superstitions of other nations, Chinese, Indian,
Egyptian, etc. ? If not originally derived from a common
source it is impossible to account for their similarity in
various points. The Trinity, the Deluge, and the Bible
description of the creation of the world and man, are
evidently the same stories told in a different way in each.
The Hindoos, like the Hebrews, have a mystic term for
God, known to but few and pronounced very seldom by
any, *Wōm*, answering exactly to the Hebrew *Jah.* . . . '

The concluding paragraphs of this letter suggest a somewhat unusual line of reading for a man of action not yet
twenty-five years old.

Shortly after this, while on a shooting excursion on the banks of the Bhavany river, he was struck down by fever in so virulent a form that for two months his life hung on a thread. But the magnificent constitution triumphed, and early in October he was convalescent. He gained physical strength rapidly and rode daily; his brain, however, remained much confused.

To his Brother.

'COIMBATOOR,
'*Octr.* 14, 1843.

'. . . I did not write, I am ashamed to say, last month, and I am fearful that unless something reaches you by this mail I may have to blame myself for causing my dearest Mother some anxiety. I am, then, quite well, but so bothered just at present by an overplus of work that it is out of my power to write anything like a letter. . . . God bless you all and love unspeakable to the Missus. . . .'

On addressing himself to the examination of the accumulated arrears of work, the mental exertion brought back the fever, but next morning he insisted on being propped up in his bed at the door of his tent and with a wet towel bound tightly round his burning, aching head, disposed of case after case with a grasp and celerity that surprised even himself. By evening the entire list was exhausted. He then turned to the correspondence and dictated answers far into the night. Not until the last letter was finished did he succumb.

He soon rallied again, but his system was so saturated with the virus that he was liable to constant recurrences. At last he acquiesced in the wisdom of the urgent advice, tendered on all sides, that he should for a time abandon all idea of the visit to England to which he had so eagerly looked forward, and try whether Africa would restore his health as completely as it had that of many of his Indian friends.

In February, 1844, he broke his decision to his mother. The task he had to perform was a difficult one; on the one hand he dared not say how very near death he had been or how ill he still was; on the other, he could not allow his patient, devoted mother to imagine he had lightly rejected an opportunity of seeing her, after seven years' separation. He anxiously awaited her acknowledgment of his announcement, writing meanwhile his usual monthly letters.

PROPPED UP IN HIS BED AT THE DOOR OF HIS TENT.

'COLLEGAL,
'MY DEAREST MOTHER,   'March 20, 1844.

'Do you remember my present place of abode? I am out in my tabernacles for the collection etc. of John Company's money, and have pretty nearly as much trouble in raising the wind, metaphorically, as the wind appears to have in raising itself literally. That "It is more blessed to give than to receive" is not translatable into any Indian language. I've been away from Coimbatoor nearly six weeks and don't expect to be back until that period has again elapsed. . . . Anything more beautiful than the tints cast upon the hills by the rising and setting sun, and the way in which the green jungle is thrown out, cannot be imagined; it is something that people in England would go miles to see, and such as even I, accustomed as I am to beautiful scenery in this magnificent world (for magnificent it is) can gaze upon with delight. Whether it was born with me or whether it is an acquired passion I know not, but I love a hill and can never see one without wishing to be upon it, and seldom if possible deny myself the gratification of a scramble. Ardent sportsman as I am I would rather shoot one head of game, with a fine view to gloat over, than half a dozen in a dense forest in which you can barely see the beast you fire at, and nothing else. The hillmen too are always of a better stamp than your low-countrymen—more simple and more savage if you like, but uncontaminated by the vices and lying propensities of their brethren (in fact not so *low*) who as always is the case with barbarians, have merely in their intercourse with civilized beings adopted the worst points of civilization and discarded the best as unworthy of a thought. . . . I've been such a wanderer for the last seven years that if I ever get back to you again, I'm afraid (although I sometimes think otherwise) you'll find it difficult to keep me stationary, and if I can't leave you all behind I must e'en carry you along with me in an *omnibus* or gipsy caravan. Talking of gipsies, they say they understand Hindustani. There is certainly a race of people in this country who answer in appearance, customs (as far as I know) habits and morals, to the dwellers under the greenwood tree of our own dear land, and, what is stronger proof still that they are one and the same race, is the fact that the Spanish gipsies who are doubtless brothers of the English are called *Zingari* and the Indian gipsies, whose relationship I think is more than probable, *Bringari*, names very similar. . . .'

When Mrs. Oswell learned that her eager expectation
of a speedy meeting with her son was not to be realized,
the cautious wording and cheerful assurances of the letter
did not for a moment deceive her. She wrote praying to
be told the truth—the worst. ' I have lost four dear
children ; am I to resign myself to parting with a fifth—
the dearest ?' To ease her mind he complied fully with
her request, and after apologizing for his ' egotism, continues :

SALEM,

July 17, 1844

'. . . I only want to satisfy you, my dear Friend and
anxious Mother, that although I have determined on going
to the Cape, no *present* necessity exists for such a proceeding in the bad state of my health, but that the voyage
is undertaken entirely with a view of avoiding ulterior
annoyances. . . . So you must not, my ever dearest
Mother, make ·yourself uneasy without cause, and me
miserable by doing so. The recall of Lord Ellenborough
astounded us all here as much as it seems to have done
you in England. Far be it from me to offer any opinion
on the subject ; what may have been his sins in the eyes
of my masters I know not, but I am exceedingly sorry
that a necessity should have arisen for recalling a man,
who, however he may have treated our branch of the
Service, was certainly one of the most energetic Governor-
Generals in every department, so far as I know, that we
have had for a long time. His silly, bombastic proclamations have been amply atoned for by the very least of the
material changes he has made for the better both in the
civil and military departments, and these, except his
apparent (not I believe real, but rather compulsory) *shonk*
as we say—or love of getting into a row, were the sum
total of his misdeeds. Say nothing however of this my
opinion to anyone. I don't wish people to suppose me a
fool anxious to talk of matters I don't profess to understand. . . . I am very anxious to hear of Ned's final

destination and location as a pastor, but shall be very sorry, although I am perfectly aware of the necessity, for a break-up of the old household. I have always regarded Uncle Ben as one of the really true friends, at whose firesides I looked forward to warming myself, and I will do so yet, please God, for a few miles distance separates not at home as it does here. God bless him and all of you. . . . Above all things don't fret yourself about me without reason, but believe me to have told you the *truth*.'

To his Brother.

' MADRAS,
' *Aug.* 20, 1844.

'. . . I sail for the Cape of Good Hope on the 2nd prox in the ship *Anna Robertson*. Since my last letter I have done nothing but improve, and am almost ashamed of going after all, but as it seems the opinion of the doctors that I should be liable to recurrences of my friend the fever, and as I find, now my appetite is returning, that my digestive organs have suffered somewhat in the war, I have made up my mind to go. . . . My next will be either from the sea or from the Cape. Hurrah for the waves and giraffes ! Think of paying a visit to Mooselakatzi, King of the Zulus. Have you read Harris's book on Africa ? If not, do so, and envy me. Give a kiss and my very best love to my Mother and tell her that I am really much better, well in fact, if I hadn't a stomach ! God bless you all.'

On the 23rd he had another severe attack, and, reduced to a mere skeleton—from twelve stone to seven stone twelve pounds—too weak even to raise his head, constantly comatose, he insisted on being carried on board, notwithstanding the assurance of the doctors that in their opinion it could be only to die.

CHAPTER IV.

AFRICA.

1844–1846. AGE 26–28.

FIRST EXPEDITION (WITH MURRAY) TO BA-KAA HILLS.— RETURN BY LIMPOPO.

Arrival at Cape Town—' I should have made a capital traveller '
—Opening of Royal Exchange—' Life of Arnold '—
O'Connell—' Lardner's Cyclopædia '—Start for the Interior—Dreary scenery—Kuruman, and Mr. and Mrs.
Moffat—Motito, M. Lemire—The first lion—The Ba-
Katla—Meeting with Livingstone, ' the most modest of
the missionaries '—Magnificent sport—Ride on a lioness—
Bushmen hunters—A Kafir nickname—Horse killed by a
buffalo—Saved by his muscles—An immense herd of buffaloes—John—The Ba-Wangketsi—Lost in the Bush; treed
by lions—A surly reception by the Ba-Mangwato—Diamond
cut diamond—The Ba-Kaa—600 starving camp-followers
—60,000 lbs. of meat in one day—Return to the Cape.

W. Cotton Oswell to his Mother.

' CAPE TOWN,
' *Oct.* 26, 1844.

' . . . We arrived here after a very pleasant voyage of
something under seven weeks, during which time I have
improved vastly, and am now quite well and *stout* again.
I am for the present living in Cape Town, but move out
in a few days to a place about eight miles off called
Wynberg. . . . I have met and been introduced to more
friends and strangers since my arrival than for the last

seven years of my life. Leaving the benefit I expect to derive from the cruise out of the question, I shall I fancy gain much from a little rubbing together with my kind, for I was I am afraid getting very rough and *junglefied*. The mere having to wear a coat seems to civilize one to a certain extent. . . . The climate although called by the residents hot at present, is by far the most delightful I was ever in in my life, and I am assured that it is something better than best out at Wynberg. The *Precursor—steamer!*—arrived last night and has created a sensation. . . . My present plan is to remain here about fifteen months and then to take Ceylon and Calcutta on my way back to Madras, for I certainly have a mania for seeing new people and places. Had it been my lot I should have made a capital traveller, and should most certainly have possessed one quality which most travellers have not—that of non-scribbling a book! . . . My constitutional idleness would have prevented me from any such perpetration. . . . God bless you all.'

For the next eleven years it was his lot to be a traveller, and for forty-eight he possessed the quality of 'non-scribbling a book.'

Mrs. Oswell to her Son William.

'WANSTEAD,
'ESSEX,
'*Oct.* 30, 1844.

'. . . I see by the papers you sailed on the 2nd of September, and we reckon you are before this at the Cape. Sincerely have I prayed that wherever you go God's blessing may be with you. . . . We had the opportunity of seeing the grand procession of the Queen's coming into the City to open the Exchange. Uncle William had seats and an awning erected at the top of the Bank,* and our places were good. Our old Duke

* He was at this date the Governor.

was so cheered. and the Queen was very well received. Uncles William and Ben went in Court dresses inside the Exchange. . . . You see by the papers Government has received Lord Ellenborough very well, and bestowed many honours on him.   There arrived a few days ago the "Life of Dr. Arnold" which I had ordered for you.   I do not know whether you will think it worth while to send it to the Cape? He was certainly a man of wonderful talents, and from his letters took great delight in his calling as instructor, but he failed in being a good Churchman, though a good man, and in many points much to be admired. . ...

' Your loving Mother and friend.'

W. Cotton Oswell to his Mother.

' WYNBERG,
' Nov. 27, 1844.

'. . . I fixed upon the Cape for many reasons in pre-ference to England. . . . I felt that the getting well at home, which it was necessary I should do before I could enjoy it, would be as it were so much time lost from the happy six-and-thirty months I hope to spend amongst you—a deduction and infringement of anticipated happi-ness I could not make up my mind to spare.   The ailing body would have chained down the spirit, and though no doubt it is pleasant to be nursed by those we love, it is far more so to be amongst them in health with a capacity for communicating pleasure rather than solicitude. . . . When I start up country I shall I think shape my course E.N.E. towards Graaff Reinet and Colesberg as this is the coolest part of the Colony and affords most sport for the gun of which I am still as fond as ever.   To an Indian whose eyes, say what they will, have been accus-tomed to revel among the beauties of fine views and a magnificent country, the appearance of Africa is not what it might be to you poor Islanders.   There is an old

Persian proverb that "Though the pains of Purgatory seem Paradise to the evil spirits, they are as Hell to the Angels," and Africa, bad as it is, does not want in bold mountain scenery, though it does sadly in vegetation, and is at all events something far superior to Wanstead Flats! . . . Let Richardson drop *Bentley* and *Blackwood*, and forward the *Quarterly* and *Edinburgh Reviews*. . . . *The Illustrated London Times* or *News* mentions O'Connell's triumph. Oh shame upon the Bar and Bench for such a bungle! There were certainly most gross irregularities and most manifest confusion in the whole trial. It appeared to me throughout that the fancied importance of the case had confounded and perplexed the Judges. They seem to have lost their heads, forgotten their true position, allowed themselves to be brought into difficulty from sheer want of tact, and ignorance of what ought to have been the mode of procedure, and then, instead of calmly retracing their steps with the dignity which ought to be inherent in such men, on finding out their error they only wallowed on and blustered; they were in short *flurried*. The acts of O'Connell should have been looked upon by the Judges at least, as those of any ordinary other man; but they were not. If Richardson could pick me up cheap the thirteen vols. of "Lardner's Cabinet Cyclopædia of Natural Philosophy," and send the account of their cost, I should be obliged. . . .'

The thirteen volumes were duly procured and despatched, and proved a great resource to him on his way up country and back again. He mastered the contents completely, and thus laid a fresh course in his education.

To his Mother.

'Greenpoint,
'Nr. Cape Town,
'*Feb.* 22, 1845.

'. . . After having lived a stirring life for seven or eight years, without some strong excitement, of which the Cape is destitute, I find it tedious in the extreme to remain in one place, and have already made two or three short trips into the country, to Worcester, the Heré River, etc. But I am now on the eve of sailing by the *Phœnix*, or rather *steaming* down in the direction of Graham's Town in company with a Mr. Murray, a brother of a brother civilian, and purpose wandering about in search of amusement and sport for some four or five months. For that period our wagons, of which I will give you a full description from Graham's Town, will be our only home, and I look forward to the trip with the most sanguine hopes of entire satisfaction, and have only one drawback in the fear that our communication with each other may sometimes be rather tardy, for posts and postboxes do not much abound in the direction we intend moving, and two or three months may probably intervene between my letters, as I shall have to trust them to the tender mercies of a Dutch Boer, whose wagon at the best moves but slowly, and whose memory is none of the best. . . . I will let you hear of me by every available opportunity you may be sure, and only warn you of the chance there is of the interruption of a regular correspondence, to save you anxiety. The *Phœnix* starts to-day and we shall in all probability reach Graham's Town about the end of the month. . . . I have not entirely shaken off my Indian friend. However, as I can be and have been twelve hours on horseback with manifest gain to my health, you will perhaps smile at my talking of my ailments !

'Your ever affectionate Son.'

To his Mother and Brother.

'LITTAKOO OR KURUMAN,
'*June* 4, 1845.

'. . . A war had broken out between the Griquas and the emigrant Boers just previous to our start, and their

disagreement prevented our crossing the Orange River at
the usual drift, as we might in that case have been stopped,
and forcibly deprived of our powder and lead. By spanning
down the southern bank of the river to one of the lower
fords—Vandervalt's—we managed to escape contact with
the belligerents and soon left them far behind to settle
their own affairs, which however they were unable to do
without the intervention of H.M.'s troops. Nothing can
be imagined more sterile and uninteresting than the country
through which we have passed. A wide expanse without
even a bush to break the monotony of the view, was the
prospect which generally greeted us morning, noon and
night. It is true this was occasionally broken by a few
straggling mimosa trees, and frequently by lines of low
rocky hills, one undulating slope succeeding another with
as little variation as the swell of the sea. You at first
fully expect that when you arrive at the top of the rising
ground over which you are moving at about two miles an
hour, you will see something to repay you on the other
side. However you soon learn that all is alike barren and
naked. For the most part it appears as if lately upheaved
from the burning bowels of the earth, bearing in nearly
every part strong marks of volcanic action. It looks more
suited for the habitation of the iguanodon than of mortal
man, who nevertheless wherever the grass is abundant,
pastures his cattle unscared by the frightful dreariness of
the scenery. However with all I like the life. I ought I
think to have been a gipsy instead of a Civilian of the
H.E.I.C.S. The only thing that puts me out at all is the
privations our oxen, horses, and I may add we ourselves,
have to put up with for want of water. We have once
or twice had to travel two days without seeing a drop
except the small quantity carried in our water casks for
our own drinking. This to an Indian is rather unpleasant,
but is still to be borne I find much more easily than I
expected. We propose being away two or three months
more and then returning to the Cape. . . . I've seen

enough of Africa already, and by far too little of wood
and water for the last six months. This is a missionary
station, and we have been most kindly received and entertained by the resident, Mr. Moffat, who has published a
book which I think would interest you. He lives here
with some fellow missionaries and Dr. Hume the most
enterprising of the traders. Kuruman is about 300 miles
N. by W. of Colesberg. I shall I think be able to amuse
you not a little, should we ever meet over a winter's fire-
side, with a narrative of my travels. A wagon, though a
wonderful thing *for a wagon*, is but a bad house if one is
very fond of one's creature comforts, which I am, among
those who know me, considered most surprisingly careless
of. The only inconvenience I find is the want of room
for dressing, and the heat which accumulates in it during
the day. My companion complains more of the cold, but
at this I laugh and delight myself. It is cool enough at
night and in the evenings, the thermometer having twice
sunk as low as 17 degrees below freezing, and a good hard
frost is generally our lot. But I actually don't feel it, and
am told that I am so full of caloric that I shall take a long
time to cool. We sit out in the open air to dinner and
breakfast before our camp fire, and experience no inconvenience, though you in England would be shivering in a
room. This I attribute to the great dryness of the atmosphere, not a drop of rain falling for many months. In
India it would be madness to attempt bivouacking in the
open air, but here as I have proved you may sleep perfectly safely rolled up in your skin blanket at the foot of
the first tree you like. The sun is just setting, and his
parting beams will afford me only sufficient light, seated
as I am in the inside of my wagon, to see to close this.
So God bless you.'

Referring elsewhere to this visit to Kuruman he says:

'We stayed a short time at the station of that grand
old patriarch of missionaries, Mr. Moffat, where we

received all the kindly hospitality, attention and advice possible from him and Mrs. Moffat—verily the two best friends travellers ever came across. I shall never forget their affectionate courtesy, their beautifully ordered household, and their earnest desire to help us on in every way. He advised us to go to Livingstone who was then stationed at Mabotsé—220 miles or so to the Northward, and obtain from him guides and counsel for our further wanderings.'

To his Brother.

'Graham's Town,
'*Nov.* 29, 1845.

' . . . On the third day after leaving Kuruman we arrived at Motito, a French Missionary station, and quitted it on the fourth, after having been most hospitably entertained by the Rev. M. Lemire. . . . You here first begin to meet with the mimosa tree in abundance, and the most uninteresting of all scenery, the open plain, is in places converted by its verdure into the most picturesque and park-like country. This description holds good up to the Ba-Katla, with the exception of the two *choois*, or salt lakes, and their neighbourhoods which were more desolate than anything we had previously passed over, and of which I can, I fear, convey to you no adequate idea, but must ask you to picture to yourself a burnt, barren, interminable plain, literally without a bush, and exposed in consequence to the full influence of the most fiery of suns. The sasayby, hartebeest, wildebeest, quagga, and springbok were now tolerably abundant though very difficult of access, and at the first outspan beyond the second or greater *chooi*, we heard for the first time the voice of Leo, within sixty yards of our wagons. It was night and dark, and though afterwards habituated to his presence, I fancy neither of us will readily forget the *anxiety* with which we listened to his serenade ; for we were unaware of the perfect unconcern shown by the horses and oxen to his roar, and even to the view of him if unaccompanied by his smell, and feared that they, one or both, would inevitably break loose from the wagons to which they were made fast. However nothing of the kind occurring, we were comforted and retired to rest. When I tell you that the loss of either horses or oxen would have been irreparable in the country in which we then were, and that our chance of sport entirely depended on them, you may imagine that uninitiated as we were, we had something of a reason for worrying ourselves. We fell in with large game one march beyond the Meritsané River, where the first elands died. The eland is a large buck of the *genus* antelope, about 18 hands in height. . . . On arriving at the Ba-Katla, the last Missionary station, the country changed its character entirely, and still for the better. Fine ranges of hills, well wooded and watered close you in on every side, and the scenery is strikingly like some parts of India. It was now that we really began to enjoy our life as sportsmen. After staying two days with the Rev. Mr. Livingstone, the best, most intelligent and most modest (a rarer virtue is modesty than you suppose) of the missionaries, and having by his advice taken a direction which led us at first rather to the westward, and eventually to the N.E., we certainly for three months revelled in the finest climate, the finest shooting, and anything but tame scenery. I shall give you no detailed account of our progress and sport, although I at first intended doing so, and therefore began this letter in your name rather than in my Mother's, fearing that the repetition of "we killed this, that or the other," probably but of little interest to you, would entirely disgust her. If you should ever wish to hear particulars of the deeds then committed, are they not written in the Chronicles, or my notes which you may read if you please. Suffice it then to say that we were fully repaid for our long journey, that we penetrated further than anyone had done before us, saw as much as we could with one pair of eyes apiece, and last, not least,

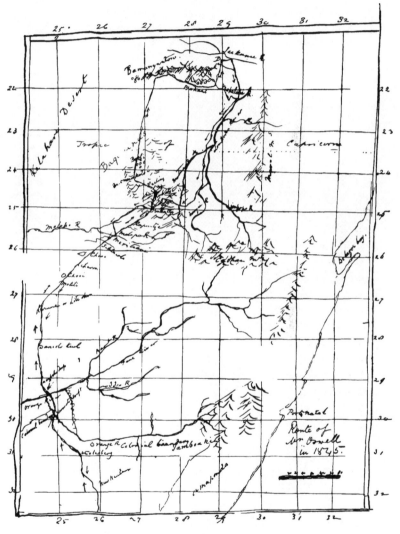

ROUTE IN 1845

slew game in abundance—elephants, rhinoceroses, hippopotami, giraffes, *et hoc genus omne.* We returned by
nearly the same route as we went, that is to say, from
Mabotsé southwards. I give you a small sketch of the
line, as from Kuruman we penetrated upwards of 400 miles
into the interior, far, far beyond the maps of South Africa,
I should much like to make another tour, and had I but
three months more leave would certainly do so ; or if you
at home would *give me leave,* I would risk the losing of my
Head Assistantship and return to India after another
delightful trip, perfectly satisfied to continue a humble
Assistant Collector for years to come. And in addition to
the pleasure I should most assuredly derive from such an
expedition I should, if I may judge from the extent to
which I have already improved in health and strength, become completely re-established and able to withstand the
insinuations of our Indian clime, unharmed. Of doing this
just at present I am free to own I have my fears, although
my term be but short. God bless you all. Kiss my
Mother for me. The nearer the time approaches the more
earnest is my wish to see you all again. Preaching nervous
work, eh ? I could manage it in Tamil, I think, but am
afraid I should break down in English, for I have for a
long time found it easier to express myself impudently and
concisely in my acquired than in my mother tongue.'

' An incident,' he writes later, ' highly creditable to
Kafir womanhood occurred just as we reached Mabotsé.
The women, as is their custom, were working in the
fields—for they hoe, and the men sew—and a young man,
standing by the edge of the bush, was chatting with them.
A lioness sprang on him, and was carrying him off, when
one of the women ran after her, and catching her by the
tail was dragged for some little distance. Hampered by
the man in her mouth and the woman behind her, she
slackened her pace, whereupon her assailant straddled
over her back and hit her across the nose and head with

a heavy short-handled hoe till she dropped her prey and slunk into cover. The man was the woman's husband! Would Mrs. Smith do as much for Mr. Smith? Could she do more?'

STRADDLED OVER HER BACK AND HIT HER WITH A HOE.

For many weeks of this journey he hunted with a party of Bushmen and gained valuable hints from them about beasts and their ways. 'They are,' he says, 'past masters in the art of hunting, upright, tall, sinewy fellows; with their skill and the abundance of game they never suffer hunger. I was very fond of them; they tell the truth, and instead of being mere pot-hunters, are enthusiastic sportsmen, enjoying the work as much as yourself.'

This experience developed his natural alertness and powers of observation, and educated his sight and hearing to such a degree that the Kafirs allowing him to be their equal in "spooring," beastcraft and woodcraft, and in the marvellous instinct of locality, gave him the name of *Tlaga*, (on the look-out, wary, as of game) which clung to him throughout his travels in Africa. He was justly proud of

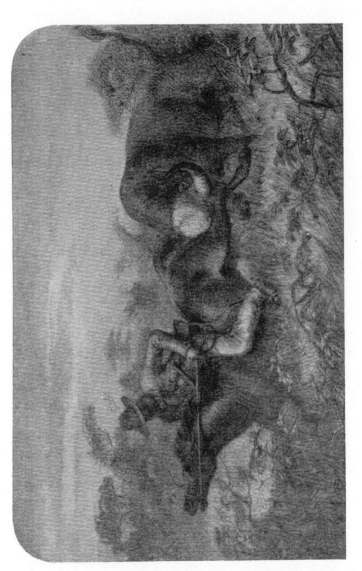

THE WOUNDED BEAST SPRANG UP AND STRUCK HIM HEAVILY.

this tribute from men who were the outcome of centuries of the *necessary* cultivation of the qualities to the highest point.

The country of the Ba-Katla swarmed with buffaloes, and he had several narrow escapes from them :

'One morning whilst the wagons were moving slowly through the low bush three bulls crossed the line of march. I was on my horse Superior, and with a shout to Murray that I meant to make sure of a bag, galloped after them, and singling out one, got alongside of him within five feet, and fired. He pitched upon his head and lay perfectly motionless. Making sure he was dead I would not give him the second barrel, and turned the horse to ride after

HORNS OF THE BUFFALO THAT KILLED SUPERIOR.
Length inside curve, 77 inches ; between tips, 24 inches.   Width, 14 inches.

the two others which were still in view; but before I could get my animal into his stride the wounded beast sprang up and struck him heavily. I felt the thud, but the horse did not fall, and cantered on for twenty yards, when the whisk of his tail dabbled my trousers with blood, and on getting off I found a hole thirty inches deep and nearly wide enough to get into, in the flank, for the horn had been driven up to its base. The bull was two weak to follow up the attack, and died where he stood; the

horse crawled a few yards and then, seeing it was a hopeless case, I put a ball through his head.'

On another occasion his life was saved by his muscles :

' Coming homeward one afternoon we stumbled into
the middle of a herd asleep in the long grass. Our sudden
appearance startled them from their dreams ; a panic
seized them and away they galloped in the wildest confusion. One old patriarch had been taking his siesta
apart from the rest in a dense patch of bush to the right ;
the sound of the gun and the rush of his companions
roused him, and with one barrel loaded, as I ran after his
relations I found myself face to face with him within ten
yards. He was evidently bent on mischief. We stared
at one another for a second and then I fired at his broad
chest ; it was the best I could do, for his nose was up and
the points of his shoulders were not exposed. He plunged
at me instantly ; I fortunately caught a projecting bough
of the minosa tree under which I was standing and drawing
my knees up to my chin he passed below me.'

' I once found myself in an immense herd. The bush
was full of them, I was surrounded and had nothing to do
but stand still. They dashed about me like rooks after the
wireworm in a newly ploughed field and I had the sensation of drawing myself in very tight about the waistband.
Till they thinned out into a tail I could not begin to shoot,
but there were such numbers that even then I knocked over
six at exceedingly close quarters. The danger was being
run over or butted down in the headlong stampede. The
same thing has happened to me, and I dare say to many
all-round shots, with elephants. How they avoided or
missed you—for they didn't seem to try to avoid—you
can't tell ; you come out of it without a scratch, and therefore as a rule think no more of it.'

Leaving the Ba-Katla after three months' magnificent
sport, the wagons made their way slowly towards the

I . . . CAUGHT A PROJECTING BOUGH . . . AND DRAWING MY
KNEES UP . . . HE PASSED BELOW ME.

8—2

Ba-Wangketsi.   Before reaching them an event occurred
which, in Oswell's words, ' coloured the whole of my
African life and will colour my life as long as I live ' :

' We were trekking through some low sand-hills covered
with scrub, when three lions crossed about fifty yards
ahead of the oxen.   Snatching up a gun I jumped from
the wagon and called upon someone to follow me with a
heavy rifle that was always kept loaded as a reserve battery.
I pressed so closely on the leisurely-retreating trio that
the largest stopped short.   I squatted, intending to take
his shoulder as he turned, looked round for my second
gun, and heard the bearer, who was close to me, whisper
in Dutch, " You can get nearer by the ant-hill."   The
move lost me the lion, as he broke away after his companions ; and then for the first time I took notice of the
cool, tall, handsome lad, who had offered me advice, and
recognised in him, at once, the stuff to make a henchman
of.   From that day forth he was my right-hand man in
the field, and never failed me.

' John Thomas was an Africander born at the Cape, of
parents probably slaves, but as a grand specimen of man-
hood, good-nature, faithfulness and cheerful endurance, I
never met his equal, black or white.   Plucky to a fault, he
was the least quarrelsome of men, the life and light of our
camp fires, and the pet of the Kafirs who seemed at once
to understand his quiet unpretending nature, and always
made their requests to me through " bono Johnny." '

He had been with the Ba-Wangketsi for a fortnight,
enjoying even better success than usual with his gun, when
he had an experience interesting and exciting enough in
itself, but particularly remarkable for having made a greater
impression on him and remaining more accurately stamped
on his mind in every detail, than any, save one, of his
numerous after adventures :

' One morning our head-man told me there was no food

for the twelve or fourteen dogs, our night-watchmen, so I took up my gun, which was loaded only in one barrel, and strolled out on the chance of a shot, but as, kill or miss, I intended to return immediately I did not carry any spare ammunition.   A reedy pond lay close in advance of the wagons, in a little opening ; beyond this, as on every other side, stretched a sea of bush and mimosa trees.   Two hundred yards from the outspan I came upon a clump of quagga and wounded one, which, though mortally hit, struggled on before falling.   I followed, and marking the place where it fell, set my face, as I thought towards the wagons, meaning to send out men for the flesh.   No doubt of the direction crossed my mind—the pool was certainly not more than four hundred yards away in a straight line and I thought I could walk down upon it without any trouble; so taking no notice of my out tracks which had bent slightly in following the quagga, I started.

' It was now about 10 a.m.; little did I think that 5 p.m. would find me still seeking three vans nearly as large as Pickford's, and half an acre of water.   In my first cast I cannot say whether I went wide or stopped short of the mark I was making for, and it was not until I had wandered carelessly hither and thither for half an hour, feeling sure that it was only the one particular bush in front of me which hid the wagons, that I very unwillingly owned to myself that I was drifting without bearings in this bushy sea.

' The sun was nearly overhead, and gave but slight help as to direction, and the constant turning to avoid thick patches of thorns rendered it nearly impossible, in the absence of any guiding points, to hold a fixed course in this maze of sameness.   I tried walking in circles in the hopes of cutting the wheel tracks, but though on a previous occasion this plan had succeeded, it now failed.

' As with empty gun I plodded on, occasional small herds of rooyebuck and blue wildebeest, evidently very much at home, swept and capered by me, and stopping

I HAD REACHED THE LOWEST BOUGH . . . WHEN . . . A DEEP
NOTE . . . TOLD ME THAT A LION WAS PASSING.

and looking at me with wondering eyes, increased my feeling of loneliness. I had no doubt of regaining my party next day at latest, and cared but little for passing a night in the jungle; but bewildered and baffled, I envied the instinct of the so-called brutes, which careless of their steps, were nevertheless quite sure of their ways.

'Twilight near the Tropics is very short. Just before the sun set, therefore, I followed a game track which I knew would lead to water, as it was still early in the season and the rain supply had not dried up in the hollows. At dusk I reached a pool similar to the one I had quitted in the morning. After a good draught, I began collecting firewood, but for once it was very scarce, and the night closed in so rapidly that a bare hour's supply was all my store. Partly to save fuel, partly in the hope that as night crept on signals would be made from the wagons, I climbed a tree which stood by the side of the water, and had not been long perched before I heard, though so far off that I could hardly catch the sound, the smothered boom of guns. Alarmed at my absence my companions suspected the cause and were inviting my return; but it required a very pressing invitation indeed to induce a man to walk through two miles of an African wood, in those days, on a dark night. This particular spot, too, was more infested with lions than any other, save one, I was ever in ; and though harmless and cowardly enough, as a rule, in the day, they were not likely to prove very acceptable followers at night.

'But I had been walking all day under a tropical sun, my clothing was wet with perspiration, and it now froze hard—for freeze it can in Southern Africa—and I was bitterly cold. I determined to come down and light my fire. I knew it would last but a short time, but thought I would make the best of it and thaw myself before attempting to return. I had reached the lowest bough of my tree and placed my hand beside my feet before jumping off, when from the bush immediately under me a deep

note and the sound of a heavy body slipping through the
thorny scrub, told me that a lion was passing.   Whether
the creaking of the tree had roused his attention and caused
him to speak so opportunely, I don't know, but without
the warning in another half second I should have alighted
on his back.   I very quickly put two or three yards more
between the soles of my feet and the ground.

'Presently from the upper end of the pool came the
moaning pant of a questing lion; it was immediately
answered from the lower end.   Their majesties were on
the look out for supper, and had divided the approaches
to the water between them.   It was much too dark to
see anything, but from the sounds they seemed to walk
in beats, occasionally telling one another of their whereabouts by a low pant ; of my presence I think they were
not aware.

'This went on for an hour or more and I grew colder
and colder; my beard and moustache were stiff with
frost; I could not much longer endure the cramped position in my scraggy tree, and I felt I must get down and
light the fire, when suddenly up came the blessed moon
and right under her the sounds of three or four muskets
fired together.   With the help of her light and partial
direction in case my companions grew tired of firing, I was
not going to stay up a tree to be frozen.   Waiting, therefore, until she was about one tree high, and until the
lions were far asunder on their respective beats as well
as I could make out from the sounds, I came down and
capping—it was all I could do, for as I said, I had started
without powder and ball—my empty gun, I passed at the
double round the end of the water, and dived into the
bush on the opposite side.

'I have no doubt my desire was to get on as quickly as
possible, but reasons for a cautious advance soon made
themselves heard on all sides.   An African forest was
then *alive* at night.   I thought only of the lions, and
especially of the two I had left at the water; but every

THE BAULKED ROAR OF A DISAPPOINTED LION RANG THROUGH
THE CAMP.

nocturnal animal that stirred kept me on the stretch—the less noise the more danger; the movement of a mouse might well be mistaken for the stealthy tread of the King of the Cats.

' Among the trees the moon gave but a scanty light, and nearly every minute I had to stop and listen as some unseen animals passed near me. Sometimes I could recognise them by their cry, but mostly it was a running that could not be seen of skipping beasts, that troubled me. The only animal I really saw that night was a rhinoceros that with head and tail up, and in a terrible fuss, crossed a few yards before me.

' A sound in front, and I strained my eyes into the shadowy darkness in advance; the rustling of a leaf told of life to the right or left; the snapping of a twig of possible death in the rear. But I struggled on for an hour I should think, when, stooping to clear a low bough, four or five muskets fired together within fifty yards, told me I was at home again.

' I hope I was thankful then; I know I am now. Two of my Hottentot servants and a batch of Kafirs had come some distance into the bush in the hope of meeting me, and escorted me to the fire in triumph. As I held my still only half-thawed hands over it, the baulked roar of a disappointed lion rang through the camp. He had not been heard before that night. " He has missed you, Tlaga, by a little this time," said my black friends, " let him go back to his game."

' They were right, for in the morning we found his spoor *on* mine for a long way back. Whether he had come with me from the water, or I had picked up a follower in the bush, I never knew. My constantly stopping and listening probably saved me, for a lion seldom makes up his mind very suddenly to attack a man, unless hard pressed by hunger. He likes to know all about it first, and my turning, and slow jerky progress had doubtless roused his suspicions.'

From the Ba-Wangketsi, he made his way to the Ba-Mangwato, and here met with a surly reception, for the first and only time during his sojourn in Africa. His pluck and determination, however, were equal to the occasion. Before sunset he sent some of his Hottentots to reconnoitre; they discovered and reported to him that three hundred yards from the camp, in the direction in which the wagons headed, there was a *cul-de-sac*, the steep hills suddenly closing in and offering no passage through them, and that the ground was strewn with human skulls. Watch was kept all night and the direction of the Ba-Kaa Hills ascertained, and as the morning broke he had the oxen tied ready for inspanning to the trek-tow, the horses to the wagon-wheels, and allotted to each man his tree, impressing on all that in case of a disturbance they were to *follow*, not *set* an example, and that he would shoot anyone who fired a shot before he did.

In the morning Secomi soon made his appearance at the camp fire, surrounded by his spearmen, and as he sat down Oswell turned himself so that the muzzle of his gun, which lay across his knees, covered the chief. Believing he had the party in a trap, he steadily refused to grant guides to the Ba-Kaa.

Wearied of the long discussion, Oswell gave the word to inspan the oxen and loose the horses; the chief and his followers evidently considered their opportunity had come. But :

'I ordered my men to turn the wagons and as the oxen slowly brought them round and faced in the direction of the Ba-Kaa, the faces of the Ba-Mangwato were a sight to see. . . . They stood stupefied and crest-fallen, and the wagons moved on without a word or sign of opposition. I brought up the rear with loose oxen and horses. We had gained three hundred or more yards . . . when I heard the sound of running behind me, and

A MAN COMING ON AT THE TOP OF HIS SPEED.

turning saw a man coming on at the top of his speed after us. He threw up his hands to shew he was carrying no arms, and I grounded my gun and waited for him. "What is it?" "I am sent by the Chief to take you wherever you like to go." "Lead on to the Ba-Kaa then." '

On arriving at the Ba-Kaa he found them in a pitiable condition; the crops had failed and they were starving. The Chief welcomed him warmly, and besought him to take his people and feed them. He accepted six hundred men, women and children, all in the most terrible state of emaciation and sickness, and started for the hunting-grounds, whence after seven weeks he sent them back to their kraals plump, well, and happy—not one missing, ill, or feeble. They had to requisition porters to help them carry the large *faggots* they had collected of sun-dried strips of meat. How enormous was the entire amount may be gathered from the fact that the one day's shooting previous to their departure had given them over 60,000 lbs. —fourteen hippopotami, two large bull elephants, a rhinoceros, a giraffe and a quagga.

The hippopotami—the first they had killed—were somewhat unexpectedly secured. Murray had made a *détour* to the north-east, intending to strike the river low down and follow it up to the encampment, while Oswell hunted in the immediate neighbourhood. Hearing, however, shot after shot from the direction taken by Murray, Oswell hastened thither, and in a few minutes came upon a kind of backwater from the main river, very deep, 150 yards long by 50 wide, with high banks.

On that opposite to him sat Murray blazing away, his after-rider loading one of the guns. 'Look at these beasts!' he cried; and, indeed, the spectacle was most remarkable. The pool was alive with monstrous hippopotami. Oswell opened fire at once, and, maddened with fright, they snorted, plunged, dived, struggled and fought in the vain effort to escape from the attack. Sometimes, as a bullet struck home, a vast head and shoulders reared themselves out of the water, and the clash of the immense jaws echoed from bank to bank.

This went on for a quarter of an hour, but not one beast appeared to die. A big bull made straight for the part of the bank on which Oswell was standing. Letting it get its forelegs clear, he fired within three feet of its head, blowing it back into the stream. 'Well, I'll swear I hit that fellow!' shouted he to Murray. 'Oh, I can swear I've hit all I've fired at!' was the reply. The evening was closing in, and just before the hunters started for the waggons *one* hippopotamus floated up dead. They looked at each other, and did not say much of their shooting. Next morning, however, fourteen huge bodies lay on the surface of the creek. They had evidently sunk to the bottom when killed, and risen when the gases distended the stomach.

For a month or five weeks longer they shot down the Limpopo, and then, as the season was drawing on, and from December to April it was impossible to keep the horses alive, the horse sickness, endemic through the old hunting-grounds, killing every one, the travellers turned southward and westward towards Mabotsé, and 'shaking the dear old Doctor and Mrs. Livingstone by the hand,' made their way to the Cape, which they reached in December.

Murray returned to England, and Oswell busied himself in refitting for the following year.

THE POOL WAS ALIVE WITH MONSTROUS HIPPOPOTAMI.

CHAPTER V.

AFRICA.

1846–1847.   AGE 28–29.

SECOND EXPEDITION (WITH CAPTAIN FRANK VARDON).
EXPLORATION OF COURSE OF LIMPOPO, AND
DISCOVERY OF RIVER MOKOLWÉ.

Gunpowder permit—Six weeks' sport on Mariqué River—An
elephant-hunt of twenty-three hours — Captain Frank
Vardon, ' the most perfect fellow-traveller —Enormous
herds of buffaloes and elephants—' That must be a lie '—
A liberal proposal—Tsétsé fly; *post-mortem* appearance of
victims — *Rhinoster Oswellii* — White rhinoceros tosses
Oswell and his horse — A gallant vengeance — Oswell
tossed by a keitloa—Return to India.

THE experience gained in the preceding season made
the laying in of fresh supplies an easy task.   When it was
accomplished he bought half a dozen horses to fill up gaps,
and halting at Graham's Town, applied for and was
granted a gunpowder permit.

' *March* 12, 1846.

' Permission is hereby granted to William Cotton Oswell,
Esquire, to purchase and convey across the Land Boundaries of the Colony, for his own private use, One Hundred and Fifteen Pounds of Gunpowder.   This Gentleman
will proceed on his journey with two wagons and six
Musquets.

' By Command of His Honour,
' THE LIEUT.-GOVERNOR.'

One hundred and fifteen pounds of powder for one gun and a seven months' expedition would seem an enormous allowance, but the event proved he had by no means over-estimated his requirements.

By the middle of April he was on his way to the Mari-qué River, a small tributary of the Limpopo, intending to

CAPTAIN FRANK VARDON.
'The most perfect fellow-traveller.'

shoot down it to its junction, and then explore the main stream as far as he was able. The number of animals was really incredible. He was out every day and all day, and sometimes all night. 'On one occasion,' he notes, 'John and I had a very long ride after a herd of elephants we never came up with; we started at 8 a.m. and only reached the wagons again next day at 7 a.m.' Five or six weeks passed thus, when one morning before he left camp, a Kafir came in with a letter fastened in a cleft stick from a Captain Frank Vardon, of the 25th Madras Native Infantry, who, hearing that an Englishman was within a short distance, proposed to join parties and shoot together.

'I had been one whole season and part of another at the work and I thought that a newcomer, of whom I knew nothing, might not be the most desirable of companions; he would very likely wish to stop when I wished to go on, and *vice versâ*, and I sent an answer in this spirit, but, thanks be praised, I repented my churlish-ness in an hour after the departure of the messenger, and wrote a second letter begging Captain Vardon to ignore the first, pardon my selfishness, and join me as soon as possible ; and to the end of my life I shall rejoice that I did so, for in three days the finest fellow and best comrade a man ever had made his appearance. . . . I will not attempt to describe him. Let every man picture for himself the most perfect fellow-traveller he can imagine, and that's Frank; brightest, bravest-hearted of men, with the most unselfish of dispositions, totally ignorant of jealousy, the light of the camp fires, the most trust-worthy of mates; a better sportsman and a better shot than myself at all kinds of game save elephants, and only a little behindhand in that, because he was a heavy weight and poorly armed with a single-barrelled rifle. Yet he was always rejoicing in my success and making light of his own disappointments—and this man I had all but missed!'

The buffaloes were in immense herds along the Mariqué:

'One bright moonlight night the report of the gun awakened the whole forest to the left of us into life, un-heard, unseen, before. I rode up to the edge. It was a mass of struggling buffaloes jammed together. The out-side ones startled by the shot, and having got sight of our party, bore back upon the main body; hoof and horn, horn and hoof rattled one against another, and for some distance I rode parallel with a heaving stream of wild life. I cannot pretend with any accuracy to guess their num-bers, but there must have been thousands, for they were packed together, like the pictures of American bison, and any number of braves might have crossed over their backs.'

Elephants, too, were in such large herds that he halted a week or ten days and shot all day long, and had the ivory as it was brought in piled up under his wagons.

One morning there appeared two wagons on the

opposite side of the river. Seven or eight of their occupants, Boers, crossed the stream and had a friendly chat, coffee and tobacco, with the travellers: when all of a sudden one of them caught sight of the ivory under the wagon. They all got up to look at it.

'"Where did it come from? Who shot it?" "I did," replied I, "and during the last few days." "Alone?" "Yes, alone." "That must be a lie—a poor lean fellow like you could never have shot such a splendid lot of tusks." They appealed to my drivers for the truth, and when we returned to our coffee-pot made the astonishingly liberal proposal that I should join and shoot with them and take half the ivory killed by the whole party. They were in earnest, and I had the greatest difficulty in getting off, but I have reason to believe it was through the account of these Boers and of another party I met at Livingstone's station, that I received a most courteous message from Pretorius, who was then their chief, that he hoped I would visit Mahalisberg, and that I should find a hearty welcome through Boerland.

'They had a wholesome dread of traders who for ivory might supply the natives with muskets and ammunition, and thus render them recalcitrant, and they had found out I didn't and wouldn't trade; indeed the story among them was that on a native bringing a tusk to my wagon for sale, I threatened to shoot him then and there!'

Whilst they were on the low Siloquana Hills, the travellers first made acquaintance with the *tsétsé* (*Glossina morsitans*):

'A dusky-grey, long-winged, vicious-looking fly, barred on the back with *striæ*, about the size of the fly you so often see on dogs in summer. Small as he is, two to three will kill your largest ox or your strongest horse; for the poison introduced by the proboscis is zymotic. The victims sicken in a few days ; the sub-lingual glands and muscles thicken, the eyes weep, the hollow above them fills up, a defluxion runs from the nostrils, the coat stares, emaciation is rapid and extreme, and in a period varying from a fortnight to three months, death inevitably ensues. We examined about twenty of our beasts after death, and the appearances were similar in all—flesh flaccid and offensive, fat, if any remained, like yellow water, membrane between skin and flesh suffused with lymph, and puffy, stomach and intestines healthy, heart and liver, and occasionally lungs diseased. The heart in particular attracted our attention. It was no longer a firm muscle, but flabby, like flesh steeped in water, blood gelatinous and scanty — the largest ox not yielding more than 18 pints. Moreover, it has entirely lost its colouring property, the hands when plunged into it coming out without stain. All domesticated animals

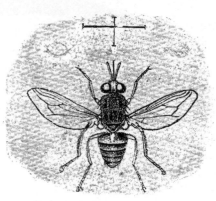

TSÉTSÉ FLY (HIGHLY MAGNIFIED).
A B, actual length of body; C D, span of wings.

are affected save the ass and the goat, and the calf as long as it sucks. Man and all the wild animals are proof against the poison. The fly infests particular spots, from which it *never* shifts. The natives herd their cattle at a distance from its haunts, and should they in changing their posts be obliged to pass through tracts of country in which it exists, they choose a moonlight

winter's night, as during the nights of the cold season
it does not bite.'

It was on the banks of the Mokolwé, an important tributary of the Limpopo discovered by Oswell and Vardon,
that the former first met with and killed the *quebaaba* :

'This beast resembles the white rhinoceros (*Rh. simus*),
except in the formation of the horn, which is longer,
much straighter, and curved, though but
slightly, in exactly the contrary direction. The two specimens which we
brought from the interior are abraded
at the points on the lower sides,

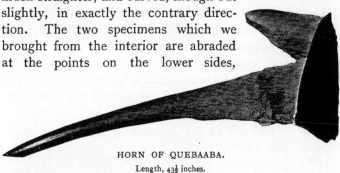

HORN OF QUEBAABA.
Length, 43½ inches.

probably from coming in contact with the ground whilst
the animal is feeding. When running at speed also, or
when alarmed, it carries the head very low, as do likewise
the other species, and the horn, then standing nearly
straight out from the nose with a trifling curve downwards, may occasionally strike or rub against the in-
equalities of the ground.

'From the circumstance of the *quebaaba* being found in
the same neighbourhood, and from its general resemblance
to the white rhinoceros, we at first supposed the pecu-
liarity of the horn to be merely a malformation, but the
fact of five having been seen, two of which were shot ;
of the Bechuana who inhabit the country in which the
specimens were obtained, knowing the animal well under
a distinct name, and describing it as frequently to be met
with, though by no means so common as the other kinds ;
and of its being unknown to the south of the Tropic

DROVE ITS HORN IN UNDER THE FLANK, THROWING HORSE AND RIDER INTO THE AIR.

though the common white rhinoceros is there found in abundance, caused us to change our opinion and to consider it as certainly a distinct species.'*

During this expedition Oswell had two terrible experiences with rhinoceros. That neither proved fatal is little less than miraculous.

He had one pre-eminently good horse, the very pick of all he ever had in Africa—some hundred and eight—fast and most sweet-tempered, and so fearless that it would without whip, spur, or any urging carry him right up to a lion and stand

HORN OF THE RHINOCEROS THAT
KILLED STAEL.
Length, 32 inches.

perfectly motionless within a few feet of the brute whilst its master fired. Returning to camp one evening on Stael, he fired both barrels at a white rhinoceros. Instead of dropping or bolting, it began to walk towards the smoke. He turned his horse only to find a thick bush was against its chest. Before he could free it the rhinoceros drove its horn in under the flank, throwing horse and rider into the air with such terrific force that the point of the horn pierced the saddle. As they fell the stirrup iron scalped his head for four inches in length and breadth. He scrambled to his knees, and saw the horn actually within the bend of his leg. With the energy of self-preservation he sprang to his feet, but tottering a step or two he tripped and came to the ground. The rhinoceros passed within a foot without

* He reverted, however, latterly to his original view.

hurting him. As he rose for the second time his after-rider came up with another gun. Half pulling him from his horse, Oswell mounted it and galloped after and caught the rhinoceros. Wringing the blood from his eyes, and keeping back the piece of scalp with his left hand, he held the gun to his shoulder with his right, and shot the brute dead. Resting for a few moments under a bush he remounted, and rode back to Stael.

' That very morning as I left the wagons I had talked to him affectionately, as a man can talk to a good horse, telling him how when the hunting was over I would make him fat and happy; and I had played with him and he with me. It was with a very sore heart that I put a ball through his head, took the saddle from his back and started wagonwards, walking half the distance, ten miles, and making my after-rider do likewise.'

It would be impossible to conceive anything more characteristic of the man than these last few words. Shaken in body by his terrible fall, in mind by the loss of his favourite horse, severely wounded and bleeding, he yet, as a matter of course, shares the ten-mile tramp home equally with his black servant. When they reached the wagons and explained what had happened, the Kafirs to a man burst into tears.

On the return journey to the Cape he met with the most serious accident of his life. Stalking two rhinoceroses of the *keitloa* variety, he was lying flat and waiting for a side chance. They came within twenty yards of him, but head on, in which position they cannot be killed except at very close quarters, for the horns completely guard the brain, which is small and lies very low in the head. Constant success and impunity in shooting these beasts induced a somewhat rash confidence, and he lay still until he saw that if the nearer of the two forged her own length once more ahead her foot would be on him. He would have shot her up the nostril, but a charging

FIRED BOTH BARRELS; BUT WITH THE SMOKE HE WAS SAILING THROUGH THE AIR.

rhinoceros always makes straight for the smoke of the gun, and he knew that if number one fell, number two, who was within four or five yards of her, would be over him before the smoke cleared. Hoping that his sudden appearance from the ground would startle her and so give him a chance of escape, he sprang up and dashed alongside of her to get her in the rear, his hand being on her as he passed. She immediately gave chase. He was a very fast runner, but in thirty yards she was at his heels. A quick turn saved him for the moment; the race was over in the next. As the horned snout came lapping round his thigh he rested the gun on the long head, and, still running, fired both barrels; but with the smoke he was sailing through the air, and it was not until three hours later that he recovered consciousness, to find a deep gash in his thigh, eight inches long, down to the bone in all its length. The limb stiffened, and, unable to get into the wagon, he made his bed for nearly four weeks under a bush, the rip healing rapidly, covered with a rag kept constantly wet.

As soon as he was sufficiently recovered he hurried down to the Cape, where an official announcement awaited him that in the event of his failing to return to India by a certain date, then two months past, his appointment would be cancelled. He accordingly secured a passage in the next ship.

HORN OF SPECIES OF RHINOCEROS
THAT TOSSED OSWELL.
Length, 23½ inches.

CHAPTER VI.

INDIA AND ENGLAND.

1847–1848. AGE 29–30.

Oswell's plans for the future — Livingstone writes from Kuruman ; the course of the Limpopo ; twenty years old, twenty children—Oswell appointed superintendent of Government catch of elephants; the *coopum ;* taming and training ; a servant over one hundred years old, with sixty years' good character ; a sound whipping ; a knock-down blow ; a dash for liberty ; the elephant in war and pageants ; as a nurse ; as a wood-cutter's assistant ; mode of capture in pitfalls—Adventure with black bears—Peter and his little ways—England re-visited—Death of Mrs. Oswell—Decision to return to Africa.

W. Cotton Oswell to his Brother.

'MADRAS,
'*April* 12, 1847.

' . . . I am going up to the Neilgherry Hills to linger out the four or five months I have to stay in this world, and then D.V. intend proceeding to Ceylon and taking my passage home from Point de Galle My appointment was, as I have already told you, lost by my overstaying my leave at the Cape. Since my return, however, I have been offered the refusal of two very excellent ones, and could I have made up my mind to remain in India after my furlough became due, should have accepted one of them. But I have always led you to expect me home at the end of ten years, and I am very anxious to see you all myself! So if I live I shall be with you D.V. about the end of the year. . . . Now that my return to England draws so nigh, I begin to fear that I have, as usual, been overcolouring the picture. It is hard for an alien to think that others do not remember him so well as he remembers them ; but this, of course, must be the case. The world, so far as Europe is concerned, has been standing still with me. I have had nothing else to think of but those it contains dear to me. The one often thinks of the many, the many but seldom of the one . . . If there is anything in this country I can bring home that you think might be likely to be acceptable to anyone, pray let me know ; you have yet time. You must tell my dearest Mother not to fancy that she will see her son such as he left her—a fine, rosy-faced, plump, cherubimish-looking boy, but rather ancient, exceedingly thin, and frightfully green and yellow. I tell you this in sober earnest for fear lest she should be alarmed at such an appearance as the glass tells me I have.'

As a result of their meetings in Africa a warm friendship had sprung up between him and Dr. Livingstone. Each recognised, and very cordially appreciated, the fine qualities of the other.

The Doctor wrote the first letter of a correspondence which continued with singular fidelity and increasing affection until his death :

'KURUMAN, 1847.

' . . . Having come out here on a visit and finding a direct opportunity to Colesberg, I hasten to give you a word of salutation. We heard from Captain Vardon that you had actually sailed for India, so we must now think of you as again in that sultry clime. . . . It will afford us all much pleasure to receive a note from you. A short time after you left, Mrs. L. and I went a long way to the Eastward. We were at least twelve days due East of Chonuane when we reached our farthest point in that direction. There we were astonished to find the Limpopo had come round and was just three days beyond us when we looked to the sunrising. When at the Bamapela we asked where the Basileka lived, and the natives pointed N.W. to them and said they lived three days (native travelling) from them; the Bamapela are a little to the South of East from Chonuane. I have felt exceedingly anxious to inform you of this, lest you should give your name to any map-maker with the mistake you seem to have made, and therefore begin the subject at once. There are a great many magnetic hills a little to the N.E. of our station, and these extend a long way Eastward; they are composed of black oxide of iron, and are so powerful that pieces stick to the wagon wheels in travelling. I have thought your compasses must have been affected by this cause, and led you astray. If the Basileka are not more than sixty or seventy miles N.W. of the Bamapela you have not made more Northing than that from the latitude of Chonuane, 24° 30'. The Limpopo, it is certain, comes round to our Latitude, for it was directly East of us at the Bamapela. It there receives a large river called the Lepinolé, then another, the name of which I forget, and then makes a sweep away back to the N.E. There is still room for discovery; the boors declare it goes into the sea only a little way North of Delagoa Bay; the natives say it becomes an immense stream—" the Mother of all Rivers "—after receiving these two rivers. We found quite a cluster of tribes situated in the bend made by the Limpopo. We visited three, and saw the habitat of four more. One of these is that which has nearly been destroyed by the boors. The country is much more densely populated the farther East one goes, than in the centre of the country. They received us like the boors, with far more fear than love. The Chief of the Bamapela has forty-eight wives and twenty children, the latter in feature all very much resembling himself; he is not more than twenty years of age. . . . . .

Cumming has shot but few elephants this year. He had
a bad attack of illness beyond the Bamangwato which
prevented him doing much execution. He intends to follow
your " spoor " henceforth. We found that the wagon
you so kindly allowed us to have, had arrived at Kuruman
before us. It had got a turn over which damaged the tent ;
but that will soon be mended. . . . We were right glad
to get it as it is. We needed a wagon, and but for your
very great kindness, should have been obliged to wait and
save for it, at least three years more. Please accept of our
united and hearty thanks for the favour. I hope to be
able to do something towards my duty by next year. We
have now resolved to move from Chonuane, and if there
is no better place to be found, our residence will be at
Kolobeng. We go on much as usual at Chonuane. Here,
all are pretty well except little Robert, who is teething.
Mr. Ashton and I went to Lekatlong, were summoned
back in a few days, and though we rode incessantly, came
only in time to look at his little boy's grave. Allow me,
my dear sir, to recommend the Atonement of Christ as
the only ground of peace and happiness in death. To His
favour and friendship I commit you. . . . Mr. and Mrs.
Moffat, Mr. Hamilton, Mrs. L. and self unite in very kind
regards to you. Should you happen to meet with Captain
Steele, you will oblige me by presenting my very kind
remembrance. I shall write again as soon as we have any
news ; probably in six months from this, when the bags
for the season have been made up. We hear nothing about
the Caffre War. Murray, we hear from a son of Mr.
Moffat, reached London safe and sound. Do remember
and write soon. This is my last request.'

On Oswell's return to India, the *Madras Journal of
Literature and Science* applied to him for some account of
his wanderings. He accordingly sent them a sketch-map
of the country traversed, which appeared in their next
issue, and some explanatory notes, which they embodied
in the following article :

'We have much pleasure in presenting our readers with the accompanying sketch map, for which we are indebted to Mr. Oswell, of the Civil Service, showing the extreme points to which he penetrated in the course of two expeditions into the interior of South Africa, made in search of game in 1845 and 1846.

'On the first occason, with Mr. Murray, he reached the Ba-Kaa mountains, and returned by the valley of the Limpopo. This line nearly coincides with the track of Mr. W. Hume in 1830.

'In his next journey he was joined by Captain Vardon, and they together explored the course of the Limpopo to a greater extent than had been done by any previous travellers. Mr. Oswell was at first led to suppose that the stream pursued a more northerly course (indicated by the red line on the map), and he had placed their turning point in the Lingwapa mountains somewhere between 20° and 21° S. Lat. But subsequent consideration, and the result of a communication from Mr. Livingstone, the enterprising Scotch Missionary in the Bechuana country, induced him to exhibit the direction of the river as it now stands.

'"This sketch," observes Mr. Oswell, "is not supposed to be strictly accurate. We laid down the course of the river Limpopo as correctly as we could from the tops of the hills, etc., with a compass, but having no other instrument, we are aware that many errors may have crept in, and only hope that others more carefully provided, may some day or other give the world a better. The present will serve to show the wanderer where water may be obtained at a distance from the river, and information such as this even, is not to be despised in Africa.

'"The lines dotted and plain mark the track of the wagons, but the country was well quartered on horseback for forty or fifty miles on either side. The Limpopo is supposed to reach the sea at, or somewhere a little to the North of, Delagoa Bay."'

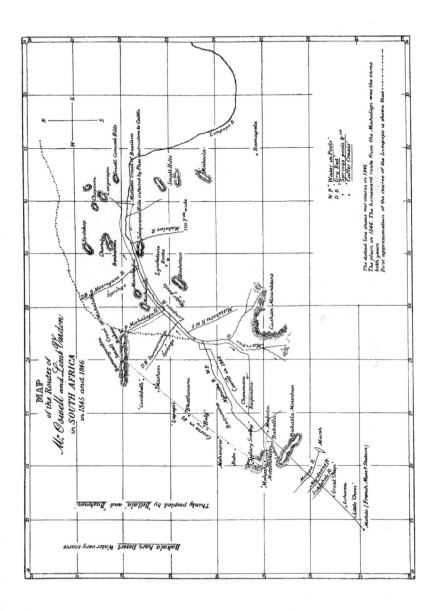

' The Bekoa and Bumungwatow tribes whom Mr. Oswell visited in his first excursion mentioned three other people as living to the north of them, viz. the Makalakka, Mancupani and Mashuna. They were also familiar with the existence of the great Lake, and had frequently visited it. They described it as lying in a W.N.W. direction from their location, at a distance of twelve or fourteen days' journey for a man on foot (which would be about three hundred miles) or a month with the wagon.'

Although, in view of his having decided to bid a final farewell to India, Oswell had declined a permanent appointment, he was unwilling to remain idle for the six or seven months that must elapse before his return to England, and on this becoming known he was at once offered temporary employment as superintendent of the Government *coopum*, a post for which inclination and qualification alike fitted him. Forty-five years later he wrote the following admirable and spirited account of this period of his life :

' Orders were out for a Government elephant hunt to fill up gaps in the commissariat and pagoda studs; messengers sped to the outlying villages under the Anay-malay* range ; shikarris† and Irulurs‡ were convened for *khabr*, and after due consideration it was decided to draw a large tract of country at the foot of these hills. Preparations began at once ; east and west, north and south, the keen-eyed scouts were sent forth to view the feeding grounds, and see by what arrangement the herds might be massed, and in what direction driven. A valley between hills, or ground with low ridges rising on either side, is, if possible, selected, and in a narrow part a *coopum* is constructed.

* Anglicè, Elephant Hills.
† Native hunters.
‡ An Indian tribe who live entirely in the jungles, and in knowledge of wild animals and their ways equal the African Bushmen.

'And what is a *coopum*? Not far from water a spot, a hundred to a hundred and fifty yards in diameter, is pitched upon, and nearly enclosed by a trench nine feet wide and the same deep, in the form of a horseshoe coming in rather suddenly at the heels, the space between which is left solid and uncut; from the shoe-ends diverging palisades of large trees felled by the jungle folk and dragged into position by tame elephants, stretch away a mile or so into the forest—very strong close to the *coopum*, and getting less and less compact as the distance increases. On the day of the hunt, outside the heavy palisades where they run into the *coopum* ditch, for a hundred and fifty yards men lie in ambush with spears, and at intervals, as the fence broadens out and weakens, others in groups of four or five make fires and watch beside them; and beyond, as the hedge dies away altogether, fires, still in diverging lines, with their attendant watchmen, stretch on for four or five miles farther into the dense jungle, till the last on one side is six miles asunder from its opposite. Four miles deeper in the wood three or four thousand beaters have taken their posts on a curve, with a chord, say, of ten miles.

'The morning of the hunt has dawned, and with the earliest streak of light the beaters advance very slowly and cautiously, gradually taking closer order, and contracting their wings as they near the line of fires. We at the *coopum* in the meantime have been walking the tame elephants backwards and forwards over the entrance to the trap to scent it, and thus if possible give confidence to the expected oncomers.

'But the sun grows hot, and as yet not a sound has reached us. We leave the rock immediately over the enclosure where we have been sitting since 5 a.m.—it is 11 now—and make for the shade.

'Suddenly a sharp-eared native lifts his head—there is a murmur amongst those close around us—they have caught a distant shout, or shot. But all is still again.

'Another half-hour, and even our duller senses are

conscious of an occasional intermittent wave of sound;
"nearer it comes and yet more near," until at length an
unbroken hum surges towards us.

'You have an undefinable *vision* of what is going on;
three or four shots in rapid succession, a storm-wave of
yells tell you that the herd has made an attempt to break
through the line of fires; the shouting grows longer and
louder, and the anxious trumpeting of the elephants
mingles with it. You feel they are between the first
palisades, and growing every instant more suspicious, are
seeking for a weak spot along the lines; but you know they
are met at every point. Shot after shot with blank car-
tridge is fired at them; as they swerve, maroons and
rockets are showered behind them. At last they are
within the heavy fence of felled trees, and only a short
two hundred yards from the trenched enclosure.

'They are fully aware of their danger now, but their
enemies are too thick behind them. The incessant ex-
plosion of the fireworks, the shots from the guns, and
the shouts from the thousand human throats intimidate
them as they again and again turn and threaten to break
back. Nothing is left save the chance of a faulty place
in the palisade. Two or three, more determined than the
rest, have partly thrust aside the large forest trees, and a
way of escape seems opening fast.

'A lithe, dark form glides along the outside of the barrier,
reaches the half-made breach, and lying sheltered by the
logs, passes his spears through the chinks, and sharply
pricks the legs of the elephants. Startled, they move on,
and *pêle-mêle* in dark mass reach the jaws of the trap.
A tusker is leading. As he comes to the narrow, uncut
way he stops irresolute, and for a moment refuses to
move. But it is too hot for him, and taking a female
between his tusks he pushes her to the front, and holding
her securely, and prodding her if she attempts to turn
right or left, he makes her try every yard before he puts
his foot down.

' The leaders have passed the Rubicon ; the others follow as sheep through a gateway. As the last clears the portal, twenty men, who have been lying concealed in a trench, spring up, each with a large truss of *cholum* straw, place it a little inside the *coopum*, across the inner neck of the bridge along which the elephants have just gone, and in a moment it is blazing furiously ; the flare is kept up by fuel, whilst two hundred men in gangs of twenty at a time toil their hardest to complete the encircling ditch.

' It is terrible work in the full heat of the sun and the scorching fire, and they can stand it only for a two or three minutes' spell ; but fresh and fresh they keep at it, until in a very short time the frightened herd, which has retired to the further side, is ringed in.

' For the last hour the excitement has been stirring enough—the sound-drawn pictures of the distance, the actual sight as the great beasts break into view, the maddening roar of humanity strung to its highest tension.

' The watching motionless by the waving grass of the *jheel* till the " sounder " breaks, and law is given, is trying, and I have known men break down under the strain ; but it is short—a matter of eagerness for the coming tussle with the spear—and is over with the first stride of the race as you settle down to the boar ; but in this other there is passive anxiety, long drawn out, a fear that the labour of weeks may all be in vain, the feeling that you must wait, wait, wait, and be content to breathe again only when the fierce blaze tells you that the quarry is enclosed and the hunt up.

' The captives stand cowed and quietly miserable for a space, then they begin to poke round for a way of egress ; but the ring is continuous, and they are not much of jumpers, so they give it up.*   They still move about

* In the hunt I am trying to describe a tusker deliberately pushed a female into the trench, and essayed to walk out over her back ; we stopped him by firing charges of powder in his face, and killed, cut up, and removed piecemeal his improvised bridge.

THE MAHOUT PASSES THE CANE · · ROUND THE HIND-LEGS OF THE CAPTIVE · · ONE OR
TWO TAME ELEPHANTS PATROLLING MEANWHILE BETWEEN IT AND THE WILD HERD.

mournfully, gather into small dejected groups, and hang their heads sadly; and so it goes on for three days. Water is once or twice run in to them through wooden troughs, but they have no food save that growing in the *coopum*, and that they won't touch; they are thoroughly down-hearted, weak in body and spirit. The headmen now decide that they may be individually secured; faggots are thrown into the trench, and a temporary bridge made, over which four or five tame elephants with mahouts up are sent in. As they advance, the wild herd retreats to the farther side, and stands in an untidy clump. Three of the tame elephants are moved up, and presently receive orders to cut off any one of the herd that may happen to be somewhat detached from the main body; and, one on either side, one at right angles across its rump, they shut up their wild sister or brother in a triangle or Greek *Δ*. It is wonderful to see how these intelligent, educated animals hold their prisoner in check, preventing its using its trunk with their trunks, and all lateral, forward or retrograde motion by the weight and strength of their bodies.

'When the struggle is over, one of the mahouts slips off the neck of his mount, with a coil of ground rattan in his hand, and crawling under him, passes the cane in a figure of 8 round the hind-legs of the captive, the tame elephants meanwhile stopping all the attempted kicks and side thrusts of the wild one with the skill of practised boxers. It takes time, but at last the rattan is securely tied, the mahout remounts, and the prisoner is freed. He tries a step forward, finds his *two* legs *one;* strains to snap the ligature, the tough siliceous-coated withy cuts through the skin and flesh, and the fettered victim moves no more.

'Throughout the operation one or two tame elephants have been patrolling between the wild herd and the one being operated on, and if a friend, moved by excitement or the cries of the triangled comrade, seems inclined to make a diversion in his favour, and singles himself out, one of the patrols bears down upon him, and striking him on the side, generally grasses him, and always knocks his wind out for the time, leaving him incapable, even if inclined, of sacrificing comfort to friendship. The tying business is a long one, especially at first, whilst all the captives are comparatively strong and fresh ; five or six in the course of each of the first days is the complement, but as they weary and lose all spirit, the work is less tedious, and there are not so many to keep at bay.

'At last they are all rattanned, and dragged out bodily over the faggot-bridge by the tame elephants, to sites prepared for them in the neighbouring forest ; they are made fast by a chain and rope round each leg to four trees—a leg to a tree—and there they are kept for some days. At first they are sulky, and will not eat, and they strain, till the fastenings cut deeply into the flesh, but they very seldom break away altogether. I should have mentioned that the rattan is removed as soon as they are securely picketed.

'When they are considered meek enough, a number of tame elephants are requisitioned to bring them into the breaking station, which is sometimes close by, sometimes, as in the instance I am writing of, fifteen miles off. Each wild one is placed between two broken ones and attached to its guards by a thick rope noose or collar, to which two other ropes are made fast— one for each attendant *hatti;* if the captive allows himself to be run in quietly, well ; if not, he is pulled along willy nilly.

'On reaching the training station they are again fastened as before, and their education begins ; each elephant is given a man, or man an elephant, which you like, and he is to do his best. Great emulation is the result, everyone coaxing his pet his own way, with the view of taming him.

'At first they are very troublesome, trying to get hold of

their grooms with their trunks, or give them a sly poke with
their legs—but tied as they are, their reach is small, and
after a few days, a bamboo burnt and scraped to a sharp
point brings them to their senses. Each man carries
one of these weapons, and if his elephant shows any
inclination to use trunk or leg, it is sharply pricked,
and in a very short time the sensible beast coils his
proboscis, and jams his legs close together, whenever his
keeper approaches. Then the hide is scratched and tickled
with the bough of a tree, which keeps the flies off, and
amuses the tender-skinned beast—for an elephant's upper

'THAT'S A BAD FELLOW, LACHMÉ—WHIP HIM.'

skin is very thin and sensitive—and all the time he is sung
to in interminable dronings, to accustom him to the
human voice, and calm his nervousness. Occasionally he
behaves himself unseemly, is violent, sets his keeper at
defiance ; and it becomes necessary to punish him severely.
An elephant schoolmistress is called in—ours was a dear
old female called " Lachmé." She had been sixty years
in Government employ, and was registered as full-
grown when taken—so she was over a hundred, for an
elephant is not grown up before fifty—but she was still
young, and very much up to her work. " That's a bad

fellow, Lachmé—whip him." Raising her trunk, she tears
down a huge bough from one of the trees, and holding it
by the small end, mercilessly belabours the recalcitrant,
until he *begs* for mercy, if ever animal did. This is generally
sufficient ; if not, and the contumacy continue, he is tied,
as I have said, to separate trees by a chain and a rope to
each foot, and, not able to move, Lachmé takes advantage
of his position, and backing at right angles to his side,
coils her trunk, lowers her head, and comes full butt against
his ribs, knocking him over. One such lesson is usually
quite enough, and henceforth the attendant, with the threat
of Lachmé in the background, is able to manage his
pupil.

'A few weeks have passed, quiet reigns in the school,
and some of the more advanced scholars have ropes passed
over their backs, one well behind, and one forward, connected with one round the neck to prevent their slipping
backwards and forwards, a kind of double surcingle. It
is the first day of mounting. If the tree under which the
elephant is tied lends itself to it, the would-be rider crawls
along a bough until he is over the animal's back, and then
gently lowers himself, clutching fast hold of the rope,
another man meanwhile preventing the *hatti* from using
its trunk by threatening it with the pointed bamboo. It
is a strange sight to witness the abject terror of the
mounted monsters. I have seen them, with their well-
known note of fear, sink till their bellies nearly touched
the ground, as in dread of the weight breaking their
back, and then, shivering and staggering, raise themselves with a mighty shake, spreadeagling their riders
into the air, till they look like performers on the trapeze.
But they hold on to the ropes, and by degrees regain their
seats. If the bough of the tree is not available the
mount is effected by a short ladder, or by climbing up
the ropes.

'Thus day by day, and little by little, education
goes on, until at the end of two or three months,

the mahouts will ride their coursers about the canton-
ment, and within the latter period I have known them
brought to our bungalows, on a begging "lay," asking
for plantains with a chuckle, and thanking you in the
same dialect.

'It does not do to take them into the neighbourhood of
the forest in which they were caught, for a long while, for
their memories are tenacious. A very well-tamed young
tusker was bought from the overplus of this hunt by
a friend of mine; some months after his purchase, his
owner, who was a great sportsman, got leave of absence,
and dived into the jungles. I put one of my tents upon
the young one, and for a time nothing could be better
than his behaviour. One morning he was rather fidgety
at starting, and after marching a mile or two, up went his
trunk, and with a shrill trumpet he bolted into the dense
wood, tent and all—he had come to a tract of country he
recognised, and stop him no one could. His tracks were
taken up that day and the next, but every time he got
sight of his pursuers, down came this three days before
perfectly quiet beast most viciously to the charge. It
would have been easy enough to shoot him, but then
there was the hope of recapture. Some of the party got
a glimpse of him the third day, and reported that the
tent had slipped down under his belly and was torn into
ribbons. His life was given him, for he was a fine young
fellow, the tent was ruined, and his tusks were nothing
to speak of. He had not been caught more than five
months, but was the most docile and gentle of the whole
catch.

'The desire of freedom generally dies out after a year
or two, and the giant becomes man's very reliable friend
and ally, and what work he does for him! He draws and
pushes his heavy guns, carries his mountain batteries, his
tents and baggage; he is the chief figure in *tamashas* and
processions; and ever since Ganesa lost his head and his
mother stuck on an elephant's in a hurry, or even before

such latter-day myths, he has been the life and soul of all
the stories of India.

'Look what a deft nurse he makes to his mahout's
children. This gentleman is from home, probably drinking somewhere, and his wife has gone to the bazaar; but
the children having once been made over to the elephant,
who is picketed hard by, once placed within sweep of his
trunk, he allows of no wanderings. That baby is crawling
away too fast, he is caught by the heel and very gently
drawn within range; two little dots, propping themselves

AN EXCELLENT, HARD-WORKING WOODCUTTER'S
ASSISTANT.

up against his fore-leg, play at "peep-bo" in perfect
safety; he smooths down their naked, tiny, oily bodies in
the gentlest way with his trunk, and would rather die
than raise his ponderous foot; he understands what is
expected of him, and the nature of his trust, and is
proud of it.

'And if good as a tender nurse, he is also an excellent,
hard-working woodcutter's assistant. The teak-fellers
are off to the hills in the morning, and some of the
elephants, who are divided into three classes—the hill-*men*,
the trolly-*men*, and the stackers—accompany them. A

tree is dropped, lopped and cut into suitable lengths if necessary, noosed round with a rope and the end made over to a *hatti*, with orders to drag it down the hill in the direction of a stacking-yard below. Pinning the rope over his tusks with his trunk, he walks steadily down the side of the hill; the ground grows steeper, and the log shows signs of coming too fast, and outpacing him. He casts off the rope, and watching as the timber bumps from terrace to terrace, deliberately follows, takes up the traction line, and recommences his descent, but always with a wary eye. When he reaches the bottom his work is done, and he *trunks* over his charge to other elephants, whose special work it is to take it to the stackyard. This, assisted by men, they do on low trollies, or rollers. At the yard it is consigned to the stackers (elephants also), who lay it straight by itself or parallel with another block on the ground. For the second course an inclined plane is constructed, up which, with the greatest care, the elephants push a second piece; three or four stand ready, and at the word of command " Push," put their heads against the log and shove in unison, moving it very slowly, with pauses, and preventing it slipping back by pressing their heads, legs, and points of their shoulders against it. Now it rests on the under balk, but it is out of line a little : " Put it straight," " Push," it is even.

' In India, elephants are occasionally taken in pitfalls made on purpose very large ; but having caught your elephant, what are you going to do with him, how get him out ? Again you resort for aid to his tame brethren and his own instinct ; green faggots are liberally supplied him one by one, and he immediately places them under his feet, and stamps them down, until he thus raises himself within a manageable distance from the surface. Ropes and chains are then passed round his legs, and, with plenty of slack, temporarily secured by double turns round trees, beside each of which a man stands with the end of a rope in his hands. When quite close to the top

of the pit, the tame elephants lug him out and crowd
him up, the men at the trees shortening the attachments
before, behind, on one side or the other, as the movements
of the captive give them opportunity, till at last he is
securely fastened by the right length of fetter to the
green posts, and then his education is undertaken after
the manner of the *coopum* curriculum.

'In his wild state the elephant does not, I think, show
any superior sagacity; he hardly needs it, for, monarch
of all he surveys, with a well-stocked vegetable garden,
the necessity for self-protection and the imperative
demands of hunger do not stimulate his instincts. But
in servitude he is the most teachable and receptive of all
animals, and very wise and thoughtful.   . .'

(The MS. breaks off at this point unfinished.)

In common with the preceding pages on the Indian
elephant, the following stories were developed by William
Oswell from notes written in 1893 for a contemplated
book of general sporting reminiscences.   They are
merely rough, uncorrected sketches, but as they possess a
certain interest, and refer to events which occurred at
this period, it has been decided to include them exactly
as they stand :

'I had dug a well for them—the hills above their village
were looked upon as my preserve, and strictly watched.
If a bear harboured among them I knew it next morning;
if a wandering bison showed himself in the jungle at
their foot, one of their best runners started for my head-
quarters at once.

'How often have I since regretted that I did not understand sooner the nature of the people I lived amongst.
Be a great man if you like, keep up a show of state—it is
well—but show an interest in them that they can appreciate, do kind acts, not only in your own way, but also in
accordance with the traditions of *their* race—you'll live

with them, not apart, and be the happier, and you and they the better—*Ah, si la jeunesse savait ! ah, si la vieillesse pouvait !*

'Bears had been run to ground and the tidings had reached me. A tent was immediately sent off and pitched under the hills, in the spot indicated by the villagers, who were quite as much delighted to do me a pleasure in my line, as I had been to dig their well. And this is as it should be—accept their returns frankly, and as they are human beings it pleases them.

'I slept at my tent, and at daybreak, after a cup of coffee, climbed the range with a couple of guides, and found men who had been on the watch the best part of the night, and earthed two or three bears as they returned from their feeding-grounds in the very early morning. They pointed to the mouth of the rocky den which, they said, they had seen them enter—they had heard *snoring* just before I came and were quite sure they had not left their *cache*. I listened, but could not hear anything. The spot was a pile of loose rocks which looked as though they had tumbled from a higher level and adjusted themselves any-how—chinks everywhere throughout, and two or three gaping holes into which the small Indian bear might well creep.

'After making a thorough examination of the surround-ings, and settling which way the occupants were most likely to bolt, I directed the men to pass a rocket or two between the crevices over the spot where they thought they had heard the hard breathing. *Whish, whish, bang !* three times over without result. The smoke came eddying from the lower recesses, showing that the fireworks had penetrated. Another and another salvo in different direc-tions, but the sounds of the discharge died away without eliciting a grunt. 'There are no bears there.' 'Yes, there are,' said the men. 'Go in and look,' said I. 'No, my lord, we would rather not.'

Ashamed of having asked them to do a thing they

evidently thought perilous, I gave my gun into my bearer's hands, and selecting the largest of the openings in the stony heap, crawled in three or four yards on hands and knees. The light came through the rifts, but I could see nothing of any bear.

' Whilst peering about, six feet in advance of me, very suddenly, the daylight was shut out as it were with a large muff, and after a moment's hesitation, with an angry growl, down came Bruin upon his joint tenant. Notice to quit was accepted without murmur at sight, and I got a good start and made the very best of my way backwards to the mouth of the den, and gained the open air a couple of yards in advance of my pursuer. As I sprang up my gun-bearer put the Purdey into my hands, and in an instant I was straddling over the hole from which I had just emerged, one foot on one stone and one on the other, and the bear passing between my outstretched legs. But he never cleared the entrance, for half in, half out, he dropped with a ball through his head. A second bear was behind him but he could not pass his dead companion, and turning, made for the exit at the other end of the run, but was stopped and shot.

' I have known the black bear come back to the charge from a distance of a hundred and eighty yards, and you may roll him over shot after shot, but you will not prevent him trying to carry out his programme, be it for a charge or for escape to his den. Whatever other bears may do I know not, but our friend does not as a rule walk up and embrace you with a hug. If you come suddenly upon him round a bush or rock he will sit up like a dog, and might, if near enough, hug you, but generally he makes a run on all fours at your legs.

' He is not perhaps a very formidable antagonist, but he is a plucky little fellow and very tough, and gives an active, quick-footed man good sport. For a certain distance you can race with him and cut him off, and your interest in the sport is thus much increased.

PASSING BETWEEN MY OUTSTRETCHED LEGS . . . HE DROPPED
WITH A BALL THROUGH HIS HEAD.

He is not by you and out of reach in a second. You cannot race with him down hill, however—here he beats you hollow—for Brer Bear rolls himself over the ledges of rock as easily and harmlessly as a football.

'He is readily tamed. Whilst I was pitched under the spurs of the Nilghirris a private note written in English, to air his knowledge of that language, came to me from one of my native heads of police, to inform me that he "sent into my Honor's presence two small *bars* which he had apprehended on the pass." Our sub-collector Murray took one and "hobbed" him up, and an amusing fellow he turned out, devoted to his master and miserable out of his sight. He always climbed up into the buggy, when Murray went for his evening drive, sat on the vacant seat and sucked his thumb, or perhaps you would say his toe, and the inside of his foot.

' Sometimes when there was a stoppage on the road, he would get out, tempted by an anthill or some such delicacy, and we occasionally left him behind on purpose, and drove on.

' Poor Peter, after an attempt to follow us, would sit down and whine piteously as a lost child ; and when we stole back again we invariably found him on his haunches on the most open part of the ground, with his nose in air, in deep dejection, crying like a baby. His joy at our reappearance was touching ; he cuddled his master, sucked his own paw in a vulgar, smacking way, rolled over and over on the ground, and by every little affectionate action begged us never to leave him again, an orphan in the wide, wide world.

' As he grew up he required correction sometimes, and took punishment meekly enough at the hands of his master, but resented outside interference. He was latterly chained, for he took to killing the chickens for fun. and one day upon my remonstrating with him on his enormities, though I did him no violence, made a rush at me, and broke loose. I had just come in from shooting, and had drawn the shot

from the gun before squibbing it off. Hoping to stop
him I fired the powder into his face, but it did not check
him, and so I ran, and Peter after me, up the steps of the
bungalow. As I reached the top, I saw Murray's switch,
caught it up, and turned on Peter, who, undaunted by the
gun, fled ignominiously at the mere sight of his rod. He
grew very troublesome afterwards. He was allowed to
come in to second course, for puddings and tarts were
very much in his line; but if not immediately attended to
he would take hold of the cloth and pull it, with all on it,
to the ground, and then revel in the sweets, until Murray
bit his ear, when he would bolt away howling.

'At last we had to shoot him, for we could not cure him
of destroying hen-roosts out of simple mischief—he never
ate the occupants.'

When Oswell reached home in November he found his
uncle hale and hearty as ever, but he was deeply concerned at the change in his mother. Though only fifty-
eight, she was a very old woman. Her hair was snow-
white, she had wasted to a mere shadow, her hands and
face were transparent; she was so weak that the slightest
exertion exhausted her, and she felt the cold acutely.
There was nothing actually amiss with her, the doctors
assured the devoted, anxious son, but she was worn out—
with grief, with nursing, with pain. He took her to Tor-
quay, hoping against hope that the soft, warm air might
revive her. Day by day the gulf of their eleven years of
separation seemed to narrow as she listened with fond
pride to his stories and adventures, and filled in the gaps
of the home letters. And when she was too tired to talk
he read aloud to her for hours at a stretch 'most beautifully, more beautifully than any one I ever heard,' as she
wrote to her sister. On her fifty-ninth birthday, January 7,
1848, the exhaustion became critical, and on the morning
of the 8th she passed away, painlessly, peacefully, happily,
thankfully, in the arms of her 'best-beloved boy.'

Her death was a black cloud on his home-coming which visits to friends and relations and compliance with the insatiable demands of society did little to dissipate. His thoughts therefore naturally reverted to Africa for the comfort of strong distraction which England failed to afford.

W. Cotton Oswell to Dr. Livingstone.

'LONDON,
'*Sept.* 26, 1848.'

' . . . I received your long letter yesterday. Many thanks for it; it has cheered my heart wonderfully. D. V. I propose being at the Cape by the middle of December next. . . . My chief anxiety is to give you to understand for certain, that with God's blessing I will be with you towards the close of May, 1849, and earlier if the horse-sickness will allow me. . . . I sail on the 25th prox. Steele will not accompany me; Murray perhaps may. . . . If not altogether incompatible with your views I hope to find you at Kolobeng on my arrival. I will bring all books, instruments, etc., thought requisite; your periodicals shall not be forgotten. Kindest remembrances to Mrs. L., and *ruméla thala thala* to Sechélé. What would the latter take by way of a present?'

CHAPTER VII.

AFRICA.

1848–1849. AGE 30–31.

*THIRD EXPEDITION (WITH LIVINGSTONE AND MURRAY) —
PASSAGE OF KALAHARI DESERT, AND DISCOVERY
OF RIVER ZOUGA AND LAKE NGAMI.*

Preparations for expedition—Prices and quantities of neces-
saries—Mrs. Moffat not forgotten—Graphic description of
Natal—Steele and Vardon write their ' God speed '—Start
made from Colesberg, April 23, 1849 — Livingstone's
announcement of success of expedition arrives February 11,
1850—Chagrin of Oswell's friends at receiving no tidings
from him—He writes his story to Benjamin Cotton and
Vardon—Vardon's generous congratulations, and intervention at the Geographical Society—Further advance
contemplated—Followers hesitate—John steps into gap
—'We will all go '—Chief hostile—Project abandoned—
Livingstone's testimony to Oswell—Gigantic horned oxen.

OSWELL reached the Cape at the end of 1848, and immediately began to prepare for the journey of exploration on
which he had set his heart, by engaging servants, and
buying wagons, oxen, horses, stores, provisions and imple-
ments. On February 10, 1849, he went on board the *Phœnix*,
and reached Port Elizabeth on the morning of the 13th. At
2 p.m. next day he started his wagons towards Graham's
Town, where he had determined to complete his purchases
and preparations, and 'hiring two little bits of rooms in a
small cottage there, I at once set seriously to work in
making ready for a start Northwards.' The actual pre-

liminary expenditure would seem to have amounted to about £600. Fortunately the rough notes have been preserved, and they will no doubt be read by sportsmen of to-day with particular interest, as affording a comparison between modern requirements and prices and those of sixty years ago :

ARTICLES, STORES, ETC., REQUIRED FOR A TRIP OF TEN OR TWELVE MONTHS WITH TWO WAGONS AND SEVEN OR EIGHT SERVANTS.

Coffee, 300 lbs.
Salt, 100 lbs.
Pepper, 10 lbs.
Rice, one bag.
Sago, two lbs.
Spices, etc., qu. suff.
Soap, a box.
Tar, two flasks.
Sugar, 400 lbs.
Mustard, three bottles.
Meal, six muids.
Arrowroot, two lbs.
Cheese.
French brandy, two cases.
Wax candles, 30 lbs.
Snuff, two dozen boxes.
Tobacco, five rolls.

One large baking pot.
One smaller   ,,
Three saucepans.
Six tin plates.
Six knives and forks.
One fryingpan.
One meat knife.
Four tin canisters for tea, etc.

Two kettles.
Two pots.
Four tin dishes.
Six spoons.
One gridiron.
One meat axe.
Three large tin dishes.
One ladle.
Two coffee pots.
One teapot.
Two lanterns.
One flour sieve.
One coffee mill.
Three water casks.
Six needles.
Half pound wicks.
Six tinder boxes.
10 lbs. brass wire.
One candle mould.
Six beakers.
One pair of bellows.
One pestle and mortar.
Two buckets.
Two lbs. of twine.
One dozen knives.
Two dozen boxes lucifers.

40 lbs. of beads.
One bale of canvas.
12 riems.
Three saddles and bridles.
Six linchpins.
One spokeshave.
Three axes.
Three picks.
One chisel.
One punch.
Two spare skenes.
Two gimlets.
One saw.
Three spades.
Three sickles.
One cold chisel.

One hammer.
Two augers.
Screws, nails, etc.
Thermometer.
Small telescope.
Sextant, etc.
Iron spoon for running bullets.
Coarse powder, 60 lbs.
Fine powder, 20 lbs.
Caps, 3,000.
Lead, 150 lbs.
Tin, 30 lbs.
Flints, 60.
Muskets, 6.

FOR BOYS.

Six beakers.
Six spoons.
12 common shirts.
Two greatcoats for drivers.
A small tent.

Six scotels.
One piece of moleskin.
Six jackets.
12 blankets.

PAID BY CHEQUE ON MESSRS. RUTHERFORD.

	£	s.	d.
Mr. James for wagon	37	10	0
Mr. James for oxen	96	0	0
Krommehout for wagon and span	130	0	0
Cockroft for wagon, etc.	57	10	0
Wedderburn's bill for stores, etc.	40	5	0
Ogilvie's ,, ,,	30	14	0
Coffee (3 bags)	9	0	0
Canvas	2	8	0
Holder, for repairs wagon, etc.	12	10	0
Godfrey, ,, ,,	6	9	0
Wagon box	0	12	0

PAID BY CHEQUE ON MESSRS. RUTHERFORD (*continued*).

					£	s.	d.
Wagon box	...		...	...	2	0	0
Twelve riems	...		...	...	0	10	0
Mats ...	...		...	...	0	9	0
Cartels		...	...	...	2	10	0
					428	7	0

HORSES.

				£	s.	d.
For 3 from Mr. James, £20, £10, £9				39	0	0
For dun pony, Trollop	...		...	15	0	0
For brown pony, Boer	...		...	15	0	0
For dun pony	...		...	10	0	0
Brown	...	...	...	20	0	0
Brown chestnut		...	...	15	10	0
Bay pony	...	...	...	15	0	0
Chestnut	...	...	...	15	0	0
'Wildebeest'	...	...	...	9	0	0
Mare ...	...	...	...	6	0	0
'Harry'	...	...	...	10	0	0
Chestnut	...	...	...	9	0	0
				178	10	0
Principal expenses as above for stores, repairs, etc.	...	...		428	7	0
For horses	...	...	...	178	10	0
				606	17	0

SERVANTS.

	£	s.	d.
George Fleming, engaged 1st January, 1849, advanced	15	0	0
Peat Frer, engaged 1st January, 1849, advanced	4	10	0
Claas David, engaged 1st January, 1849, advanced	1	0	0
John Thomas, engaged 1st February, 1849, advanced (15s. a month to be drawn by his family)	8	0	0

SERVANTS (*continued*).

	£	s.	d.
John Scheimen, engaged 26th February, 1849, advanced	3	0	0
Ruyter, engaged 26th February, 1849, advanced	0	10	0
Hendrick, engaged 26th February, 1849, advanced	0	10	0
Claas Henry, engaged 9th March, 1849, advanced	1	0	0
Christian, engaged 7th April, 1849, advanced	1	0	0
Willem Kurt, engaged 7th April, 1849, advanced	0	17	6

There is then an entry :

' FOR MRS. MOFFAT.

' Cauliflower, peas, broccoli, cabbage, spinach, carrots, turnips, Jerusalem artichokes.'

Contemplating a shooting expedition in Natal on his return, he made inquiries in various directions as to the nature and possibilities of the country. Among the replies he received one which gives so graphic and minute an account as to be of real historical value :

Octavius Fordham to W. Cotton Oswell.

' PIETER MAURITZBURG,
' *Feb.* 28, 1849.

' DEAR SIR,
' As you were so flattering as to ask me to send you my opinion of Natal, I sit down to do so. Owing to the bar the trade is carried on by small vessels from 100-150 tons. Along the South Coast there are very strong currents running westward, often four knots an hour. From this and the frequency of South-easters,

vessels have often to run a long way out to sea and make passages of about twenty or twenty-five days. The bay is large, but the greater part too shallow for ships, and the entrance is narrow and inconvenient. The country looks well from the sea, green and wooded, gradually rising in ranges of hills, and mountains far inland bound the view. D'Urban, the village at the bay, has very poor one-storeyed houses with dirt floors, poor accommodation at the inn (Macdonald's) and is a most untempting place altogether. The roads are a deep, dry sand, and the

DURBAN IN 1899.
From a Photograph by G. W. Wilson and Co.

population very small—some hundred and fifty whites besides a hundred soldiers.

'The world at large should believe but little that they hear about Natal *from* Natal, as it is the fashion with some of the inhabitants to sit about, drink brandy and water, and extol the country to the skies for its productiveness, while they are importing flour, etc., for the consumption of its small population ; and because one man has in his garden ten or a dozen tobacco plants which (probably by high cultivation and perpetual attention) look flourishing, and another has noticed wild indigo and sugar-cane, it is set down to produce all these things and fifty more in perfection ! I don't say it is *not* so, but

there is no *evidence* that it *is*.   In the immediate proximity
of D'Urban and along the coast there is wood and thick
bush loaded with creepers, in which are elephants, tigers,
wolves, etc., and there are many bucks in the neighbourhood ; alligators and sea-cows are also to be seen, but
nobody goes after these wild animals, and I have not seen
any of them.   About twelve days (with a wagon) North
of Mauritzburg, there are said to be immense numbers of
every kind.   From D'Urban to Mauritzburg is about sixty
miles, which I travelled in a wagon.   When three or four
miles from the village there is one extensive view of green
hills and vales chequered with small trees and bushes—fine
picturesque scenes for the artist.   Many of the hills which
we as—and des—cended, although not so bad, force me to
believe in the truth of Cradock Pass.   There are a few
Dutch grazing farms on the road, at which there are three
or four hundred head of cattle kept ; and there are also the
Cotton Company's estates, which are not, I think, likely
to do much good for their shareholders.   Mauritzburg
is a pleasant village of neat houses with a tolerably comfortable inn (the Crown) at 5s. per day.   Nobody here
makes more than a subsistence by trade or agriculture ;
but I think it is well suited for a person with £1,000 or
£2,000 to bring up a large family in health and plenty ;
for beef is from a penny to twopence a lb. and of very fine
quality, and likely to be cheaper rather than dearer, as
the whole country from one end to the other is one extensive pasture field of rich grass.   I do not think it is any
use for labourers to come out here, as the large number of
Caffres will prevent the farmers from giving high prices.
Blacksmiths, shoemakers, etc., would earn 6s. to 7s. per
day.   The temperature is hot in the summer, which is the
showery season, and cold and dry in winter.   The climate
is reported to be, and I think is, extremely healthy.   The
soil is very good, and will grow three crops of oats in
thirteen months ; but a great part is not well adapted for
wheat.   Indian corn and beans grow well, but sheep do

not thrive.   What is wanted are active, industrious farmers with some capital.   By their mediation the country might support many millions of English labourers much better fed and in better health and greater ease and enjoyment than at home; and so the country might be the means of adding to the amount of happiness in the world—a consummation devoutly to be wished!   The Boers trecked to

PIETERMARITZBURG IN 1899.
From a Photograph by G. W. Wilson and Co.

Natal* and each took possession of the land which he fancied, often twenty or thirty miles from each other; they

* The fifty-six years that have elapsed since the annexation of Natal have been productive of marvellous changes and developments.   Thus, whereas in 1843 the imports were £11,712, and the exports £1,348, they were in 1897 £5,983,589 and £1,621,932 respectively.   Sugar, coffee, indigo, arrowroot, ginger, tobacco, rice, pepper, pineapples, tea and cereals are extensively cultivated; horses, cattle and sheep are reared in immense numbers; while the last returns showed an output of £182,223 worth of gold and 243,960 tons of coal.   Timber and iron exist in vast quantities, and are now attracting considerable attention.   The population of the colony was in 1896 631,000; of Pietermaritzburg, the capital, 20,000.

protected their property in these solitary regions by main
force, unhesitatingly shooting Caffre or Bechuana thieves
on the spot. By this means and holding a sharp hand
over the Caffres they got work out of them, grew produce, and trade flourished. The English Government
took possession of the country, established tribunals to
decide between man and man, be he black or white, and
forbade the Boers to take the law into their own hands.
The Government practically takes away from the Boers
the protection which from their isolated position it is itself
unable to extend to them. The Boers again treck to find
other regions out of the pale of British interference ; trade
decreases, and the country is not at present flourishing.
The laws suitable to preserve order and protect property in
a thickly-populated country, are applied to an opposite state
of things and produce opposite results, but perhaps time
will set this right, as English emigrants are more likely to
go where law has authority, and population will remedy
the evil. The view of the Government is in my opinion
the long-sighted one. . . . Wishing you a pleasant and
successful excursion,
                              ' I remain, dear sir,
                                     ' Yours very truly.

' If I can ever do anything for you in England I shall be
most happy. My address is Odsay, near Royston, Herts.'

At Colesberg Oswell received a hurried note of good
wishes from Vardon. ' What about the Lake,' he begins
' —to be or not to be ?' and a long letter from Captain
Steele :

' MY DEAR OSWELL,   ' *Jan.* 26, 1849.
        ' I must not allow much more time to slip by
without sending you a line to reach you before quitting
civilized life, and I hope you will get this about the time
you are starting for the interior. I wish I could fold
myself up in the envelope and appear by your side at the
same moment you open this, all prepared for a trêk. Of

your movements since you left me in that hurried manner at Windsor, I have as yet heard nothing. I did not even know the name of the vessel you sailed in, so that I could not see by the shipping reports of your safe arrival at Capetown. On all these subjects I hope to be enlightened one of these days. I was however glad to hear from Richardson, the Colonel of the 7th Dragoon Guards, that Mr. Murray had sailed to accompany you. I did not at all like the idea of your starting off for such a trip by yourself, and there are not many men you would care to undertake the expedition with ; but an old friend, and particularly one who had already been up with you, makes quite a different thing. . . . I am living now in a retired little roadside inn at Brixworth, a small village in Northamptonshire. I have four very good hunters and get my four or five days a week with the Pytcheley and Quorn hounds. I am quite convinced now that it is A.1 in the list of sports. A good run such as we often get in these grass countries is far more exciting than walking up to an old *huttee*, riding down a *keitloa* or spearing a hog. If one could always have such a day's sport as you, Gifford and I had after the tiger near the Karity Waterfall, well then, that's another thing. But, take one day with another, the delight of rattling across country and finding oneself one out of four or five who have been riding to hounds, is not to be surpassed in any part of the world. I do wish you had remained for one season and had been living with me in this snug little inn. I am sure you would have enjoyed it, and in the course of one fortnight I could have introduced you to half the people in the county. I hope however to be here every year, so that I may yet have the chance of talking over your last *shikar* in Africa over a good fire in old England. . . . You will most likely have much later Indian news than we have. Up to this time nothing very brilliant appears to have been done. The action at Ramnugger with the loss of poor Cureton and Havelock must have been a blundering, mismanaged affair.

I am afraid Lord Gough will not shine on this occasion. It is quite astonishing how very little people seem to care in England about what is going on in India. I was staying at a house the other day and announced at breakfast the death of those two men. The only remark was, "Dear me, how very sad! I wonder where Sir Richard Sutton meets next Monday." What a consolation to a man fighting in India to know that it is pretty nearly a matter of moonshine to most of the people in England whether the Punjaub is annexed or not! Gifford is, I see by the papers, with Lord Gough, so he will see more soldiering than I am likely to do. . . . And now God bless you, my dear fellow. I sincerely hope you may have good health— good sport you are sure of—and that you may return safe and sound to this country with the great Lake with you!

'Ever your sincere friend.'

In April, 1849, Oswell wrote home from Colesberg, and then nothing was heard of him until February 11, 1850, when extracts from two letters from Dr. Livingstone, announcing the complete success of the expedition, were read before the Royal Geographical Society. The papers of the day took up the subject, and discussed it with much interest. But no word arrived from Oswell, and his relations, jealous of his reputation and eager for his fame, chafed at the delay and at his supineness in claiming his share of the credit and honour of an expedition and a discovery of which he had been the leader and moving spirit, and all the world was talking:

Rev. E. W. Oswell to his Brother.

'Bonchurch,
'Isle of Wight,
'*Mch.* 9, 1850.

Week after week we have been in expectation of hearing from you, without avail, and all the intelligence we have had has been gleaned from the newspapers which have mentioned the discovery of the great inland Lake. The last account from the *Athenæum* induced me to make application to the Secretary of the Royal Geographical Society in London (in which Society was read a paper on the subject of your discovery) for more information than I possessed. He writes me word this morning that you are in good health, for which intelligence I am most thankful, and that you have gone to the Cape for a boat to navigate the Lake. Would that we might hear from you from there! It may not be too late yet. But how the Secretary has obtained this news I have not learnt, and have to-day written to enquire, as I feel entitled to know all that is known of you. We all rejoice in the success of your expedition most heartily, and only want a letter from you to feel quite happy. Some gentleman is about to leave from the Geographical Society to join you, and I hope to induce him to take charge of this, and to come and see me before he goes. I rather envy you on the banks of Ngami—is not that the name of the Lake?—surrounded as we are just at present with fog and haze. I do hope you have kept regular notes of your proceedings. The Secretary of the Geographical Society regrets in his letter to me that you have not sent him such in order that he might have the pleasure of putting your name down as a candidate for one of the two gold medals given by the Society for discoveries. *I* hope you may have kept them for other reasons. I want to find out Captain Vardon's whereabouts, as I fancy he knows something about you. Has Mr. Livingstone any relations hereabouts? There is a clergyman of that name residing in this place. I feel an intense desire to hear from you, and I sincerely trust that if you are detained at the Lake you will devise some mode of communicating with me. And looking forward in great hopes of seeing you ere very long in England, and with very kind love from all here,

' I am ever, with every earnest prayer,

'YOUR VERY AFFECTIONATE BROTHER.'

At last, on March 20th, 1850, to the proud delight of all the family, the long-delayed, eagerly-desired letter arrived.

W. Cotton Oswell to Benjamin Cotton.

'CAPE TOWN,
'*Jan.* 16, 1850.

'MY DEAR UNCLE,

' I owe many letters and am but one man having but one subject to write about—self. It would be hardly worth while to tell one that I went *here* and another I went *there*, one I did *this* and another I did *so*. My creditors are all your nephews and nieces and look upon you as their joint property. Surely, such being the case, they will consider a letter to you as theirs also. I'll take this for granted, though I think I can hear cries of "Idle fellow!" and "I'll never write to him again!" When they have waded through this perhaps they will change their minds, and congratulate themselves that I have not bored them individually.

' I wrote to Edward just before leaving Colesberg in April last, but no second opportunity has offered until now, as I have but just returned to the land of Post Offices. When I started I had a definite object, but did not mention it, as it would not have enlightened or interested you much in England, and my failure would have gratified some of the good folks here. There have for many years been reports received through natives from time to time of the existence of a Lake in the interior of Southern Africa. In 1835, I think, an expedition was fitted out by Government, and headed by a Dr. Smith, purposely for its discovery. They grew discouraged and turned homewards. Many others have since *talked* of making the attempt, and the Griquas, a mixed race living to the North of the Orange River, have repeatedly tried it, but always failed for want of water. Two hundred miles beyond Dr. Smith's farthest point I had pushed in my former wanderings, and heard of the existence of this Lake and its direction, from

many of the natives ; this time I determined to make for
it, for I felt persuaded the difficulties were not insurmount-
able, and the more arduous the task, so long as we accomplished it, the better. With horses, oxen and wagons I
waited four weeks at Colesberg, the last of the frontier
towns, for Murray, and inspanning immediately on his
arrival, passed onwards to Kolobeng, the most Northern
Missionary Station, situated in 24° 30′ S. Lat. and about
25° 30′ E. Long. Here our party was increased by Mr.
Livingstone, the Missionary, and a Mr. Wilson. A party
of the Baquaina, the tribe residing at Kolobeng, accompanied us, and one of them who had in former years been
at the " Great Water " was appointed guide through the
pathless wilds. For the first hundred and twenty miles,
to the hills of the Bamungwato, a people whom we all
had previously visited, the course took a N.E. direction.
From this point the road was unknown save by report.
Two days' travelling through heavy sand covered with low
bush and clumps of mimosa, in a N.N.E. line, brought
us to a spot called by the natives Serotli.

' It was here our first difficulties began. Serotli stands
on the extreme verge of the Kalahari Desert. Our oxen
had already been without water for two days on our
arrival, and there was no apparent probability of their
obtaining that necessary. The place itself was a sand
hollow with no signs of water save about a pint in one
small hole. We had eighty oxen, twenty horses and
thirty or forty men, all thirsty. Unpromising as was the
appearance of the spot, the old guide assured us that if
we dug we should obtain a supply. Spades and land-
turtle shells were accordingly set to work, and at the
close of the day we had sufficient to give the horses a sip
each. For two days longer the poor oxen had still to
remain without, but four pits being at length opened to
the depth of eight or nine feet, a sufficiency for all our
beasts was obtained. Watering them, we once more
moved on. The sand was distressingly heavy and the

sun fiery hot. The oxen moved so slowly and with such
difficulty that I was at times afraid we should fail even in
the very outset, but fortunately, considerably before we
expected it, on the third day we came by chance upon a
small pool of rain-water. The poor beasts were nearly
exhausted, but a day's rest and three or four good drinks
recruited them. The most trying, because the heaviest,
part of the Kalahari was behind, but a hundred miles was
still between us and any certain supply of water. Another
small rain-water pond and a little spring, however, furnished us with what we wanted, though not without our
having to go twice, three days without. You will perhaps
wonder at our being so long in covering so short a
distance, but a wagon is not a steam-carriage. Water
was excessively scarce, its whereabouts unknown, and the
sand, occasionally for miles together, over the felloes of the
wheels. I shall never forget the pleasure with which,
whilst riding out ahead of the wagons, on the 4th of July,
we came suddenly upon a considerable river,* running, as
we struck it, N.E. by E. The wagons reached it the
same evening, and our troubles were looked upon as past,
for we were informed by the natives, with whom we
managed after much trouble to open a parley, that the
water flowed from the Lake we were in search of. Their
information was correct, and holding up the course of the
stream for two hundred and eighty miles, and meeting
with no difficulties to speak of, save from the denseness
of the bush and trees in particular tracts, through which
we had to cut our way, we at length reached the object
of our expedition, and were fully repaid.

   'None save those who have suffered from the want,
know the beauty of water. A magnificent sheet without
bound that we could see, gladdened our eyes. Animal
life, which had in the Desert been confined to one or two
of the deer tribe which do not require water, and Bush-

* The Zouga.

A MAGNIFICENT SHEET OF WATER . . . GLADDENED OUR EYES.

men, who inserting a reed some three or four feet below
the surface, suck it up, was here and there along the river,
greatly increased. A new nation, speaking a language
totally distinct from the Bechuana, inhabited the islands,
moving across the water in their canoes and living principally on fish, and animals taken in the pitfalls which
lined the banks of the stream. Among the *feræ* the
elephant and buffalo were the most numerous, the latter
roaming in immense herds, and every accessible drinking
place in the river being trampled with the spoor of the
former. I had not much spare time to shoot, but a few
capital specimens fell to my gun.

' The scenery generally along the river was magnificent.
Trees of great size, rich in foliage, fringed it on either
side ; now it is shut in between high steep banks, and
runs black and deep ; now it opens out into a broader
and shallower bed dotted with banks and islands. Its
vegetation is distinct from that of the country from which
we came ; palms, flowering trees something like lilacs,
and a species of the *ficus indica* were abundant ; in places
that giant the mowanah or baobab was found. Of this
tree I have spoken to you before, but those seen this year
exceeded our old friends in size ; the largest measured
was upwards of seventy-five feet in circumference at
four feet from the ground. The lake is situated in
S. Lat. 20° 19' and about 24° E. Long. We had to make
a long *détour* to the Eastward to obtain water, and consequently the distance from the last Missionary station
was about six hundred miles. From knowing where to
dig for water, our route back was not so harassing as our
inwards one, though want of water made us longer than
we otherwise should have been. I could write at much
greater length to you on this topic, but will spare you.
My African mania is apt to run away with me. . . .
You mention £270 having come to me by Mrs. Harrison's
death. Ask Lou Cotton to take £25 of it, and after
deducting my share of *our picture* (£20) to spend the

remainder as seemeth good to her, in *soup!!* or flannel waistcoats. £45 I should like you to hold and dispose of in charity as you will, for one who is too indolent and selfish to think sufficiently of others himself. The remaining £200 you can either pay into Colvin & Co.'s hands or keep in your own, as you like best. Tell Dr. Acland I have tried hard to get him specimens of Bechuana and Bushmen skulls, but the former bury their dead so close to their houses, and are so touchy as to their being disturbed, and the latter are, when dead, so soon devoured by the birds and beasts, that I have hitherto failed. The scales tell me that notwithstanding the hard work we have undergone, rather better than 14 lbs. have somehow or other been added to my English weight. You will think it about time that I should say how I intend disposing of myself for the current year, and will, I am afraid, be rather disappointed at my persisting in a life of vagrancy; but the accounts from home are so good, and my love of vagabond life so unsatiated, that I purpose again diving into the interior and trying to reach the Portuguese settlements on the Zambesi, by an overland route.

'Mr. Livingstone, the missionary, will again accompany me, Murray will not. Of our intended course I will give you some idea in a letter which D.V. I will send to my brother from Colesberg. My furlough is up on the 13th of September next, and whether my Honourable Masters will give me an extension, is, I am afraid, doubtful, but I shall solicit it. It is my sincere wish to return to India if I can conscientiously believe I can *live* there, but of this I am very doubtful, for although now in this country I am much better than in England, my *interior* is not altogether as it should be, especially during the hot weather. You must not think I wish to complain, for this is not the case. I thank God that I am much better than I was. Before deciding upon trying Madras again, I shall take the advice of the best medical authorities here, and be guided by their opinion. Love to my very dear brother and to all. God bless you.

'Yours most affectionately,

'W. Oswell.

'P.S.—Did Joe Cotton ever get his bulbs ? . . . I am sending you home half a dozen skin dresses of the Kafirs, with a few ostrich feathers for the cousins. The thick " caross" please hand over to the Parson to keep him warm in the carriage during the winter. Do what you wish with the others—the leopard skin makes a handsome cover for a table. If I do not go to India on my return, you may expect me home again. The worst part of Cape Town is its want of obedience—the inhabitants still refusing to receive Her Majesty's convicts. Sir Harry Smith's conduct is considered to have been very weak.'

Oswell had made no mistake in addressing his letter to his uncle :

Miss Louisa D. Cotton to her Cousin W. Cotton Oswell.

'Gloucester Terrace,
'*March* 23, 1850.

'My dear William,—

'Your long-expected and capital letter of January 16th, from the Cape, which reached us a few days back, gave us all very great pleasure, and perfectly satisfied all parties that it was addressed to our dear, good Uncle. You would hardly believe what true pleasure and interest he took in trying to find out something about you from the Secretary of the Geographical Society, who was very close with his information, and seemed only to care to increase the fellows of the Society, regretting very much you had not corresponded with them and become a member. Edward, in consequence, empowered Uncle to nominate him a Member, that thus he might be entitled to all the information they gained. However, I do not think Uncle will have him proposed now we have had your letter, and a promise that you will write again from Colesberg. Uncle has seen Mr. (or perhaps Captain) Frank Vardon, and many were the regrets you had not written to him. But now he has seen your letter he intends himself to be at the next Geographical Meeting and put in a few words for you, the prime mover in the great discovery, whereas, through the London Missionary Society, Mr. Livingstone seems to have more than his due. I intend sending this letter to Captain Vardon to give to a Mr. Galton, who is going out, we hear, to join you next week. . . . Robert always mentions you in his letters and says he has seen your name as having made the discovery of the large inland lake. . . . Uncle says you will have a bonus from the London Insurance this year of £75, but he adds "Much he cares for this"! . . . .'

Before setting out William Oswell had promised to write details ·of his journey at the very earliest opportunity to his dear friend Captain Vardon, whose romantic feeling for Africa and all things African equalled his own. The sweetest-natured of men, Vardon was incapable of taking offence at anything his friend did or failed to do; but with this promise in mind, and with more intimate and accurate knowledge of the country and the explorer than any man then in England, it was a bitter disappointment to him to hear the first accounts from another source. But he did not allow it to interfere with the heartiness of his congratulations :

'33, OXFORD TERRACE,
'HYDE PARK,
'March 25, 1850.
'MY DEAR OSWELL,—
'. . . I have come to the conclusion that a denizen of the mighty Lake looks with ineffable contempt on a Limpopo plodder, and that one who once crept along the

sandy margin of the crystal Mokolwé, is not henceforth to
hold communion with him whose foot has left its print
on the banks of the noble *Zouga*! Be this as it may,
however, I cannot allow Mr. Francis Galton to leave
England for Kolobeng without giving you a line or two
and congratulating you from the bottom of my heart on
having at length reached the " Groot Vater." Your good
uncle, Benjamin Cotton, called on me not long ago to ask
me if I had any tidings of you. Then your worthy brother
wrote to me from the Isle of Wight, to the same purport.
Since then, however, your letter to the former has arrived,
and he very kindly came over here with it, and made me
acquainted with its contents. . . . Livingstone's letters
have been read before very full meetings of the Royal
Geographical Society and he has acquired immense renown
in consequence. I was present when his very long letter
to Steele was read. It is a thousand pities no production
of yours was likewise forthcoming. You are indeed
wasting your sweetness on the desert air! I long to
hear more about the lake. What about the liché ? Is
there such a buck ? Did you fall in with him or not ? I
hope you may meet with Galton. He is an enterprising
fellow and has seen something of the White Nile. His
present expedition is to be quite a boating one on the Lake
and its rivers, and he takes up with him a beautiful craft
for the purpose. I hope he will succeed and so circum-
navigate the Lake and determine its extent. It will be a
most interesting trip indeed. Again and again have I
wished I was entitled to a pension from our worthy
masters. I would wish them good-bye, and set to at Africa
in earnest. I hope you will succeed in your *Zambesi* expedition. . . . Cumming is here in England. I believe he
intends exhibiting all his trophies by and bye—in London
of course. They say Dr. Smith lost money by his, but I
cannot fancy Cumming losing by anything, can you ? . . .
My brothers are all well and repeatedly ask me if I have
heard from you, and how you are getting on, but an ominous

shake of the head is all that I can favour them with.
I have written to Livingstone by this opportunity. No
doubt he is as good and kind a little fellow as ever. I
should like to have a chat with him once more. I sometimes think I've a great mind to stay my five years away
from India and to rush off to Kolobeng at once, but I am
not the rich man, Oswell, that you are, and my exchequer
don't at all keep pace with my gigantic ideas. Had I only
the means, I would resign the service, join you in South
Africa, and if we didn't go ahead together it would be a
pity! . . . I am having *such* a rifle made by Willon—
a 2-ouncer of course, very similar to the one you no
doubt remember, and the Chokooroos won't soon forget.
. . . I hear from Steele he intends travelling in South
America. I wonder he don't stick to poor old Africa.
We are still all doubt and uncertainty here about our old
friend the Limpopo. What do you think of it now?
Have you gleaned any more particulars about it? Delagoa
Bay or not? Were I to go out again my plan would be
to construct a boat at the junction of the Lephalala and
Limpopo and so go down it to the sea, or at any rate till
I knew whether it was the Manice or not. . . . Do you
remember a point where it made a sudden bend South by
East after running very nearly due North? Dr. Smith
got as far as this, and fancies it makes no more Northing.
But we came on no such turns which lasted for any distance, I think. The opinion here is that it does go into
Delagoa Bay. Something tells me I may yet see that
river again. Would that I could get another lesson or
two in elephant shooting from you, on its banks! Whenever you have an opportunity be sure you write to your
uncle or brother. They really seemed quite distressed at
not having heard from you, and I am sure you wouldn't
like them always to be applying to different people for
scraps from Livingstone's letters, etc., in hopes of gaining
some information of you. You are fortunate indeed in
having friends who do take such interest in you, and it is

no very desperate labour to concoct a few lines during an idle hour, is it ? I know you will pardon me for mentioning this, but I didn't like to see your good old uncle so entirely destitute of information, especially when the Secretary of the Geographical Society (to whom he and your brother applied) was not particularly communicative or obliging. So spare him the mortification of having to apply in that quarter again. And now, my dear Oswell, farewell. May God bless you and bring you once more home, where no one will be more happy to welcome you again than

'Your affectionate friend,

'FRANK VARDON.'

It is pleasant to know that two days later he received a minute account of the expedition, which in every particular amply fulfilled his most sanguine expectations :

W. Cotton Oswell to Captain Frank Vardon.

'CAPE TOWN,
'*Jan.* 10, 1850.

'On the 10th of March I left Graham's Town for Kolobeng. with three wagons and five of my old servants, and, picking up horses as I went, outspanned at Colesberg for four weeks waiting for Murray. Inspanned on his arrival (23rd of April), and reached Kolobeng on the 25th or 26th of May. The town stands in naked deformity on the side of and under a ridge of red iron sandstone—the Mission-house on a little rocky eminence over the river Kolobeng. Murray and I left it the day after our arrival, and, trekking to a water called Shokuan, there halted for Livingstone. The whole party left the water of Shokuan on the morning of the 2nd of June. To Mashué the road is much the same as other African roads—sometimes flat and open, sometimes bush and camel-thorn, and is besides the high road to the Bamangwato. From this we struck

13—2

off at nearly N. as a general line, and journeying forty miles over heavy sand ridges and flats sparingly covered with scrubby bushes, reached on the third morning (having watered our oxen once on the way at Lobotani) a place called Serotli.   I look upon this as the portal of the much talked-of desert, and will therefore try to give you some idea of it.   Imagine to yourself a heavy sandy hollow with half-a-dozen such holes or depressions as a rhinoceros would make by rolling himself as he usually does.   In one of these stood about two pannikins of water, and at this spot, we were told, was the last chance of water for seventy miles (three long days with a wagon).   A quart is but short allowance for eighty oxen, twenty horses, and as many human beings.   We had in coming thus far been once three days without water, but our oxen were quite fresh then, and rattled over sixty three miles in style. But the natives, who busily engaged themselves imme- diately on their arrival with throwing out the sand from the little hollows, assured us that there was plenty of *metsé* (water) within.   By the evening of the first day we had two pits opened, and sufficient to give the horses a bucket apiece ; but as there appeared no chance for the oxen until more pits were opened (nor even *then* if the water did not flow in more quickly than it was doing), we determined to send them back twenty-five miles to Lobotani, to remain there until we could ascertain whether the supply could be made to equal the demand.   Late on the morning of the fifth day the poor brutes reached their drinking place, having been four full days (ninety-six hours) thirsting.   The horses remained with us, for we foresaw a sufficiency for them, and a deficiency of food for ourselves without them.   The holes we had emptied the preceding evening were con- siderably fuller the next morning, and this we afterwards found invariably the case : time seemed to be required for the water to clear its way through its sandy bed.   The oxen returned from Lobotani on the fifth day, after a variety of mishaps which I will tell you some day when we meet

—they are not worth writing. We had a good supply of drink ready for them, and letting them have it at once, we inspanned, but, what with the heat and the sand, could make but six miles by sundown. The next night, with a little application of the whip, we reached a spot called Mokalāni (the camel-thorn trees). Our trocheameter told us we were twenty-five miles from the Serotli pits, and our guide seemed to hint that, if we went so slowly, it was a matter of doubt whether we reached the next watering place at all. It will be long if I ever forget this night at Mokalāni. We were fairly away, and no one, I really think, would have turned back for any consideration ; but the anxiety as to whether we should accomplish our intentions or not was pretty strong within *me* at all events. The want of any knowledge of the road, save that it was by repute very heavy and nearly waterless, coupled with the difficulty with which the oxen had dragged the heavy wagons through the sand on the preceding day, greatly tended to increase this, and, regarding the poor brutes as the means through which I was to gain my point, they were objects of constant care ; for I had determined, if possible, that *my* wagon should take me there.

'After breakfast, on the second day from Serotli, the horses were sent on ahead with our guide : *they* could travel faster than the oxen, and might come to water the latter would never live to see. We followed on their trail, which led for the most part through dense bush and heavy sand. Whips and screeching could get but nineteen miles out of the poor beasts ; they were beginning to feel the want of water sadly, for although hardly two days without, it had been no colony-travelling over hard roads, but right harassing work. Forty-four miles had been accomplished with *great* difficulty in twenty-one hours ! Murray was with the horses, Livingstone and myself had remained behind. The dinner-party was not a merry one, for the members were all too well aware that the poor bellowing beasts around them could not drag on the wagons *very* much farther, and the next spring was believed to be still some thirty miles in advance. We determined to go on as long as the animals were able to work, and then send them on. Half an hour in the morning brought us to the edge of the thicket in which we had passed the night, and upon entering the hollow immediately beyond, the steeds came into view. Was it water? No. The guide had lost his way in this pathless wilderness, and Murray very rightly had halted at once. With the sun, our guide's perceptions seemed to brighten, and he again walked confidently forward. Eight miles were hardly crawled, when the waddling gait of our oxen warned us to outspan. The natives said they would follow the little path we had been coming along, as long as it led in the right direction, in the hopes of finding what we stood so much in need of. It appeared afterwards that they had been told of a small marsh, and of this they now went in search. Breakfast was not over when one of them returned with the intelligence of a large pool close at hand. The oxen, which ten minutes before had been considered as all but exhausted, were now yoked at once. Two miles brought them to Mathuloāni. On Wednesday we had quitted Serotli—it was now Saturday. Giving our cattle Sunday's rest, we again proceeded, though with no very distinct idea when we were to see water. Our guide indeed assured us that even our horses would never thirst more, that we were in the bed of a river, though *we* did not perceive it, but we knew the old fellow's notions of the distance a wagon could travel were rather vague—the marsh we had just drunk at too was a godsend he never calculated on, and how far it still was to Mokokonyani (the first *certain* water from Serotli) was a mystery. For the next four days we fared well enough, finding on the first and third a sufficient supply of rain water, and on the fourth reaching the *first* surface-water in Mokokoong*

* These sand rivers are puzzles to me. Water has evidently, from the height of the banks, *once* flowed in them, but *when* and

(the river of the guide) at a place called Mokokonyani, signifying "my little brindled gnoo."

'After leaving Mathuloāni we had followed the course of this said sand river, which presently became defined enough, but was to all appearance dry. It, however, yielded us an abundant supply, though not without considerable labour in the way of digging. At Lotlokani (another small spring in the Mokokoong, three miles from Mokokonyani) we left the river, and touching it once again on the morning of the second day, left it where it spreads out into a large lagoon-like marsh, now dry. Beyond this our pathfinder wandered a second time, and had I not captured a Bushwoman whom I saw skulking off in the long grass, I am not quite sure we should have reached our goal so well as we did. We had been two full days without water, and were going in any but the right direction when I discovered her. A few beads and mortal terror induced her to confess that she knew of a spring, and offer to conduct us thither. After passing through a very thick belt of trees we came suddenly on an enormous saltpan, or rather succession of saltpans. It was evening, and the setting sun cast a blue haze over the white incrustations, making them look so much like water, that though I was within thirty yards of the edge, I made sure that I

---

why has it ceased to do so? It still runs under the surface. Dig to a certain depth, and, as far as I know, you invariably find it ; but never *on the surface*, except in a few particular spots where the limestone appears above the sand and there is a spring. The Mokokoong is but a fair specimen of a class ; there are many such to the westward. The whole desert, so called, from Serotli to the Zouga, partakes of the character of its rivers, inasmuch as it has no *surface-water*, but innumerable sucking-holes, which supply the Balala and Bushmen. The Serotli pits are a good specimen of the whole. A reed is sunk two or three feet down in the sand, and the water drawn up by the mouth. I have tried it, and found it come readily and abundantly ; but I shall take up small pumps next time with me.

had at last reached the Lake, and throwing up my hat in the air, I shouted till the Bushwoman and Bakuains thought I was mad. I soon discovered my mistake— many made it after me. By the side of the first pan was a small spring of very brackish water. Our oxen reached it next morning. From this point towards the W.N.W. and N.E. we could see dense columns of black smoke rising, and were assured that it was the reeds of the lake on fire! Little thought we that the lake was still some three hundred miles from us. Livingstone and myself had been climbing up the little hillocks in vain, to get a "first view," for the last three days; but all doubts of seeing it eventually vanished on the 4th of July, when riding out from our night's resting place a little beyond Chakotsa, to search for a path, we came upon the *real water* river (the Zouga) running, as we struck it, towards the N.E. A village was nearly opposite us, and we were naturally anxious to open a communication, but the people had all made over to the other side. I tried to drive my horse through a place that looked like a drift, but got him swamped and very nearly lost him. Livingstone and two of the Bakuains managed to get through, and we were gladdened on their return by the news that the water we saw came from that of which we were in search, the Great Lake. We felt all our troubles were over, and next morning, when our wagons stood on the banks of the Zouga, all anxiety for the result was at an end. We might be a long while; the natives said a moon; but we should at last see the 'Broad Water,' for we had a river at our feet, and nothing to do but to follow it. I shall mention this river again presently, so I will not detain you on it now. We followed it up stream for ninety-six miles from the point at which we struck it, and were then told that we were still a considerable distance from the Lake. Our oxen were getting tired, and could make but short journeys with such heavy loads. Emptying my wagon, therefore, and selecting a span from the freshest,

we determined to make a push for it.   Leaving the other
wagons and the remainder of the cattle with the greater
part of the servants, we started on the 16th of July, and
after twelve hard days' work arrived at the half tribe of the
Bamanguato, who call themselves Batouani.   We outspanned nearly abreast of the town at the lower end of
the Lake.

'A tongue of land or an island, I could never discover
which, jutting out in a peculiar way, and sand ridges,
prevented us from getting a fair view of the water
where our wagon stood, so we mounted the horses and
rode five or six miles along the bank, and then I was fully,
fully satisfied, and more than repaid.   One broad sheet
of water lay before us.   To the N.W. and W. you looked
in vain for shore.   To all appearance in those directions
it was boundless as the ocean.   Straight across, that is
N.N.E. from where we were standing, the shores were,
as we thought, about fourteen miles apart.   The eye could
follow their tracery for a short distance to the N. and
N.N.W.   Towards the E. they continued slowly but
gradually approaching each other, and contracted suddenly at the place where the wagon stood.   What was
an expanse of water eight miles across, is now, just
below, but a moderately broad river (say two hundred
yards).   The bank on which we stood was very flat ;
probably the opposite one may be so too, and therefore
not visible at any great distance.   Of the actual breadth
I, of course, can form no correct notion.   The canoes
never *cross* it, but some coast round and along the shores.
Of its extent we may perhaps arrive at an approximation
from the accounts of the Batouani, who assert that a man
walks two days (fifty miles) along its bank to the S.W.,
one day (twenty-five miles) to the N.W., and then finds
the lake a river coming from the N.N.E.   We were
obliged to be content with hearsay, and so must you for
the present.

'During the expedition some of our day's journeys were

short enough, often not more than ten miles; but the
work was nevertheless hard from the thickness of the
jungle and the heavy sand. In one five and a half mile
stage upwards of a hundred trees were cut down, from
the size of *my* arm to that of a blacksmith's—the distance
took six hours and a half to accomplish. Another heavy
sand-rise thickly covered with bush, of about a mile and a
half in extent, kept us for two hours. I was on this occasion just ahead of the wagon trying to find the most practicable line, and very often could see nothing but the fore
oxen's heads, and knew not by sight where the vehicle
might be, till all at once I would behold it tearing its way
through the thicket. A small dwarf thorn-bush also
caused us no inconsiderable annoyance, tearing the noses
and legs of the oxen, and preventing them from pulling
together.

'The Noka a Batlatli, Noka a Mampooré, Nğami,
Inghabé (for it has all these names), is situated in 20° 19′
S. lat., and about 24° E. long., at an elevation above the
sea of 2,825 feet. The latitude you may consider correct.
The longitude, in consequence of our having no watch
that would go, is merely worked out by courses and
distances. The height is an approximation only, as
ascertained by one of Newman's barometric thermo-
meters.

'The distance traversed from Kolobeng was six hundred
and three miles, measured by a good trocheameter. Kolobeng is about five hundred and seventy miles from Colesberg, or nine hundred from Algoa Bay. Now that we
know the "short cuts," we might perhaps make the
journey in five hundred and fifty miles. The direct course
would be N.W. from Kolobeng, but there is no water for
a wagon; men walk it after rains.

'The Batouani have no communication with the
Portuguese. The only other large tribe on the Lake, of
which I learnt the name, was the Maclumma, of Damara

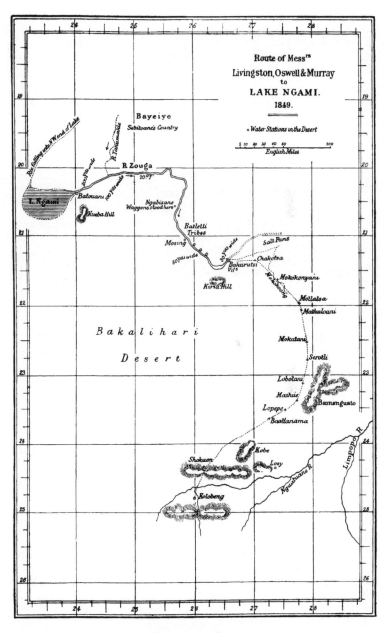

ROUTE IN 1849

descent, I fancy.   Sebitoané is said to live on one of the
tributaries of the Tamunaklé, which flows into the Zouga.
His country is called that of "large trees," or "many
waters."   He *has* communication with the Portuguese;
but through another tribe, *not* direct.   Don't you envy
me my trip in perspective ?   The tsétsé is spoken of in
particular spots; but as the chief is a kind of Moselekatsé
of the west, and very rich in oxen, it cannot, I should
suppose, be spread over any large tract.

'A few words on the Zouga, its inhabitants, etc., etc.,
and I have finished.   Its course is, as you see, at first
nearly E., then S., S.E., N.E., and E.N.E.   From two
or three days from the Lake it is broad, varying from
two hundred to five hundred yards, with flat and rather
swampy shores.   It then narrows, and flows through
high banks of limestone for six days—again opens out,
and at its most southern point spreads into a little
lake four miles or so across; then divides into two
streams, one of which (the most southerly) is said to
lose itself in the saltpans to the eastward, while by
far the largest branch, on the authority of the natives,
runs away N.E. and E.N.E. through the country of the
Matabelé.   I should mention that all this part of the
banks of the river, so far as we saw it, is excessively
thickly edged with high reeds, and bears evident marks
of inundations.   May it not take a bend S.E. and unite
with the Limpopo ?   For the first ten days the banks are
very picturesque, the trees (most of them unknown to
the Bakuains) magnificent, for Africa; indeed the mochu-
chong, one bearing an edible fruit, would be a fine
specimen of arboreal beauty in any part of the world.
Three enormous morlwānahs grow near the town of the
Batouani: the largest is upwards of seventy feet in girth;
but they are not common.   The palmyra is scattered here
and there amongst the islands, and on the banks of the
Zouga, and is abundant along the Mokokoong (the sand

river of the desert). In appearance it is exactly the same as our Indian ones, but bears a smaller fruit. I have brought some down with me. A tree very like the smaller banian of India grows on the bank of the river. The natives said it had, occasionally, "drops"; but I did not see any. It would seem, however, to have some kindred affinity to the Indian one; for in cases where a branch had been taken and bent downwards, I noticed that it had frequently shot up again. Wild indigo is abundant in places. The Makalakka or Mashūna (I think them to be the same) do really make cloth, and dye it with this blue. Don't you remember our being very sceptical on this point? They use the cotton of two kinds of bushes and one tree—the latter is of inferior quality. The Bakoba are the principal dwellers on the islands and banks of the river, though there are a few scattered Bushmen and Baharootzi kraals towards the lower end, where we struck it. The word Bakoba means slave, and is only applied to them by others, they styling themselves Bayéiyé, that is pre-eminently men. They are fine intelligent fellows, much darker and larger than, and in every respect superior to, the Bechuanas. Their language is distinct, with a click; but *not* Bush. They must come from the Damara side I fancy. They are not by any means confined to the river *Zouga*, but "fish and float," as Livingstone's letter says, in all the neighbouring waters. Their canoes are but roughly fashioned out of whole trees, and, so that one end can be made to counterbalance the other, they do not care whether they are straight or not. Many of them are quite crooked. Paddling and punting are their only means of progression; sailing is unknown. They live chiefly on fish (that abomination of the southern Bechuanas), which they catch with very neatly made nets, manufactured from a species of wild flax. Their float-ropes are made of a flag, and the small floats on the nets of a kind of reed with joints, so that, although one may become saturated, the others still remain buoyant. I have pieces of rope, net, twine, hemp or flax, which you shall see some day. To prevent their rotting, the nets are dyed with a tan prepared from the bark of the camel-thorn. The Baharootzi have no canoes or nets, but spear fish with the assegai, standing on rafts made of bundles of reed tied together. The fish are in great abundance, and of immense size, our old Limpopo flathead among the number. The Baharootzi, Bakoba and Bushmen have also another way of providing themselves with food, hardly so unobjectionable in my eyes. From end to end the banks of the Zouga are lined with pit-falls. Eleven of our horses fell in—one only died however ; but two of the oxen managed to bury themselves —fortunately we had a few spare ones. We ourselves were all caught—the trader twice or thrice in the morning whilst searching for and opening the holes to prevent mishaps amongst the cattle. They are most artfully concealed ; loose sand is sometimes thrown over the covering reeds and grass, and the impressions of animals' feet, together with their dung, placed on the top. They make the game very wild. One animal falls in and alarms the whole herd. They retreat far off, and only return again to drink, and flee. From the elephant to the steinbuck nothing escapes.

'We had hard work enough without much hunting; but I have killed some fine bull elephants. These and buffaloes are abundant — rhinoceroses and other game (except in one or two particular spots) very scarce. Hippopotami are so hunted by the Bakoba, that they hardly ever show themselves. The elephants are a distinct variety from the Limpopo ones; much lower and smaller in body (ten feet is a large bull) but with capital tusks. I saw two quebābas (straight-horned rhinoceroses) and wounded one, but did not bag him. Eight or nine léché fell. Piet (my wagon driver) shot the first,

Livingstone the second, Murray the third. The horns of the léché are very much the same as a male waterbuck's, and his habits are precisely similar. Two other species of antelope are mentioned by the natives— one we saw; something of the koodoo kind, but lighter and smaller — the other is yet to be seen. Lions are very scarce along the river and by the lake. We never heard them but once, and at one time used occasionally to let our oxen run loose at night. The day, however, that my horse fell into the pitfall and died, we found there *were* such things. The trader rolled one over, and I the other, rather disgracefully it must be allowed, from a tree; but had we been particular as to our honour, we might as well have left them alone, for we could never have seen them for the bush. I slew two others, and this was the whole of the bag, though I never missed but one chance, and that was from being greedy and trying to make too sure. The only thing like an escape I had was with the first. We had lost the road coming into Kolobeng, and, cantering along through some rocky hills to look for it, I heard a grunt behind me, and, turning round, saw a lion within eight yards of me in full chase, head and tail up. My old hat, torn off by a tree, and a shot fired Parthianwise satisfied him till I had got fifty yards ahead. I then jumped off, with the intention of loading the empty barrel, and bringing my friend to account. My foot was not clear of the stirrup when he was on me. *This* time I was on the look-out for him, and a lucky shot dropped him amongst some low bushes and masses of rock, about fifteen or twenty yards from where I stood.

HEAD OF LÉCHÉ.

'There is now a great point to be ascertained, namely, whether it be not possible to reach the Portuguese settlements on the Zambezi by an overland route. I hope to do something towards elucidating this, and have therefore made up my mind to leave Cape Town towards the close of the present month. I have letters of introduction to the Portuguese authorities should I happen to fall in with them, and anticipate no danger from the natives. We shall not, in all probability, reach the stations on the Zambezi, but we may be able to prove the possibility of subsequent travellers doing so. Livingstone will accompany me.'

With affectionate promptitude Vardon set about replying to this letter the instant he had finished reading it:

> ' 33, OXFORD TERRACE,
> ' HYDE PARK,
> ' *March* 27, 1850.

' MY DEAR OSWELL,

'. . . Your long and welcome epistle has gladdened my eyes. Your good uncle sent me the enclosed last night and I have run up to Galton's with it to hand it over to himself *in propriâ personâ*. I shall take care you have your due share of fame in this part of the world, and will put pen to paper for you if need be, and see that you stand right with the Geographical Society, of which, were I you, I would certainly become a member. Steele, I see, has just been proposed as a candidate. I have attended two meetings. . . . On the 8th of April we are to have a South African night again. I shall certainly go, and shall perhaps say some few words for you. I direct this to you at Kolobeng, but when Galton gets there I suppose you will be on the Zambesi drinking coffee with the Portuguese Governor !! Mind the fever, that's all! I hear the coast there is very unhealthy indeed. . . . I hope soon to see the skin and horns of a liché . . . That passage over the Kalahari is an awful affair apparently. Couldn't men go *in advance* to dig out the sand-holes, so that water

would be ready when the oxen arrived ? Now that you
have pioneered the way it will be much easier for those
that follow. Would that I could again try the veldt with
you ! . . . It was too bad of that old fellow Macqueen
saying that Parker had reached the Lake, and now he
tells us that the Boers have followed the Limpopo to
the sea ! And so it is with everything else. If you were
to discover an enormous range of snowy mountains he
would be sure to declare he knew of them years ago.
This is so unfair and ungenerous, that I cannot bear it. I
like to see all men reap the benefit of their labours, and so
no doubt do you. Can I do anything for you in England?
What can I send out to Livingstone ? I shall be so glad
to give him anything he wants. Would he like any
medical books, do you think ? Try and find out, there's
a good fellow, and tell me, when you write. I believe he
does know something of surgery, so he can name what
sort of books he wants and I will get them. I jog on in
the old way at No. 33, heartily sick of England, and dream-
ing of South Africa almost every night. I have two lovely
rifles, and hope to lay low some specimens of various
Indian fauna when I rejoin the gallant 25th next cold
weather. The *Times*' City article, 6th of March, tells us
there are no hippopotami or crocodiles in the Lake ! Such
nonsense has got abroad about it, you have no idea. I
placed on record your discovery as fairly as I could the
moment I saw it dimly alluded to and doubted by the
Athenæum. I must send you a copy if I can, merely a
few lines, but quite enough. I couldn't write more as I
had not heard from you, but I determined to put the
saddle on the right horse. I shall see Steele and have a
chat with him over your letter. Once more farewell, and
God bless you. My Mother and all my Brothers desire
their kind regards and best wishes,

                                    ' Affectionately yours.

  ' Your letter has made me quite a different man !'

'WHAT YOU EAT, I CAN EAT; WHERE YOU SLEEP, I CAN SLEEP; WHERE YOU GO, I WILL GO.'

Whilst the travellers were at the Ngami an incident occurred which united Oswell still more closely to his henchman John:

'Before starting on the expedition, we had held out to our followers that if we were successful we would not attempt to press on further. They were, as a rule, a timid folk, dreading the unknown, too ready to listen to any tale of danger and difficulty that might be in the world beyond, and always eager to turn Colony-wards. Success, however, inevitably bred a wish to do more, but we were of course bound to stand to our agreement. At last, the desire of penetrating deeper into the land became so strong that I suggested calling a meeting of the servants and trying what our eloquence might effect. After putting before them that we fully recognised our promise of not constraining them to go with us any further, I told them that the Doctor and I had made up our minds to give them one of the wagons with sufficient stores, supplies and ammunition for their homeward journey, while we ourselves had decided to push on ahead. I further explained to them that they would have no difficulty in reaching the Colony as they knew the waters and had the wheel-tracks. I paused for a moment, and then added that though we could not *ask* them to accompany us, yet if any one of them was willing to do so, we should be very glad. I rather enlarged upon our ignorance of the country in advance, for we did not wish to influence them unduly to join us. For a few minutes there was silence and blankness of face; then out stepped John, and speaking in Dutch, as he always did when his feelings were touched, though he at other times spoke English perfectly, said, "What you eat, I can eat; where you sleep, I sleep; where you go, I will go; I will come with you." The effect was instantaneous. "We will all go!" was the cry. Do you think after that it was much matter to us whether our brother was black or white?'

They had reached the lake by following the course of the *Zouga* on its southern bank, and proposed now to cross over and make their way to the great Sebitoané, visiting on the road the chief of the tribe living on the northern bank. He however showed a passive hostility by keeping all his men with their boats on that side. Thereupon, writes Livingstone to Captain Steele:

' I endeavoured to construct a raft to pass over where the river was only fifty or sixty yards wide, but the wood was so heavy that it sank immediately. Another effort was equally fruitless, and though I could easily have swum over, the landing in a state of nudity, as I must have done, to obtain the loan of a boat from the Bakoba, would have been scarcely a becoming appearance for a minister of peace, setting aside the risk of an alligator meeting me on the journey. I did not like to give up the attempt, but was finally dissuaded from it by my kind friend, Mr. Oswell, with whom alone the visit to Sebitoané was to be made, and who settled the matter by nobly offering to bring up a boat next year at his own expense, from the Cape, which, after visiting the Chief and coming round the north end of the Lake, is to become missionary property. To him and my other companion, Mr. Murray, I cannot sufficiently express my obligations. The chief expenses of the expedition have been borne by them.'

Speaking elsewhere of this journey, he says:

' I believe Mr. Oswell came from his high position at a very considerable pecuniary sacrifice with no other end in view than to extend the boundaries of geographical knowledge. . . . He undertook to defray the entire expense of the guides, and fully executed his generous intention.'

On the shores of the lake there existed a gigantic long-horned breed of oxen which had been stolen in a raid from the Ba-Wangketsi in 1819. They were originally remarkable for their heads, but in four or five generations, from feeding on the siliceous-coated reeds and succulent grasses that grew near the water, had developed to an astonishing extent in horns and height.   Oswell purchased one which, though not three years old, stood eighteen hands two inches, and measured from tip to tip of the horns eight feet eight inches, and thirteen feet seven inches round from one point to the other, taking in the base of the skull. He hoped to bring it home alive and present it to the Zoological Gardens, but the difficulties in the way were too great.   In many places the path cleared for the wagons through the bush on the journey up had to be widened for it to pass, and when the lake and the Zouga had been left behind, the grass grew so short that the poor beast could not feed, its horns coming to the ground before its nose ; it was practically impossible to cut a sufficient quantity, and at last, at the end of eight hundred miles, it became necessary to shoot it.   The extraordinary head was preserved.

CHAPTER VIII.

AFRICA.

1850. AGE 31–32.

FOURTH EXPEDITION (UNACCOMPANIED) —EXPLORATION
OF RIVER ZOUGA.—SECOND VISIT TO LAKE NGAMI.

Takes boat to Kolobeng—Livingstone already started—Meeting on Zouga—Impossible to obtain guides—Visit to
Sebitoané deferred—Peerless sport—Native dogs outwitting
alligators—Gemsbok, remarkable horns—Nakong, swamp-
shoe—Lead runs short—Mr. Webb's courtesy—Sir Harry
Smith suggests negotiations with Ngami tribes—Narrow
escape from wounded bull—' Night-elephants.'

TRUE to his promise, Oswell purchased the boat, and at
the beginning of the next hunting season left the Cape to
join Livingstone and carry out with him the programme
arranged between them five or six months previously.
But on reaching Kolobeng he found the heat and drought
had warped and injured the boat to such an extent as to
render it impossible to launch it in a serviceable condition
on the inland waters; and that the Doctor, unable to resist
the desire and opportunity of being the first to visit Sebitoané, had started a month before.   There was no chance
of overtaking him ; he resolved therefore to shape his
course towards the *Zouga*—the river they had discovered
in the previous year—and shooting at his leisure along its
banks, ultimately, if he could obtain guides and an interpreter, bore his way through to the chief.   He followed
the south bank on his way up to the Ngami, and then,
passing round the lake, returned by the north.

After seven or eight weeks' sport, hearing that Living-stone and his party were within fifty or sixty miles of him, he hastened to them, and escorted them on their home-ward way as long as he could be useful to them. 'Met Oswell,' writes Livingstone; 'he brought supplies for us from the Colony, and returned a bill for £40 which was to be spent on purchasing them.'

W. Cotton Oswell to his Cousin, Miss Louisa Cotton.

'BANKS OF THE ZOUGA.

'. . . I rode to meet Livingstone, who was returning, having given up all hopes of proceeding further at that time. He had, perhaps rather unwisely, taken with him his wife and children, and the latter together with many of his camp-followers, had been attacked with fever. He told me that he did not believe I should be able to obtain guides as the Ba-Towana, from whom I hoped to procure them, were afraid that Sebitoané might take offence at their showing the white man the way through his dominions, and as he is a chief of great power they were unwilling to anger him. This I found to be the case, for later, messengers came from them telling me that some of his people had arrived there with orders from their captain not to return without seeing a *makooa* or white man. I was not above a hundred miles from the Ba-Towana when the news reached me; inspanning, therefore, at once, I rode thither in four or five days. I was at first in great hopes that these men would show me the way themselves, but they asserted, whether truly or only awed into saying so by the Ba-Towana, that their chief wished to hear their report of the white man before seeing him. I remained three or four days with them, but the same story was per-severed in throughout, and finding it useless to tarry longer, I, through them, sent a present to Sebitoané, bidding them tell him that I should attempt to reach him after the lapse of six moons. Without guides the road would be im-

prácticable for wagons and oxen, or even on
horseback, as in particular spots, which unless
you had someone to tell you you would
not find out until too late, the tsétsé
(the fly so destructive to horses and cattle)
is abundant, and even if I were luckyenough
to escape the tsétsé and find the *road*,
without an interpreter — I had counted
on Living- stone for this— I was hardly
likely to be able to make Sebitoané
understand, and should then in all
probability have been looked upon
as a spy. I was thus forced to turn
hunter again.'

Game was incredibly abundant, the
sport peerless, and he thoroughly enjoyed himself. The Zouga swarmed
with alligators, and it was a constant
amusement to him to watch the native
dogs outwitting them.

'Three or four,' he writes, 'would wish
to cross, either for better fare, or to see
their friends on the other side; but
though alligator is very partial to dog,
dog is not so fond of alligator. Assem-
bling on the banks, they would run, barking violently, a quarter of a mile up
stream, in full view; halt; join in a chorus
of barking, yelping and baying; suddenly
pull up in the middle of the concert, dash at
the top of their speed, absolutely mute, and out
of sight on a lower level, to the point they
had started from, and then jump into the water
and swim across, thus selling the alligators, who,

HEAD OF GEMSBOK..
Length of horns, 44 inches.

THOUGH ALLIGATOR IS VERY PARTIAL TO DOG, DOG IS NOT SO PARTIAL TO ALLIGATOR.

hungry after their "course of bark," were eagerly expecting their dinner at the spot where they had had the
largest dose.'

One day, whilst watching the beasts come up from
drinking, his attention was attracted by the remarkably
fine head of a gemsbok.   He at once gave chase on foot,
and waterlogged as she was, succeeded in running down
and shooting her.   The horns proved to be just forty-four
inches long, and are, Mr. Selous declares, with a single
exception, the largest known.*

At Lakes Kamadou and Ngami he secured several
specimens of the nakong—the new antelope seen during
the expedition of the previous year.

* He had an interesting theory with regard to this antelope
which he thus states : ' In many of the Bushman caves the head
of the oryx is scratched in profile, and in that position one horn
hides the other entirely.   In Syria, even up to the present day,
I am told, a very near relation of the *Oryx capensis* is found.   It
is the habit of man in his hunting stage to try his hand at
delineating the animals he lives upon.   Probably the rocks or
caves of Syria show, or formerly may have shown, glyphs of
the oryx resembling the work of the African Bushman, and an
early traveller may easily have taken them for representations
of an animal with one horn and have thus started the idea of
the unicorn, Biblical and heraldic.   With regard to the former,
the word in the Hebrew in our version rendered unicorn is
reem ; in some old English Bibles indeed *reem* has been pre-
served in the text, untranslated.   Again, I am told that the
Syrian congener of the Cape oryx is called by the Arabs of to-
day ريم *reem*.   Is it not likely then that the Biblical unicorn is
the same as the *reem* of the Arab ?   As an heraldic beast the
gemsbok lends himself most gallantly to the theory ; he is a
strongly marked equine antelope, and is the one of his family
that frequently lowers his head to show fight, it is said even
with the lion.'

To the foregoing the following note is appended : ' Since
writing the above I find this subject has been discussed by the
learned, and a decision arrived at unfavourable to the oryx ;
but I let my remarks stand, for I do not know that anything
has been said on the glyphs in profile theory.'

' It is a veritable swamp liver, about the size of a goat, with long brownish hair, and horns resembling those of the koodoo in miniature. The abnormal elongation of its hoof enables it to skim over the surface of morasses into which other antelopes would sink. I have the hoof of one which is very nearly four inches long. If it were in the ratio of the animal's size, one and a half inches would be the proportion. On hard ground the nakong runs with difficulty—the swamp shoe is a hindrance. Instead of escaping by flight or concealment in the bush on being disturbed, it makes straight for the water, sits down in it, and submerges all but the nostrils, until the danger be overpast.'

HORNS AND HOOF OF NAKONG.

He wandered on, shooting every day and all day among the teeming herds of animals that peopled the higher reaches of the river, when he suddenly discovered that he had almost run out of lead. There was nothing for it but to start immediately back to the Cape, husbanding jealously the small store that remained.

One morning he came unexpectedly upon the wagons of Mr. Webb of Newstead Abbey, Captain Shelley, and a companion who was travelling with them and trading on his own account. Exchanging friendly greetings he held on his way : 'for though I knew they were amply provided, I had not the face to ask them for metal more valuable than gold, in the middle of Africa.'

Next day, however, he shot three elephants, and it occurred to him that he might barter their tusks for lead with Mr. Webb's companion. He accordingly sent John on horseback with a note to Mr. Webb, asking for his mediation, and telling him that the bearer would put

the Kafirs on the tracks of the elephants.   John overtook
the party twelve or fifteen miles off, and came back to
camp with his horse laden with bars of lead—' a bounti-
ful supply, and the prettiest and most courteous letter
from Mr. Webb, who would not hear of my buying lead
with ivory.   It was a most generous help most graciously
rendered, and enabled me to enjoy my homeward march.
Without it I should have been troubled to feed my followers for fourteen hundred miles.'

He was far on his way to the Cape when a letter was
brought into camp which, in view of the recent visit of
Khama, Sechélé and Bathoen to this country, and its
object, has a very special interest.   Mr. Chamberlain
would seem to be the avatar of Sir Harry Smith.

> ' COLONIAL OFFICE,
> ' CAPE TOWN,
> ' *July* 11, 1850.

' SIR,

Understanding that you are now engaged in a second
journey to the Lake discovered by you, in conjunction
with Messrs. Murray and Livingstone, in August last,
His Excellency Sir H. Smith has directed me to request
your co-operation in establishing friendly relations with
the native Chiefs in that neighbourhood, in case this letter
should reach you before you arrive at the Lake or while
in the adjacent territory.   Feeling confident that you will
yourself be anxious to promote the objects which he has in
view, His Excellency has directed me to request that you
will, if possible, explain to the Chiefs that by establishing friendly relations with this Government, they will
obtain a favourable opportunity of disposing of the pro-
ductions of the interior.   They should also be made to
understand that the Government have no wish to acquire
land in those parts, but that their object in proposing these
arrangements is public, and designed as much for the

benefit of the Natives themselves, as for the promotion of trade and discovery ; whereas any body of private individuals banding themselves together to settle among them and deprive them of their territory, can have only private ends in view, opposed to the happiness and interests of these Native Tribes. His Excellency is the more anxious that these matters should be clearly explained to the Natives about the Lake, because he has reason to suspect a design on the part of some of the Emigrant Boers North of the Vaal River to effect a settlement on the shores of the Lake. It appears that a Mr. McCabe, a Trader, and his companion Mr. Baines, with their party, have been stopped by the Boers, and turned back, and it is reported, but not certainly known, that the same course has been adopted towards another party of English travellers.

' Mr. McCabe conjectures with considerable probability that the object of these vexatious proceedings is to prevent the Government obtaining information of the proceedings of a Commando of five hundred Boers who were about to proceed to take possession of the country near the Lake. His Excellency does not deem it expedient by force to interfere in the designs of the Boers in that distant region, but trusts that if the Natives are warned in time, and induced to establish friendly relations with the British Government, they may be able to resist machinations, the success of which would seriously impede the progress of commerce and Geographical research in Central Africa, to which you have rendered such signal service by your recent discovery.

> ' I have the honour to be, Sir,
> ' Your most obedient Servant,
> ' JOHN MONTAGU,
> ' *Secretary to Government.*'

He was of course unable to execute the behests of the Government, or reply satisfactorily to this letter at the

tIme, but he bore it in mind, and answered it during the
expedition of the following year.

Rev. Edward Waring Oswell to W. Cotton Oswell.

'ABBEY VILLA,
'GREAT MALVERN,
'*July* 11, 1850.

'. . . I have just heard that a certain Mr. Dolman
would take charge of a letter to you if I can manage to
get it to him in time, but as his ship is said to be about
to sail to-morrow, I only write on the chance. . . . I
saw Captain Vardon when I was in Town, and hear he is
to be married to-day, and to sail for India soon after.
He told me Mr. Livingstone was not to accompany you
this time. This I am sorry for, as the assistance of a
companion must be very desirable. . . . Your services
seem to be appreciated by the Geographical Society,
though I hardly know whether sufficiently so. We are
all intensely interested in the accounts you send us of
Africa. . . . You may have plenty to occupy you now,
as I make no doubt your discovery will lead to important
results; it seems to create general interest. . . .'

Towards the end of this season Oswell nearly lost
his life whilst elephant-hunting. He thus describes the
incident:

'The ground to our right with its sea of thorns rose
in a long swell, and as it sank into the little hollows
beyond, five or six colossal bodiless legs stood out like
bare tree stems amongst the closely-woven branches. I
slipped from my pony, and crawling on hands and knees,
got within twenty yards of the legs without being able to
see anything more of the owners. A large tree was in
advance, round whose stem the thorns did not press quite
so pertinaciously as elsewhere. Slowly and cautiously I

gained its side.   An elephant was close to me, but though
I could now see his body, he was stern on.   I broke a
twig to attract his attention; his head swung half round,
but was so guarded by the bush that it would have been
useless to fire at it.   His shoulder was more exposed.
There was no time to wait, he was on the move, and the
dust flew from his side as the heavy ball struck him.
Screaming angrily, he turned full front in the direction of
the tree by which I stood motionless.   I do not think he
made me out, and the bush was too thick for me to risk
giving him further information by a second shot.   For
a moment we confronted one another; and then the
rumbling note of alarm uttered by his companions decided him on joining them, and the stiff thorns bent before
the weight of seven or eight bulls, like a cornfield in the
wind.   I regained the path and rode along the line of
their retreat, which, as shown by the yielding bush, was
parallel to it.   After a time the thorns thinned out and I
caught sight of the wounded elephant holding a course of
his own a little to the left of his fellows; and when he
entered the tropical forest beyond I was in his wake and
very soon compelled to follow where he broke a way.
Lying flat on my pony's neck, and guiding him as I best
might by occasional glimpses of the tail of my now
slowly-retreating pioneer, I laboured on in the hope that
more open ground might enable me to get up alongside
of him.   A most unpleasant ride it was; my constrained
position gave me but little chance of using my hands to
save my head; I was at one time nearly pulled from the
saddle by the heavy boughs and at another nearly torn to
pieces by the wicked thorns of the wait-a-bit, which
although no longer *the* tree of the jungle, was intolerably
scattered through it.   I have killed elephants on very bad
ground, but this was the worst piece of bush I ever rode
into in my life.   A little extra noise from the pursuers
caused the pursued to stop; and while clinging like
Gilpin to the calender's horse, and peering at the broad

DEPOSITING ME IN A SITTING POSITION IMMEDIATELY IN FRONT OF THE UPLIFTED FOREFOOT
OF THE CHARGING BULL.

stern of the chase, I saw him suddenly put his head where
his tail ought to have been ; the trunk was tightly coiled
—an elephant nearly always coils his trunk in thick bush
for fear of pricking it—forward flapped the huge ears, up
went the tail, and down he came like a gigantic bat ten
feet across.   Pinned above and on either side, by dis-
mounting I could neither hope to escape, nor kill my
opponent.   I therefore lugged my unfortunate animal
round and urged him along.   But I had not taken into
account with what great difficulties and how slowly I had
followed the bull.   He was now in full charge, and the
small trees and bush gave way before him like reeds,
whereas I was compelled to keep my head lowered as
before, and try and hold the path, such as it was, up
which we had come.   I was well mounted and my spurs
were sharp.   Battered and torn by branch and thorn, I yet
managed a kind of gallop, but it was impossible to keep
it up.   The elephant thundered straight *through* obstacles
we were obliged to go round, and in fifty yards we were
fast in a thick bush and he within fifteen of us.   As a last
chance I tried to get off, but in rolling round in my
saddle my spur galled the pony's flank, and the elephant
screaming over him at the same moment, he made a con-
vulsive effort and freed himself, depositing me in a sitting
position immediately in front of the uplifted forefoot of
the charging bull.   So near was it that I mechanically
opened my knees to allow him to put it down, and
throwing myself back, crossed my hands upon my chest,
obstinately puffing myself out with the idea of trying to
resist the gigantic tread, or at all events of being as
troublesome to crush as possible.   I saw the burly brute
from chest to tail as he passed directly over me length-
ways, one foot between my knees and one fourteen
inches beyond my head, and not a graze !   Five tons at
least !   As he turned round chasing the pony, which
without my weight and left to its own instinct escaped
easily to my after-rider's horse, he swept by me on his

way to rejoin his companions, and I got another snapshot at his shoulder. As soon as I could I followed his spoor, but must have changed it in the thick bush, for in five minutes I had run into and killed a fresh elephant in a small open space. The Bushmen found the first, next morning, dead. Out of all my narrow escapes this is the only one that remained with me in recollection for any time. On four or five other occasions I was half or wholly stunned, and therefore not very clear about my sensations ; but on this I was well aware of what was going on and over me. One hears of night-mares—well, for a month or more, I dare say, I had night-elephants !'

CHAPTER IX.

AFRICA.

1851–1852.   AGE 32–34.

FIFTH EXPEDITION (WITH LIVINGSTONE).—VISIT TO
SEBITOANÉ.—DISCOVERY OF RIVERS MABABÉ,
SOUTA, CHOBÉ, AND ZAMBESI.

Object of expedition—Arrival at Kolobeng—Livingstone and
party doubtful starters—Oswell gives them wagon, and
precedes to dig wells—Adventure with a lioness—Notes
en route from Livingstone's journal—His views on the
drink question—Discovery of Mababé, Souta and Chobé—
Sebitoané reached—A royal reception—An all-night sitting—The chief tells his life-story ; wars, cannibalism,
slave-trade—He dies suddenly—Livingstone's lament—
Discovery of Zambesi, ' a most important point '—British
commerce to oust slave-trade—Return journey—Is it right
to accept stolen cattle ?—The general rights and duties of
missionaries—Oswell replies to Sir Harry Smith's despatch
—His testimony to Mrs. Livingstone ; ' David, put it out '
—Letter from Vardon ; Gordon Cumming's exhibition ;
léché skin sent to British Museum ; ' a fearful extinguisher
on Mr. Parker'—Oswell's sketch-map and notes of country
traversed—He orders outfit for Livingstone family—' The
best friend we had in Africa '—His brother advises him to
claim share of credit of expedition—Livingstone's gratitude
—John accompanies his master to England.

AT the beginning of 1851 Oswell left the Cape for the
interior, for the fifth and last time.

To his Cousin, Miss Louisa Cotton.

'Motito,
'*April* 4, 1851.

'. . . Before this I should suppose that my letters to
Edward must have reached their destination, and you will
by them learn that our last year's expedition was a failure
so far as doing what we intended is concerned, and that
I have in consequence determined to attempt it again,
throwing up my Indian appointment.   Had I believed
that I could have flourished or even done my work there
effectively, I should have returned.   On my arrival at
Kolobeng, Mr. Livingstone's station, on my way Colony-
wards, I found four or five men had also been sent to
Sechélé—the chief of the Ba-Kwaina, with whom he resides
—and he had had many conversations with them before
I reached, and gathered much information.   From what
he learnt, they live on a river a little to the south of the
Zambesi, having formerly lived on that river itself.   On
this Zambesi, as perhaps you know, the Portuguese have
considerable trading stations.   Sebitoané has only seen
one of them, who came seeking slaves, but with the under
slave-dealers he has had traffic for the last three or four
years.   Without wishing to appear philanthropic overmuch, if we can open the way, *viâ* the interior, to the slave
country, will it not be easier to put an end to that trade
at the fountain-head, than on the coast, whither the poor
wretches have been brought many hundreds of miles ?   If
we can reach the Zambesi, others may go further, and
eventually, by persuading the great Chiefs of the interior
not to dispose of their people or captives to the merchants
from the coast, do something to end this sale of human
beings.   Don't misunderstand me, I would not have you
think that such are the only motives that influence me in
again making the attempt—nothing so praiseworthy—I
have a love of wandering and have been once foiled.   I

have got, so far, about three hundred miles from Colesberg and on my way again. Livingstone will, I believe, accompany me, and, should it please God, we shall reach Sebitoané somehow or other. The people are now willing to show us the path, and we will not abandon our project without a struggle. How we fare you will hear when I return. The greatest difficulty we shall have to fight against is too much water—too many rivers! To reach our present point it has been against *thirst* we have had to stand up. The fly may also annoy us, but we shall see.

' I have received no letter from you or anyone for a long time . . . the accounts of Edward are good, thank God. I was in hopes Uncle Ben would have given me a line. . . . My best love to him and *all*. Keep my letters to yourselves. . . .'

The hope was realized, for a day or two later a letter arrived from him which presents incidentally, and quite unconsciously, a charming picture of the sense of responsibility and of the generosity of the family :

' 8, GLOUCESTER TERRACE,
'LONDON, N.W.

'. . . I have used your *chart blanc* to apply a portion of the interest of the money of yours in my hands in favour of N. C. He is settled in a Curacy at —— and I have engaged to make up an income for him of £200 beyond his stipend, by contributions among his family. . . . I have charged your account, and shall do so, with £25 per annum. Kitty Clarke contributes £50, Uncle Bowdler £50, Mary, William and I, £25 each. . . . His sisters are thus relieved from giving him any of their small means. They have had heavy calls on them. . . . I did not ask Edward, for I know that he considers L. as requiring all he can spare. Nothing has been obtained for L. He has a pupil, and seven children to maintain. I shall be very glad to have your orders to send him a present. . . . I am going to write to-night to one of the Fyvies, and send our contributions for the Pieter Mauritzburg church. . . . Your liberality and kindness to them were deeply felt by their friends. . . . I am now looking out for a second theodolite to send to James Fyvie, who means to practise surveying also. I am as usual, or rather heavier and more stupid. What think you of seventeen stone seven pounds for horseman's weight? You will come and see us I trust the end of this year. Though I do not expect you will remain in England, there are many here warmly attached to you. The Geographical Society sent me five copies of your letter to Captain Vardon, and of Mr. Livingstone's; they have been much enjoyed by many. We promised to let Captain Vardon hear of your progress and welfare; we were much pleased with him. God bless you and let nothing tempt you to believe that I am not your loving and very attached uncle, and friend,

'BENJAMIN COTTON.'

Passing on his way northwards, when Oswell reached Kolobeng, he found that though the inclination of the Livingstones was strongly in favour of accompanying him, there were two serious obstacles to their doing so—the lack of a wagon, and their unwillingness to expose their children to the privations entailed by the scarcity of water for the first three hundred miles of the journey, which experience had taught them to expect. He removed the one objection by presenting them with a new wagon, and the other by volunteering to precede them by several marches over the driest part of the route and clear the old wells and dig fresh ones. The offer was gratefully accepted, and the Livingstones followed on April 24.

'Mr. Oswell,' writes the Doctor to the London Missionary Society, from Boatlanama, on April 30, 'is unwearied in his kindnesses, for all which may God bless him.'

Meanwhile he had arrived at Lupapi and dug wells

there for the Livingstones. Whilst waiting for them to come up with him he had an adventure which nearly cost him his life :

'The dogs had brought a lioness to bay, and I got within thirty yards, but from the thickness of the bush could see neither them nor her. I shifted my position once or twice in the hope of making out what was going on, standing up in my stirrups and looking for an opening,

DROVE HER FRONT CLAWS WELL INTO THE HORSE'S QUARTERS.

that I might dismount and get a shot. Suddenly the barking of the dogs and the snapping snarl of the lioness ceased, and I thought she had broken bay and gone on, but in a second I heard a roar on the horse's right quarter, in a different direction from that into which I had been peering, and looking round, saw her, with her mouth open, clearing a rather high patch of bush twenty yards from me. There was no time to get off the horse and no possibility of a shot from his back, for the charge was on his *right* flank, and you cannot shoot to the right. I did the only thing that I could—jammed the spurs in and tried to make a gallop of it ; but my follower was too close, and before I could get up full speed I heard her strike the ground heavily twice in her bound, and with the third she sat up behind me. She jumped short, however, and failed to get hold with her mouth, but drove her front claws well into the horse's quarters, and a hind foot underneath him, and so clung, but only for a moment, for the poor beast, maddened by fright and pain, and unable to stand under the extra weight, became unmanageable, threw his head up, and swerved under the projecting bow of a tree which, striking me on the chest, swept me from the saddle against the lioness, and we rolled to the ground together.

'A sharp rap on the head, from my having fallen on a stump, stunned me for a minute or two, and I woke to life to find John kneeling alongside of me. . . . "What's the matter ?" I said ; but at the same instant I heard the dogs again baying fifty yards off, and recollection came back. Rising to my feet, I staggered like a drunken man, rather than walked, towards the sound, and propped myself up against a tree, for I was still weak and dazed ; indistinctly I could occasionally see both dogs and lioness. Presently something broke through the thinner part of the bush, and I fired and wounded one of the dogs. And the lioness, tired by the protracted worrying, and startled perhaps by the sound of the gun, bounded off, and escaped without a shot.'

'Thank God for preserving his life!' is Livingstone's comment in his private journal. 'May He have mercy upon him and save him !'

From the same source are taken the following notes of the next stages of the journey :

'When we reached Mashué we found Oswell waiting for us. Had very kindly taken the trouble to clean out

the watering places for us.   This kindness enabled us to
water at once and proceed in the direction of Sekhomi.
. . . Mr. O. went by way of Lobatané.   Reached Sekhomi on the 8th. . . . He has a bad name, but we have
always experienced kindness at his hands.   He has in his
intercourse with strangers been more sinned against than
his detractors like to say.   Those who have behaved well
to him, as Mr. O., etc., have no complaint to make. . . .
Reached Mr. Oswell at Lettochwé.'

' 14th May.—Passed Kanné after having found water at
a pond. . . .   The pleasantest music in Africa is that
made by the merry frogs.'

' 15th, 16th.—In the desert, and in the evening of 17th we
reached Nkao-ana. . . .   Mr. Oswell's   men   opened
another well which from long disuse had become filled up.
. . . This well on being re-opened afforded an abundant
supply for all our cattle.'

' 20th.—Left Nkao-ana.   At Kokonyane Mr. Oswell again
opened the wells.   Though I can't repay, I may record
with gratitude his kindness, so that if spared to look upon
these my private memoranda, in future years, proper
emotions may ascend to Him Who inclined his heart to
show so much friendship.'

' 27th.—Left Nchokotsa and proceeded N. to Maritsa. A
party of traders had preceded us by a few days, and being
desirous of going to Sebitoané s they offered Tsapoé, the
Bakurutsé chief, three or four guns if he would furnish them
with guides.   But he declined.   The gun of a Bamangwato man called Kamati was accidentally broken after he
parted with the traders.   Coming to us at Nchokotsa, he
offered to give us a guide to lead us Northward instead of
going to the Tamunaklé, if we would give him one of
our muskets in exchange for his broken one.   To this we
gladly consented, as the course he proposed was shorter
than the other and it would enable us to reach Sebitoane
before the trading party.   This was of great importance,
as first impressions are always strongest. . . . Mr. Oswell

furnished a gun for Kamati, and though we subsequently found that he had no power among the Bushmen to whom we were going, as a link in the chain of events which led us to go directly North, he is entitled to some share of gratitude.

'We ascertained too that the traders had found a man at Tsapoé's who was left by Mahalé (Sebitoané's messenger to Kolobeng) sick, but declined his guidance, thinking him a fool. We found however from Mahalé that he would have been an excellent guide. God seemed kindly to re-serve the honour of reaching Sebitoané first for us. I thank Him for His unmerited favour.

'Crossed the dry bed of the Zouga about 15 miles N.N.E. of Nchokotsa—the bed was stony, and there were small dykes of stones in it which are used for catching fish. Road hard—country terribly scorched.'

'Reached Koobé on the 27th. Several wells of fine fresh water at which great numbers of game drink. This water is about 25 miles from Nchokotsa.'

'28th.—Left Koobé at mid-day, and in the evening 12 miles distant arrived at the well of the Mochweeré tree. . . .'

'On 29th.—Still going nearly due North, we entered on the Saltpan of Ntwétwé, which is 15 miles in diameter, and about 100 long. At one part it is soft, and the wheels sinking through the dry crust on the surface up to the naves, rendered it difficult to get them extricated. The crust breaking before the wheel, the weight was equal to a plough 2,000 lbs. weight, working at subsoil ploughing of 2 feet deep. . . .'

'30th.—Reach Tloantla, the cattle post of Moachwé. Here we found that we could not have Bushmen in con-sequence of our having given the gun to Kamati and not to Moachwé—the latter being the true owner of the country. . . . Here Moremi stood boldly forward and advocated our cause, stating among other reasons for our being supplied with guides the entire approbation of

Sekhomi to our proceeding to Sebitoané. After producing another gun it was arranged that a Bushman guide
should go with us.

'We spent *Sunday* at Tloantla. . . . then on *Monday*
started for Horoyé's. About 12 miles beyond Tloantla
came to the spring of . . . Rapesh.'

'*Morning of Tuesday.*—We reach Horoyé's spring. . . .
about 11 miles beyond Rapesh. The whole of the adjacent country is hard, and covered over with Mopané
and Baobob trees ; the underlying rock is white tufa,
and springs abound in it. There are so many to the
East of Horoyé's place the country receives the name of
Matlomaganyana, or the " Links " as of a chain. . . . The
people of Horoyé, and indeed all the Bushmen, were
strong well-fed looking men. The game abounds and
they are reported to follow it in its migrations, and live
on the zebras, gnus, etc., as if they were their domestic
cattle. Furnished with a Bushman guide from Horoyé's,
and with a glad heart that our difficulties had so far been
removed or overcome, we set forward on *Wednesday, the*
4*th* (June) and after travelling about ten miles we reached
Maila. . . . Found a Makalaka (Mashona) who had
fled from Moselikatzé living here. The Mashona are interesting, for they are always spoken of by the other tribes as
superior to them both in the arts of peace and war, and
they always prefer the former, unless attacked. Turn to
the West at mid-day, and after travelling another ten miles
we reached Unko. Water from another of these springs
excellent. Many buffaloes drink there. . . .'

'*Friday, the 6th.*—Pass through ten miles of thick bush
and heavy sand, and next morning after going 5 miles
more we reached Kamakama, a fine pool of rain water. . . .
Leaving Kamakama we passed by a dried-out. . . stony depression similar to the other springs—a long tract of bush,
then three miles of a perfectly level and bushless flat
covered with very short grass, the distance in all being
about 12 miles. . . .'

'*On Saturday the 7th*, passed through 10 miles of well-wooded country and reached a chain of ponds in a depression like the bed of an ancient river. I counted 15 of them—there was a village of Bushmen near . . . named Goosimjarrah. . . . What a wonderful people the Bushmen are! always merry and laughing and never tell lies wantonly like the Bechuana. They have more of the appearance of worship than any of the Bechuana. When will these dwellers in the wilderness bow down before their Lord? No man seems to care for the Bushman's soul. . . . The most difficult part of the whole journey lay between Goosimjarrah and the river Mababé. The first 20 miles were heavy sand and thick bush. The axes were kept going constantly, and the course cut through was so winding we could scarcely ever see the front oxen. . . .'

'*On Monday the 19th* we were in 19° 38′; on *Tuesday* Shobo wandered, and as he followed the paths made by the elephants in passing from one clump of mohonono bush to another, our course was zigzag enough. We travelled chiefly at night, and felt contented when we had our heads towards the Northern Bear in Charles's Wain, but it was annoying when we found Shobo turned away round to the Southern Cross. Not a bird or insect could be seen during these three dreary days. As far as the eye could reach it was a vast plain of low, thorny scrub. It was perfectly still. On the third day a bird chirped in a bush and the dog began to bark at it.

'*On Wednesday the 11th* . . . we had been travelling about 65 miles from Goosimjarrah in a Norwesterly direction. Shobo refused to go on at night, and to our coaxing he replied with a good-natured smile. . . . "Do you know where you are, Shobo? perhaps we are at Bitalé, perhaps somewhere else, *I* don't know," and then doubled himself up like a dog on his side to sleep, leaving us to look on in utter dumbfounderment at his coolness. At last we began to observe the presence of birds, then

the footprints of animals, particularly of the rhinoceros
which we knew never lives far from water; then a broad
footpath made by animals in going to drink—so we unyoked the oxen and put them on the path. They went
off at a hard trot, and never stopped till they reached the
water in the River Mababé. Some of them diverged into
another path and we have reason to suspect that they
were bitten by the tsétsé in consequence. We never saw
the animals so much distressed by thirst, though we
have seen them go longer than three days without a drop
of water. Mr. O. and I remained with the wagons while
all the people went after the oxen. As is always the case,
the children drank more than usual as the water became
less, and their mother sat crying over them as she saw
the precious fluid drawing to the bottom of the bottle. It
was no wonder; we did not know for certain that the men
would return with water, and the very idea of little ones
perishing before one's eyes for thirst is dreadful.

' *On Thursday morning* Mr. O. and I went forward in
search of the people, and after walking three or four miles
met them returning. No one knows the value of water
till he is deprived of it. We never need any spirits to
qualify it or prevent an immense draught of it from doing
us harm. I have drunk water swarming with insects,
thick with mud and putrid from rhinoceros urine and
buffaloes' dung, and no stinted draughts of it either, yet
never felt any inconvenience from it. Have those who find
that good water does them harm, not wasted their stomachs
by fermented and other liquors, so that they are incapable
of bearing their natural fluid? Are their stomachs in the
same state as diseased eyes which cannot bear the stimulus
of light? . . .'*

* Later in his journal he writes: 'The introduction of
English drinking customs and English drinks among the
natives of this country inevitably proves the destruction of
soul and body.'

'12th.—After the people returned with the cattle we turned from our westerly course to the N.N.E., and went parallel with the river. . . .'

'13th.—Went about two miles and came to the village of Chombo . . . the people live on the banks of a swamp 10 or 11 miles in breadth into which the Mababé flows . . . they build their huts with a sort of second storey in which they sleep. When mosquitoes are troublesome they make a fire below and lie in the smoke. . . . Chombo volunteered to be our guide to Sebitoané and informed us that there were two paths, one of which was short, viz., only three days, but it had tsétsé; the other was longer, but we should be three nights or four days without water, and no tsétsé. Understanding from him that we could travel in the tsétsé district by night in safety, we chose the shorter path, and after spending *Sunday the 15th* with the Bomagoa, crossed the swamp. . . sleep 8 or 9 miles beyond the marsh under Mopané trees.

'After travelling other 16 or 17 miles we reached a fine large pond called Tsatsara, in all from Chombo's 34 or 35 miles.'

'18th.—Went to a small pond called Tsara. In approaching the tsétsé district in the evening saw, for the first time, the tsétsé. We unyoked and sent the cattle back till it was dark, and then rode forward, crossed the river Souta about 8 miles beyond Tsara. . . . The Souta was about 3 feet deep and about 40 yards broad. . . . 27 miles from Tsara we struck the Chobé river, and found ourselves still in the midst of the tsétsé. . . . As our cattle would not swim over they were kept in the reeds during the day, it being believed that the tsétsé does not fly thither. Next day some of the beautiful little cattle of the Makololo or Basuto were brought to precede our cattle in crossing the river—they take to the water readily.

'*On the 20th* Tonuana, one of the chief men of Sebitoané, was sent with Mahalé to us.'

They stated that Sebitoané, who had come more than four hundred miles to meet the white men, was on an island thirty miles down stream. He had sent his own paddlers to bring them to him.

For the present, at all events, they deemed it expedient to go to him alone. Accordingly they settled Mrs. Livingstone and the children with the wagons, on the south bank, and the oxen and horses, to escape the tsétsé, on the north, and on the next day—June 21—paddled down stream with the current at the rate of eight miles an hour, and landed at their destination at 3 o'clock in the afternoon.

'Presently,' writes Oswell, 'this really great Chief and man came to meet us, shy and ill at ease. We held out our hands in the accustomed way of true Britons, and I was surprised to see that his mother-wit gave him immediate insight into what was expected of him, and the friendly meaning of our salutation. Though he could never have witnessed it before, he at once followed suit, and placed his hand in ours as if to the manner born. I felt troubled at the evident nervousness of the famous warrior (for he had been and still was a mighty fighter with very remarkable force of character). Surrounded by his tribesmen he stood irresolute and quite overcome in the presence of two ordinary-looking Europeans.

'Livingstone entered at once into conversation with him; but throughout that day and the next a sad, half-scared look never faded from his face. He had wished us to visit him,* but the reality of our coming, with all its

* 'He told us,' writes Livingstone, 'that having been informed by the messengers he had sent to Mr. Oswell and me of our vain attempts to penetrate into his country in the preceding year, he had in the present instance, in his eagerness to make our acquaintance, not only despatched parties to search for us along the Zouga, but also made considerable presents of cattle to different chiefs on the way, with the request that they would render the white men every assistance in their power, and furnish them with guides.

possibilities and advantages, seemed to flit through the man's mind as a vision. He killed an ox for us and treated us right royally; he was far and away the finest Kafir I ever saw. Beloved of the Makololo, he was the fastest runner and the best fighter among them; just, though stern, with a wonderful power of attaching men to himself, he was a gentleman in thought and manner. He had allotted to us a bright clean kotla for eating and sleeping in, and after supper we lay down on the grass which had been cut for our beds by the thoughtful attention of the Chief.

' In the dead of the night he paid us a visit alone, and sat down very quietly and mournfully at our fire. Livingstone and I woke up and greeted him, and then he dreamily recounted the history of his life, his wars, escapes, successes and conquests, and the far-distant wandering in his raids. By the fire's glow and flicker among the reeds, with that tall dark earnest speaker and his keenly-attentive listeners, it has always appeared to me one of the most weird scenes I ever saw. With subdued manner and voice Sebitoané went on through the live-long night till near the dawn, in low tones only occasionally interrupted by an inquiry from Livingstone. He described the way in which he had circumvented a strong impi of Matabili on the raid, and raised his voice for a minute or two as he recounted how, hearing of their approach, he had sent men to meet the dreaded warriors of Umsilegas, feigning themselves traitors in order to lure them to destruction by promising to guide them to the bulk of the cows and oxen, which, they said, in fear of their coming, had been placed in fancied security on one of the large islands of the Chobé; how the Zulus fell into the trap and allowed themselves to be ferried over in three or four canoes hidden there for the purpose; and how when the last trip had been made, the boatmen, pulling out into mid-stream, told them they could remain where they were till they were fetched, and in the meantime might search for the

RECOUNTED . . . HIS WARS, ESCAPES, SUCCESSES AND CONQUESTS.

cattle; how after leaving them till they were worn and weak with hunger, for there was nothing to eat on the island, he passed over, killed the chiefs, and absorbed the soldiers into his own ranks, providing them with wives, a luxury they were not entitled to under Zulu military law until their spears had been well reddened in fight.

'Then he waved his hand westward and opened out a story of men over whom he had gained an easy victory, " away, away, very far from the bitter waters"; and to whom, when they asked for food, wishing to bind them with fetters of kindness, he sent a fat ox, and, "would you believe it, they returned it, saying they didn't eat ox. ' Then what do you eat ?' I asked, ' we like beef better than anything.' ' We eat men,' said they. I had never heard of this before; but they were very pressing, so at last I sent them two slaves of the Macobas, the river people, who, as you know, are very dark in colour, but they brought them back, saying they did not like black men, but preferred the redder variety, and as that meant sending my own fighting men, I told them they might go without altogether." This was the only intimation we ever had that cannibalism existed in our part of Africa.'

Many of Sebitoané's followers were dressed in green baize, red drugget, calico and cheap, gaudy cloth, some in garments of European manufacture ; and the travellers were at a loss to account for this, as the country was in 18° S. lat., fifteen to eighteen hundred miles from the sea, until, from the explanation given them by the Chief, they found they had reached the southern limit of the slave-trade.

When they had spent a day or two with him he asked to be allowed to accompany them back to their wagons to be introduced to Mrs. Livingstone, and remarking, on his arrival, that their cattle had been bitten by the fly and would certainly die, he begged them not to trouble themselves, 'for I have plenty more, and I will give you as many as you need.' He was very anxious that the camp should be moved to the north bank of the Chobé, where there were no tsétsé, and pitched as near as possible to his town of Linyanti, but when he saw that the wagons were too large for his canoes he ordered the people of that town to remove to his guests' halting place, and in a few days a new village had sprung up there. He had realized his most earnest desire, that of meeting and conversing with Europeans, and he exerted himself to the utmost to prove the sincerity of his appreciation of the dangers and difficulties they had confronted on his account. Every wish of theirs was anticipated, every request immediately granted. A crucial instance of this is noted by Livingstone in his journal:

'When Lechwee came from the Bamangwato on a visit, he enticed one of Sebitoané's wives to follow him. She had ten attendants, and after wandering about among the rivers for some months they were discovered in the reeds unable to get away. Eight of them were put to death, and then the wife was delivered to her father. He replied that she was no longer his daughter, and he must just do to her as he had done to the others. She too was executed. But the tenth person—a woman—came while we were at the Chobé. She refused to go near until I offered to speak to Sebitoané on her behalf. She was in wretched plight when she arrived, and in despair wished to jump into the river. When I besought Sebitoané to spare her, he said, " Shall I kill her after you prayed for her ? Oh no." '

This hearty friendship, as heartily reciprocated, afforded splendid promise of future development in the direction of civilization and commerce—' It is,' writes Livingstone, 'impossible to overstate the importance we attached to Sebitoané '—when suddenly, on July 6, he fell ill of pneumonia, set up by the irritation of some old spear-wounds in his chest.

Journal.—' After my preaching on Sunday, the 7*th*, he called me to see, as he said, " if he was still a man." I went to the door of the court—he lifted himself up, saluted, and then when we parted told one of the people to " take Robert (Dr. L.'s little son) to Maunko's (his favourite wife) house and get some milk for him." I saw him no more, for on the same evening his people removed him towards the Linyanti town, and when still on the way, just at the clump of date bushes at which we stood, he expired in his canoe. . . .'

' Poor Sebitoané! my heart bleeds for thee, and what would I not do for thee now that nothing can be done ! Where art thou now? I will weep for thee till the day of my death. Little didst thou think, when in the visit of the white man thou sawest the long-cherished desire of years accomplished, that the sentence of death had gone forth. Thou thoughtest that thou shouldst procure a weapon from the white man which would be a shield from the attacks of the fierce Matibele, but a more deadly dart than theirs was aimed at thee ; and though thou couldst well ward off a dart—none ever better—thou didst not see that of the King of terrors. I will weep for thee, my brother, and I would cast forth my sorrows in despair for thy condition, but I know that thou wilt receive no injustice whither thou art gone. Shall not the Judge of all the earth do right ? I leave thee to him. Alas! Alas! Sebitoané! I might have said more to him. God forgive me, free me from bloodguiltiness. If I had said more of death I might have been suspected of having foreseen the event and being guilty of bewitching him. I might have recommended Jesus and His great atonement more. It is however very difficult to break through the great crust of ignorance which envelopes their minds. . . .

' I do not wonder at the Roman Catholics praying for the dead. If I could believe as they do I would pray for them too. . . . In the afternoon Mr. O and I went over to the village to condole with the people. They received our condolences very kindly and took our advice in good part. " Do not leave us ; though Sebitoané is gone his children remain, and you must treat them as you would have treated him." '

The death of Sebitoané rendered it necessary that permission to proceed should be obtained from his successor in the chieftainship—his daughter Mamochisané. She was, however, living far to the North, and the tribesmen feared that owing to the difficult nature of the country to be traversed, five weeks at least must elapse before her answer could arrive. Livingstone decided to wait, but Oswell had announced to his family his intention of returning to England early in 1852, and he doubted whether with this long delay he should be able to keep his promise to them. He discussed the matter with Dr. and Mrs. Livingstone, who represented to him very strongly that, having come so far and being so nearly in sight of the goal, it would be a grievous pity to turn back, and that in any case a few weeks more or less could make no difference. Admitting the force of these arguments, and bearing in mind the extreme pride and pleasure all his relations and friends took in discoveries made, or participated in, by him, he allowed himself to be over-persuaded.

Journal.—' Very glad that we urged our friend Oswell to stay; the pleasure of seeing the Seshéké will be so much increased by his presence, and he, who is so liberal with his means, never sparing if he can promote discovery, ought to, and I hope will, be gratified.'

Meanwhile, whilst waiting, the Doctor and Oswell learned what they could of the country in advance :

Journal.—' Mokontju* has a great deal of knowledge. He was of much use in drawing maps, and Mr. O. and I

* A trusted follower of Sebitoané.

WE . . . THANKED GOD FOR PERMITTING US FIRST TO SEE THIS GLORIOUS RIVER.

drew, or had drawn for us, upwards of sixty. The tablet was frequently only the ground, but the agreement of different individuals in their delineations of rivers, etc., shows that what we furnish on their authority is worthy of credit.'

' *Saturday, 25th July.*—Went over to the town of Linyanti, about 12 miles distant N.N.W., crossed Linyanti river, at the town about 5 feet deep and 35 yards wide. Contains a good many people. The poor wives of Sebitoané in deep mourning ; theirs seems no fictitious sorrow.'

' *Thursday, 31st.*—Receive a message that it was the will of Mamochisané that we should be treated exactly as if Sebitoané were alive, and that we should be taken wherever we wished to go. The men who went express to tell her of her father's death, slept nine nights and reached the Borotsé town on the tenth day. It must be 350 miles from where the wagons stood.'

In the direction in which they wished to explore, the numerous small rivers made wagon-travelling almost impossible. Livingstone therefore decided to leave his wife and children behind at the Chobé camp, while he and Oswell pressed forward on horseback. On August 1 they left Linyanti and struck out in a N.E. direction. The country was generally flat and dotted with clumps of palms and gigantic euphorbia. Evidences of extensive inundations were abundant.

Nearing their destination they had to pass through fifteen miles of marsh, covered with rank, tall grass reaching to their shoulders as they rode.

Journal, August 4, 1851.—' Mr. O. rode down a quagga or zebra in the morning, to the very great delight of the spectators. . . . In the afternoon we came to the beautiful Seshéké,* and thanked God for permitting us first to see this glorious river. All we could say to

* The river here known as the Seshéké proved to be the Zambesi, ' a most important point,' observes Livingstone, ' for that river was not previously known to exist there at all.'

each other was . . . How glorious! How magnificent! How beautiful! And grand beyond description
it really was—such a body of water—at least 400 yards
broad, and deep; it may be stated as from three to
five hundred yards wide. There are numerous banks of
white sand, and on these we saw crocodiles. One hippopotamus appeared in the middle. The town of Sesheké
appeared very beautiful on the opposite bank. The waves
were so high the people were afraid to venture across, but
by-and-bye a canoe made its way to where we stood. . . .
In crossing, the waves lifted up the canoe and made it roll
beautifully. The scenes of the Friths of Forth and
Clyde were brought vividly back to my view, and had I
been fond of indulging in sentimental suffusions, my
lachrymal apparatus seemed fully charged. But then the
old man who was conducting us across might have said,
" What on earth are you blubbering at? afraid of those
crocodiles, eh?" The little sentimentality which exuded,
was forced to take its course down the inside of the nose.
We have other work in this world than indulging in sentimentality of the " Sonnet to the Moon" variety.

   ' On landing, we were welcomed by many. The pre-
vailing idea was that our presence was a sure precursor
of abundant intercourse with Europeans, and peace or
" sleep" by the possession of firearms. One of the chief
wives of Sebitoané saluted us rather too freely—she
seemed tipsy. Between three and four hundred persons
collected around us. Moriantsané, the principal person,
shewed us round the town, shewed us also three English
guns which they had procured from the Bajoko . . . who
are either bastard or true Portuguese. . . . They gave
about thirty captives for them. . . . As we had tasted
nothing since the night previous to this, and then only
two biscuits each, we were rather hungry. The question
was at last put, " What do these people eat?" " Everything except an alligator," being the reply, they had latitude enough, but still they sat and feasted their eyes while

our stomachs were starving. At length Sebitoané's sister brought some milk ; then a sickly-looking man gave a piece of meat, and the drunken lady a dish of *mothu'ohatsi*. With these we returned to the other side and prepared to sleep on account of the horses being there.'

Livingstone spent many hours in making exhaustive inquiries as to the nature and extent of the slave-trade in those regions, and ascertained that a flourishing and increasing traffic was carried on by the Mambari, of whom Sebitoané had spoken.

Journal.—' Pity this market is not supplied with English manufactures in exchange for the legitimate products of the country. If English merchants would come up the Zambesi during the months of June, July and August, the slave-traders would very soon be driven out of the market.   That the country drained by the Seshéké is not a small portion of the slave-producing region, may be inferred from the fact that the Borotsé town is situated about 8 days beyond the town of Seshéké, and the people know it as a very large river, at least 8 days, or other 200 miles, beyond. The natives too mention the existence of a water or lake called Sebola mokoa, and if this is Lake Maravi, most of the slaves exported on the East Coast come from that part. . . .   Mr. O. thinks that Agents or Commissioners situated in different parts in that region would, in the course of ten years, extirpate the slave trade. I imagine that the existence of a salubrious locality must first be ascertained, and, if that is of easy access by the Seshéké, then mercantile men may be invited to carry their enterprise into that region. If it is profitable for those who are engaged in the coast trade to pass along in their ships and pick up ivory, bees-wax, etc., those who may have enterprise enough to push into the interior and receive the goods at first-hand, would surely find it much more profitable. The returns for the first year might be small, but those who for the love of their species would run some risk, would assuredly be no losers in the end. The natives readily acquire the habit of saving for a market. Honey abounds in the country, but all the wax is thrown away. Ivory has only been used to form armlets, and the saw employed is so thick it destroys an inch each time it passes through the tusk. Ostrich feathers are only used for adorning the head in the dance. All these and other articles would be pre-served for the legitimate trader. The people have abundance of cattle; they are unlike the poor starvelings of the South, whose every thought must be directed to "What shall we eat and what shall we drink, and where-withal shall we be clothed?" Give a people the oppor-tunity they will civilize themselves, and that too more effectually than can be done by missionary Societies. The slave-dealer must have his due. All the Mambari come decently clothed; we never saw a party of Bechuanas or Griquas of whom so much could be said. Perhaps civilization as the duty of Missionaries is a thing taken for granted, yet still requiring to be proved. We ought to preach the gospel—some will believe, and some will reject. If we are faithful we shall stand in our lot in the latter day, and hear the sentence which will wipe away all tears from our eyes.'

'Our plan,' writes Livingstone to the Royal Geogra-phical Society, 'was that I should remain in pursuit of my objects as a missionary, while Mr. Oswell explored the Zambesi to the East. For such an undertaking I know none better suited than my friend Mr. Oswell. He has courage and prudence equal to any emergency, and possesses moreover that qualification so essential in a traveller, of gaining the confidence of the natives while maintaining the dignity of a gentleman. . . .'

Both projects, however, proved unattainable. Living-stone could not hastily decide on a suitable spot for a settlement among the Makololo, and Oswell found the immense marshes and the tsétsé, which abounded in every direction, insuperable barriers to his speedy advance; and though they recognised the possibility of ultimate success, the former was anxious to rejoin his wife, who was expecting her confinement, and the latter was unwilling further to prolong his absence from England. Accordingly they made their way back to Linyanti, where they heard that Messrs. Edwards and Wilson, the traders whom they had outdistanced on the way to Sebitoané, had arrived on horseback. On the same evening they proceeded to the camp on the Chobé, and finding all well, resolved to turn homewards on August 12.

Journal.—' People very anxious for our stay—promise to return . . . they propose to fulfil Sebitoané's intention of supplying us with cattle in lieu of those killed by the tsétsé. Is it right to receive them ? they have probably been stolen. . . . If they offer, I shall receive without reference to the source from which they have taken them. Ministers of the Church of England take their tithes, although many of those from whom they are exacted believe themselves robbed.'

The consideration of this point provokes a curious little excursus in the journal on the general rights and duties of missionaries :

' Jesus came not to judge—κρινω—condemn judicially or execute vengeance on anyone.

' His was a message of peace and love. " He shall not strive nor cry, neither shall His voice be heard in the streets" — Missionaries ought to follow His example ; neither insist upon our rights, nor appear as if we could allow our goods to be destroyed without regret. For if we are righteous overmuch or stand up for our rights with too great vehemence, we beget dislike, and the people see no difference between ourselves and them. And if we appear to care nothing for the things of the world, they conclude we are rich, and when they beg, our refusal is ascribed to niggardliness, and our property too is wantonly destroyed. "*Ga ha tloke*"—they are not in need—is the phrase employed when our goods are allowed to go to destruction by the neglect of servants. The principle propounded in the Bible ought to be kept in view—"The labourer is worthy of his hire." "They who preach the gospel should live of the gospel." In the South Seas the first question put to a chief who applies for a missionary is "Can you support him?" In Africa the idea somehow or other has become prevalent that he who allows a missionary to live with him confers a benefit upon the missionary. In coming among a savage people we ought to make them feel we are " of them."—" We seek not yours but you "—but while ever careful not to make a gain of them, we ought to be as careful to appear thankful and appreciate any effort they may make for our comfort or subsistence. " When you enter into a village eat such things as are set before you." Acting otherwise in order to feel that you are independent, or because the people are impure, or may have lifted the cattle they slaughter, seems like " stand by, come not near me, for I am holier than thou." " Whatsoever is sold in the shambles, that eat," ' etc.

When they reached the Zouga, there is this entry, under date September 15 : 'A son, William Oswell Livingstone, born.' 'He had intended,' says Blaikie, 'to call him Charles, and announced this to his father ; but finding that Mr. Oswell, to whom he was so much indebted, would be pleased with the compliment, he changed his purpose and the name accordingly.'

Whilst waiting at the Zouga, Oswell wrote to his brother, and replied to the despatch sent him by Sir Harry Smith on July 11, 1850. The subjoined rough notes of his letter appear in one of the MS. books he took with him through Africa :

' The insignificance of tribes, with whom friendly relations to be opened; their total inability to resist Boers.
The country visited this year with its inhabitants—end of
Bechuana proper—dense population—connection with
Portuguese—slavery; custom *now* easily stopped because
recent—people were averse ; show them that European
goods can be obtained by other means, and it will cease,
but otherwise the temptation will be too strong.—200
taken away by the Mambari last year—Portuguese met
on Bashukolompé R. by Sebitoané's people.—The map
has no great pretension to correctness, but may serve to
throw a glimpse of light upon the darkness of the interior.
—Natural barriers, rivers, fever and fly.—Fever frightened
Boers.—Seshéké or Zambesi probable termination of
Boer immigration.—Country of Mosilakatsé.—Death of
M. probable dispersion of tribe.—Regret for death of
Sebitoané.

Livingstone had no secrets from his friend, and at night
over the camp fire poured into his most sympathetic ears
his ambitions, his troubles, his anxieties.   The experiences
of the journey on which they were now engaged, and of
those of the two preceding years, had forced him to the
conclusion that he would not be justified in allowing his
wife and young family again to accompany him in his
wanderings in unknown countries, thus necessarily ex-
posing them to constant difficulties, dangers and privations ; and this view Oswell shared, and cordially approved.
No word of complaint ever passed Mrs. Livingstone's lips ;
on the contrary, she was eagerly desirous of being at her
husband's side wherever his duty called him.   Some years
later, at the British Association, Oswell said of her :

' After spending two years in the company of Mrs.
Livingstone I am qualified to speak of her courage, her
devoted attention to her husband, and her unvarying kindness to myself.   I saw her fail on one occasion only—
when her husband wanted to leave her behind.   In regions

thousands of miles away from a white person she cared for her children, and encouraged the prosecution of the expeditions. To myself she ministered many acts of kindness with a delicacy and consideration which only a woman could exhibit.'

As an instance of her courage he used to relate that during the Ngami journey the wagon in which she was travelling caught fire. There were, as she knew, more than a hundred pounds of powder in it, but she did not stir, contenting herself with calling to her husband, who happened to be near, ' David, David, put it out !'

Against her own inclination, therefore, for her children's sake, and to ease her husband's mind, she acquiesced in the wisdom of the proposal that they should all make their way to the Cape, and that she should thence take her little ones to England by the next ship. But was this practicable ? The clothes that served well enough for the wilds of Africa would not be suitable for a voyage with civilized people, and in any case they were few, and nearly worn out. A complete new outfit for the family would, obviously, be imperative ; then there was the passage money to be provided, and the missionary's meagre salary for the past year was all spent. He anxiously discussed with his wife the possibility of borrowing sufficient for their requirements on the security of his future income. At length he yielded to his friend's advice not to meet trouble half-way but to defer the consideration of the subject until it became actually necessary, and meanwhile to journey southwards with all speed. ' We return,' he writes, ' as we have hitherto travelled, together, he assisting us in every possible way. May God reward him !'

It had been agreed that a general halt of a few days should be made at Kolobeng, and it was a surprise and a disappointment to the Livingstones that Oswell, without vouchsafing any explanation of his change of mind, expressed his intention of pushing on immediately, alone.

At Colesberg he found awaiting him a letter from his brother, and one of the long friendly chats from Vardon which always gave him such pleasure :

The Rev. E. W. Oswell to W. Cotton Oswell.

' MIDHURST,
' *Aug.* 14, 1851.

' The last report of you was from a letter to Louisa, which we were not a little glad to receive as it had been a long time since we had had any tidings, and the warlike state of South Africa made us, and still makes us, very anxious about you. You seem determined to pursue your object there, and I trust you may succeed, though it keeps you away so long from England. . . . I wish you would write a book and send it to us for our amusement. . . . Had I a permanent residence I should petition you to let us have your African horns, etc., which I believe are in a warehouse at present. I see notice was taken in the newspapers of *your Lake* and the country about it. . . . I sincerely trust your discoveries may tend towards decreasing the Slave Trade.'

Captain Frank Vardon to W. Cotton Oswell.

' KURNOOL,
' *Aug.* 12, 1851.

' Your letter from Motito has just come in and I set to at once to give you a long stave in reply. . . . I have lately heard from Moffat and Livingstone. I am as fond of poor old Africa as ever and my thoughts are constantly on the Limpopo. I can never hear too much of it, that is very certain. . . . When you get this I hope and trust you will have shaken hands with the great Sebitoané ; he must be a fine fellow by all accounts. . . . Cumming's

Exhibition still goes on, and Methuen tells me that a black
fellow parades up and down in front of it in a leopard skin
kaross, to attract visitors ! !   I never thought any of us
African wanderers would have come to this. . . .   I think
I told you that he wrote to me for the skin of the leche
you sent me. He offered me various things in exchange
for it, but I thought you would prefer its going to the
British Museum, where Mr. Gray assured me it should be
well set up, and placed in a conspicuous spot. May you
soon return to see that it is so. So you have got the
skin of another buck. The nakong *must* look a rum un
indeed with such long hair. . . .   I often think of you
and wonder whether you have any of your old servants with
you. Where is George ?   I should much like to know.
Have you Piet or Claas or John ?   What did you do in
the fishing way ?   Did you haul out many more of our
huge friends the barbers ?   How about the hippopotami ?
Have you shot any since we blazed at their noses, with the
Boers, on the Limpopo ?   What did you bag besides the
thirty bull elephants and the two quebaabas ?   I am always
curious to know the exact bag. I shall look forward with
such pleasure to your next letter ; pray mind it is a long
one ; it cannot be too full of the wonders of the new
land.

' Although you won't give me credit for it, I am really to
be depended on in the letter way, and I know no friend
for whom I would sooner employ my pen, than yourself.
. . . I am only so sorry I have no stirring incidents
by flood and field to tell you of. *You* have so much to
tell *me*, that *sheets* wouldn't tire me, and even the names
of your men and horses would interest me !

' Did you ever fall in with any of the gigantic-horned oxen ?
The pair of horns I purchased of Hume hold twenty pints
each. He didn't know from what country they came. . . .
How miserable were my attempts at the elephants. Do
you remember my worrying that unhappy old cow to death
in the neighbourhood of Lynchituma ?   I am a sad spoon

at an elephant, I must confess. I think I could manage one better on foot, as I could then make sure of *hitting* him at any rate, which I am certain I could never do from the saddle. . . . When you go to England you will find Arrowsmith, the map man, well worth knowing, and he will make any corrections in his South African map you tell him. He saw Cumming once or twice, but could get no additional information out of him as to the part of the Limpopo *beyond* where we went. . . . And now when do you think we have a chance, should we both be spared, of meeting again? I fear not for many years to come. . . . But never mind; we will scribble to one another now and then, and have a chat together on paper; and in after years we may perhaps say " Dare is nix spoor." I certainly was the worst Dutch scholar that ever owned a wagon, but I must say I never *tried* to learn, as I had no fancy for Mynheer von Dunk. . . . I so hope Galton will get his large boat to the Lake, but I very much fear he will not. . . .

'I am sure I offended old Macqueen mortally, for I made a speech in front of a very full meeting of the Society one evening and put a fearful extinguisher on his friend Mr. Parker. He will never forgive me, but as you were *all three* absent and there was no one to take up the cudgels for you, I determined to try my luck, and I think I succeeded. I know nothing more illiberal or ungenerous than to take from *absent* parties the credit due to them for any discoveries they may make. You may find out whatever you please, but Macqueen is sure to say he knew of it years ago. I was cruelly disgusted with the old fellow, and so were nearly all the Members. . . . . We shall hear no more of Mr. Parker. I said that Mr. Parker had not been to the Lake, or Mr. *Walker* or Mr. *Barker* either! The old fellow richly deserved it, for the offence is a most unpardonable one. . . . The Earl of Derby you see is dead. What a loss for zoology! If his son only cared as much for animals as Protection, he would have lechés, nakongs, and I don't know what all, tame at Knowsley. And now farewell. . . . Give me a minute account of your visit to Sebitoané.'

W. Cotton Oswell to Major Frank Vardon.

'COLESBERG,
'*Jan.* 14, 1852.

' I will answer your long letter when I have more time, and give you an account of this last journey   In the meanwhile I send you a rough sketch of the country we saw and *heard* of.   I wish you to show it to any one you may please, but to allow no one to copy or publish it; I am returning to England next month or in March, but you shall hear from me from the Cape.

' Do you ever see anyone in India who remembers me— Major Fred Cotton, Brooke Cunliffe, Mayne, Nott?   If so remember me most kindly. . . . A quebaaba was shot last year, though alas! not by me, with a horn four feet nine inches long.'

On the back of the sketch-map the following notes appear :

' It is not pretended that the accompanying sketch is correct, or even near correctness.   The dotted line shows our course, and this we have laid down as well as we were able ; let others prove us wrong.   The greater part of the whole is on hearsay evidence, but this was as good as such could be, and tested to the best of our ability ; it must, of course, be looked upon merely as an approximation to the truth.   The courses and directions of the larger rivers together with the names of the people are probably tolerably correct ; but for particular bends and exact position of tribes, etc., etc., we do not hold ourselves responsible.   In some particular instances, however, remarkable windings as in the Chobé and river of Libabi have been attempted to be shown.

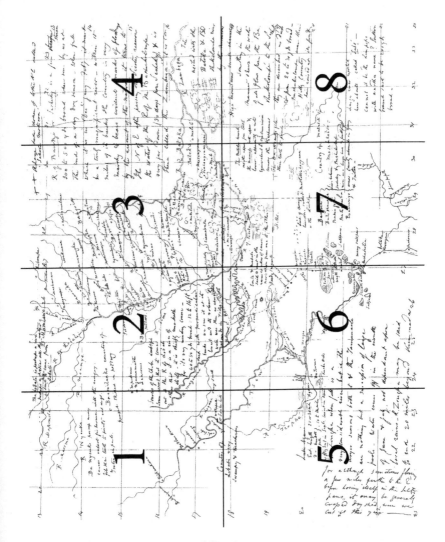

Key to following pages.

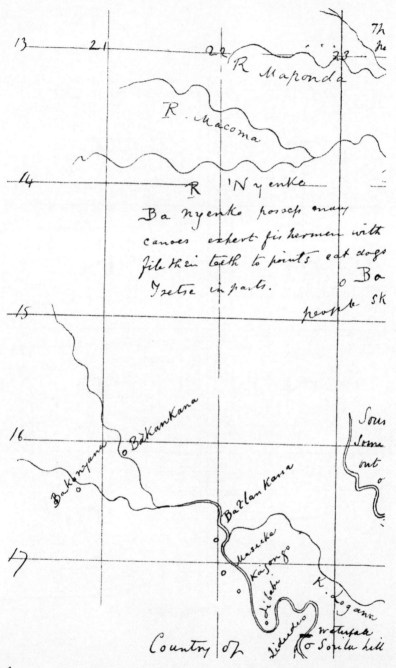

13 — 21 — 22 — 23 — 7h
    R Maponda
    R Macoma
14 — R 'Nyenke
    Ba nyenke possess many
    canoes expert fishermen with
    file their teeth to points eat dogs
    Tzetze in parts.   o Ba
15 —   people sk
16 —   o Bakankana   Sous
    Bakanyana o   some
                           out
                    Bazlankana   o
17 —   o Maseeka
                  o Kasongo
                    Libata   K. Logann
    Country of Lidudwo waterfall
                      o Soula hill

1

he LoBali is perhaps a river
perhaps a lake all the water
is said 24 to come from 25 Mambowe 26
"Lobali"

R. of Lobali (water from)

R. moenye

to the assyay.
25.
a milanko country of
"killed in pottery"

R. Liambai (water from)
R. Liambai (water from)

o India
o mashawan
o nangompe

Baerioka
R. Loe na o motondo
R. Loe na
o Mariam
o de Kwama
R. Loama o mor
o de bello bello

Chief town
R. Loe
Pebitoan's Siloka R.
Inbalti Siamba
o nalgatom
o Elicka
o chinango
o nam

o mpukani
o nguana mother
o de acomo

o Basima
potters.

R.
rivers of the Chobe doubtful
a assert that it comes R.
t of the R of Lobali Sima o ng
others that it is a river of o ngaan
itself - it is chiefly rema-kath
for its very winding course - o Rapids of
R. mazamene 40 to 50 yds broad: 12 to 14 ft. Seoma
deep with perpendicular Kale o
banks. we saw it at its Imbowa
very small lowest. and its volume + Tou
water was then as above stated 17
abounds in hippo.

2

Libompa
(route)
20
25
30

+ + Rkaye
Sebola

R. of Bar
300 to 50
The end of
which it
be a truly
miles of i
marshy &
by the acc
The N of
the water
very far
Thence Ca

Makuana   Matamalama
ananangka   Bangoia
matonao
rabisa   Bapingola   malea
moema
namacampa   moshukwage
nguanaloshe   mombalu
Barima   sesoe
sompe   namoyana   namola
nyampoho
okowhema   siamabi   R. Kakenke
matala   R.   nguanaloncilo   Liambae
R. molomo
siamabi
Djampa   namiala
Bariman   nasikalamba   mayubi
Tloiwae   Basaka
siam Loiwa   sampsa   Maminpa   R. 2. Ba
wai   Baloka   Moitsi
mojela   mokobelu   Port   Baloka
mojopa
mosanya
Sechety   siamolonka   Kabanka   Siakanyium
17 26.5   manyoti   nyati
(smiths)   molondari   Hilly Country   mataba
moshaba

3

. have spoken of to the N E called
ta Mokoaa '——————

rotzi or Sesheke is a fine <del>steamer</del> 13
                                    stream
oo yds broad when seen by us at
of a very dry season — When full
— is in Decr Jany Feby it must
' magnificent river — within 15— 14
its banks the Country is very
& bears evident marks of floodings
<del>ccount of the natives</del> it turns to
of E after passing the Sicota, receives .15
, of the R of the Bashukolompe
down (30 days from Sesheky) & is
called the Zambeza '— it is Con. 16

atoka   R Zambega   " Tete.
"a 'melale'   nected with the
<del>ana</del>   Batoka & BD
neriri   Shukolombe river
                      by the numerous

4

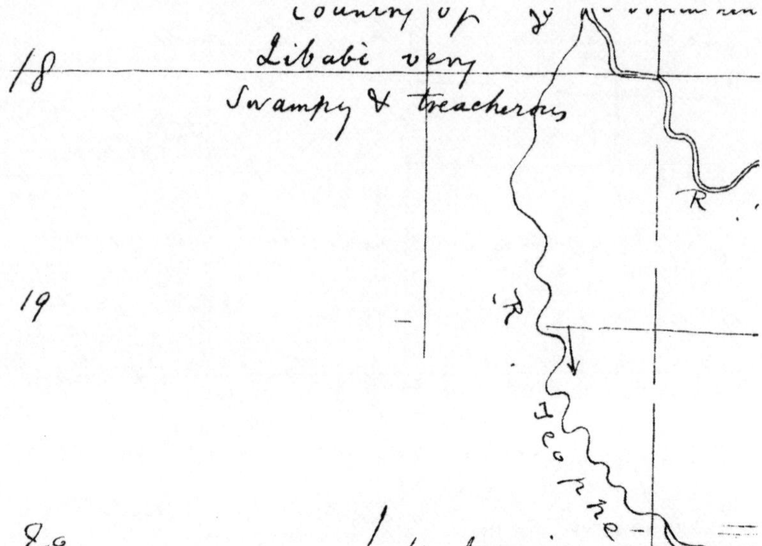

country of ...
Libabi very
Swampy & treacherous

R

'R'

Teoghe

Lake Ngami
Ext: Length. 25 or 3d miles
d.. breadth } . 10 to 12 miles
when full
Highest in Septr. lowest in Ap
The Zongka when fu
very considerable riv
dryer seasons both
are nothing but a
pools — Water comes
of June & July, not
local rains — R. Zong
to end 20 miles

or a though I sometimes flows
a few miles farther to the E')
before losing itself in the salt
hams, it may be generally
Cape) Dry bed seen on
but it this y up

22   23

a goun os in
R deyant ?.
... Route ...
R.
Tishuani
R. Chobe
Waggon left
Tselse
mpetla R
T S G N
R. South. Small
Sonta &
said to
rains
navi
Tlitse
Reedy
R. Mababo
Goosing
Kanuma K
R. Boro
Route out. 51
R. Tamanacle
unk
R.
Strings
R. Zougha
Ngami
Ba Jowana
Ngabisan
Saltpan
5 iise
miles ac
length
Kueba Hills
...pul.
... creek
... is a
... but in the
... it & the Tamanacle
... succession of large
... off in the months
... dependant upon
...gh a may be said
... beyond Kummad w 26
24   25
Kummalow
Small Lake of
Saltpan

6

o moshoba o diombu o Ramashobotyane o tunya
o mosianang
Zwange   waterfall nosi o
                          spray seen
Itsetse   16 miles off
R. of Sicota   Tietie R.

& mababi
to meet in the
& allow of canoe
ation from one to the other
swamp   Hills.

o mayeela
o Horoye.   o o o o o   Line of springs in
Rapossho   o o   limestone called Maatomahanyana
o springs   o   or The Links
Tlomtle
well
N'Toe
15   Saltpans
o koober   Saltpans.

Bangoia   Country of
Baloshangke   Mose
Bakingola   live between
Baliwamba   Serheky & Bashukob
Baemariyo   river are large but
                arrow. County aboun
                & Tsetse

many saltpans
o Mchakotia

o Soltokau
o Kowonyani   Limpopo R.

o Mchoenie.

The Batoka
out the upper
The mamepe
lower appa
Equivalent t
Among the
The Ba N
their teeth to

28   29   30

7

by the numerous

High mountains small channels

Something in the
manner shewn — the water
of all flows from the Ba
Shukolompé to the Seshek
they are described as deep
& from 20 to 30 yds broad —
Bashukolompe wear their
Hilly Country
hair raised up in front

ka knock
er fore teeth
both upper &
aren't a rite
to circumcission
Bachuanas
try & file
to points —

matabili
likatse
lompe
& feath
nds in honey

Large river reported
here abouts — called Sabé —
Cannot it be the Limpopo
with another name? Southron
branch said to be 200 yds
broad —

High mountains small channels

97
2.0
21
22

3/   32   33   23

8

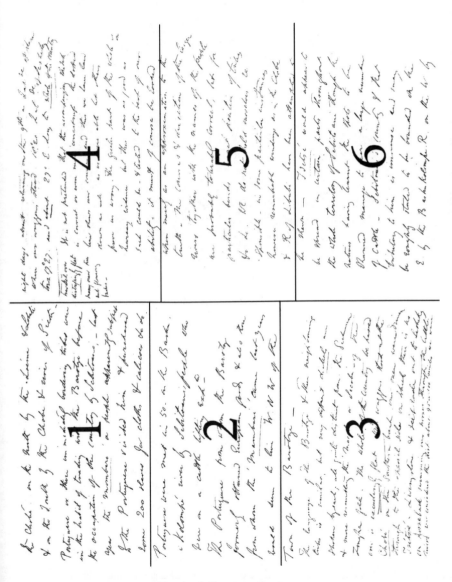

Key to following pages.

the Chobe ... on the South by the Loema & Shokole

& on the South by the Chobe & river ... of Sieste —

Portuguese or others immediately bordering tribes were in the habit of trading with the Banotze before the occupation of the country of Schitane, — last year the *Mambare* a people apparently subject of the Portuguese visited him & purchased some 200 slaves for cloths & calicoes &c &c.

Party were met in '50 - on the Barku.
'Kolombe' river by Sebitoani people who
were on a cattle lifting expo —
The Portuguese from whom the Baroty
formerly obtained European goods & also those
from whom the 'Mambare' came last year
would seem to live N. N. W. of the

2

Two of the Barotze —

The language of the Barotze & these rough roaming tribes is similar, but very different & dialects are spoken by each; all quite distinct from the Schimona & more resembling the Macoba or Lecoba — of the Zanzya folk. The whole of the country be passed over is exceedingly flat. Our waggon stood while Chobe' in the southern bank our men never drove through to the Shhnid side on which there is no Teetze'. I imagine & self each out to Lehely on horseback swimming our horses through the little river we considered the first about 95 or 100 miles we were

eight days absent, returning on the 9th an Lat. to it place
when our voyage stood) 10°20. Lat. Longitude
from 17°27. and about 27° E. along the whole of the country

Travelled over   It is not pretended that the accompanying sketch
distressing flat.   is correct or even near 'concerning' the different
many new fun   line throw our cross and thus we have been able
and flowers   down as well as we were able let them
fishes.   prove in wrong. The greater part of the whole is
Survey evidence but this was as good as good as
such could be - & tested to the best of our
ability - it must of course be looked)

4

when viewed as an approximation to the truth. The causes & direction of the larger errors together with the names of the people are probably tolerably correct, but for particular bends exact position of tribes &c &c. We do not hold ourselves responsible – in some particular instances however remarkable windings as in the Chobe & R. of Libebe have been attempted &c

be shewn — Tsetse would appear to
be spread in certain parts throughout
the whole territory of ? and though the
natives having learnt the spots to be
shunned manage to rear a large number
of cattle – Zebritone...) (really of ?
tributary to him is immense and may
be roughly stated) to be bounded on the
S. by the Bashukolompo R. on the W by

'Tsétsé would appear to be spread in certain parts throughout the whole territory of Sebitoané, though the natives, having learnt the spots to be shunned, manage to rear a large number of cattle.

'Sebitoané's country and that tributary to him is immense, and may be roughly stated to be bounded on the E. by the Bashukolompé R., on the W. by the Chobé, on the north by the Loéma and Lobali, and on the south by the Chobé and river of Secota.

'Portuguese or their immediately bordering tribes were in the habit of trading with the Barotzi before the occupation of the country by Sebitoané. Last year the Mambari, a people apparently subject to the Portuguese, visited him, and purchased some two hundred slaves for cloths and calicoes, etc., etc.

'Portuguese were met in 1850 on the Bashukolompé by Sebitoané's people who were on a cattle-lifting expedition. The Portuguese from whom the Barotzi formerly obtained European goods, from whom too the Mambari came last year, would seem to live W.N.W. of the town of Bi Barotzi.

'The language of the Barotzi and their neighbouring tribes is similar, but very different dialects are spoken by each, all quite distinct from the Sechuana, and more resembling the Macoba and Secoba of the Zougha folk. Our wagons stood at the Chobé on the southern bank; our oxen were driven through to the opposite side, on which there is no tsétsé.

'Livingstone and I rode out to Seshéké on horseback, swimming our horses through the little rivers. We considered the distance about ninety-five or a hundred miles. We were eight days absent, returning on the ninth. Latitude of place where our wagons stood 18° 20′; of Seshéké Town 17° 27′ and about 27° E. longitude. Whole of the country travelled over distressingly flat. Many new trees and flowering bushes.'

Vardon replied to this letter on the day of its receipt :

'. . . Don't you fancy I ever forget you, old fellow,
even if you didn't hear from me for the next five years.
I never forget an old friend, especially a *shikar* one, who
has wandered so far with me and with whom I passed so
pleasant a time.   I was delighted to hear you had reached
Sebitoané. . . .   What a river you discovered! and as
for the cataract of Mosio-atunya I've been thinking of it
ever since! . . .   An opening on the West Coast is what
you now want.   The land journey must be a fearful
undertaking, all one's time being consumed in going in
and coming out again.   But couldn't one go up the
Zambesi at certain seasons of the year?   You get to the
missionaries by sea, and they get you guides, and away
you go!!   Famous indeed!   How I should like to try it
with you.'

The Livingstones had not to wait long for the clue to
Oswell's action in preceding them:

Journal, March 16, 1852.—'Reach Cape Town.   Find
our friend Oswell here before us, the outfit ordered, and
he presented £50, £20, then £80, £20=£170, with the
remark that as the money had been drawn from the
preserves on our estate (elephants) we had as good a
right to it as he.   God bless and preserve him! . . . the
best friend we had in Africa.'*

Just before Oswell set sail for England, in the *Harbinger*,
a letter reached him from his brother:

'CLIFFDEN, BONCHURCH,
          'ISLE OF WIGHT.

'The mail packet shall take this as an acknowledgment
of a few lines received from you dated four months back
whilst you were on the Zougha.   I was delighted to hear

* Referring to this incident in his 'Missionary Travels,' he
says that he had not 'a penny of salary to draw' at that date,
and adds that 'the outfit for the half-naked children cost about
£200.'

of your welfare and of your having accomplished your object in penetrating to the Zambesi. I could have wished you had given us further details, as your few lines did not satisfy the cravings which so long a silence on your part has excited. I suppose however you were pressed at the time. I do not gather whether you are on your way to the Cape, as you speak of the journey " in advance," without further explanation. I trust however that this is the case, as we have learnt from Mr. Livingstone's letter to the Missionary Society that this is *his* intention. Uncle Ben, I believe, has seen this letter. But I know next to nothing more on the subject. It appears to me that if you wish to have any of the credit of the discovery, and hope that it may lead to anything else, you should represent your share in it to the quarter you may think most desirable. Otherwise, from everyone's ignorance of your proceedings (at home) there is no chance of your benefiting by it. All the notices I have seen of it, have certainly attributed the greatest, if not the sole merit to Mr. Livingstone, and necessarily so, as he alone reports the proceedings. Not that I at all mean he acts unfairly towards you, but only that your silence necessarily brings this about. I hope you will pardon what may appear advice. But I cannot but feel that you would scarcely have undertaken such an arduous enterprise and have gone through so much, without wishing to have a share of the credit, and to be placed in a position, perhaps, where you may be the means of conferring a real benefit to civilization and commerce. Your note to Mr. Macqueen also came to hand ; but as yet, no chart has made its appearance. Uncle Ben is *at* them in London about it. But it ought to have been delivered ere this, as it is more than a week ago since the *Hellespont* arrived. I do most sincerely hope that when (if you are) at the Cape, you will come on to England, if only for a visit. The packets make such short work of it now, that this might readily be done, and it is a very long while that you've been away. . . . Thank God we are all well. I am tolerable, not quite so well perhaps as usual just now. With our united kindest love,

'Ever your most affectionate Brother.'

Edward Oswell was mistaken in his estimate of his brother when he suggests that he 'would scarcely have undertaken such an arduous enterprise and have gone through so much without wishing to have a share of the credit.' Having done the work and undergone the labours, William Oswell was quite content to stand aside and let another enjoy the fruits, and this was characteristic of him through life.

Livingstone, however, made no secret of his indebtedness to his friend and fellow traveller. Thus in his journal he gratefully acknowledges 'the kind attentions of Mr. Oswell,' and 'his request that we should draw as much money as we should need from him'; to the Geographical Society he mentions that 'all the guides of this expedition were most liberally rewarded by Mr. Oswell'; while to the London Missionary Society he enters frankly into details:

'But for the disinterested kindness of Mr. Oswell we could not have come down to the Cape. He presented supplies for last year's journey worth £40, for that to Sebitoané upwards of £20, also a wagon worth £55. . . . . Most of our oxen are dead, and but for Mr. Oswell's presenting a number worth about £60 we could not have come down to the Cape.'

'Had Mr. Oswell not presented us with £170 since we came here I should have been in a fix. He clothed Mrs. L. and family in a style we never anticipated. This I state in confidence to you; it would offend him to make it public, but it makes me comparatively easy in mind.'

After his eleven years' quiet sojourn in the interior, the unrest and turmoil of the Cape struck Livingstone very forcibly and provoked the following interesting note in his journal :

'The Cape heart is chafed and irritable. Its rancour and rage are sometimes directed against Earl Grey, or the Hottentots, or the Caffres, or Mr. Montagu, or the Missionaries, or Botha. The blame of everything wrong is hurled everywhere. In the meantime merchants become rich, and England must pay the piper, the natives generally learn to despise us, the follies of Government officials, over which we have no control, teaching the natives their own power. The mass of the people and natives too are stumbling on to developments which God alone can plainly foresee.'

John had, of course, accompanied his master to the Cape, and the time came to say good-bye. Both men were strongly affected. They had shared the perils and privations, the pleasures and excitement, of five stirring years, and were friends in the truest sense :

'I told John in part how I valued his services, and asked him if I could in any way repay my debt of gratitude. I had taught him to read in the Bush, but that was the only good I had ever done him. His answer came after some hesitation. He had heard so much of England that he should like of all things to go with me there. Two days later we were on board ship together. He, as usual, was everything to everybody, helping the steward, attending the sick ladies, nursing the babies, the idol of the sailors, to whom he told stories of bush life, the adored of the nurses ; for John with all his virtues was a flirt, the admirer and admired of all womankind.'

END OF VOL. I.

BILLING AND SONS, LTD., PRINTERS, GUILDFORD

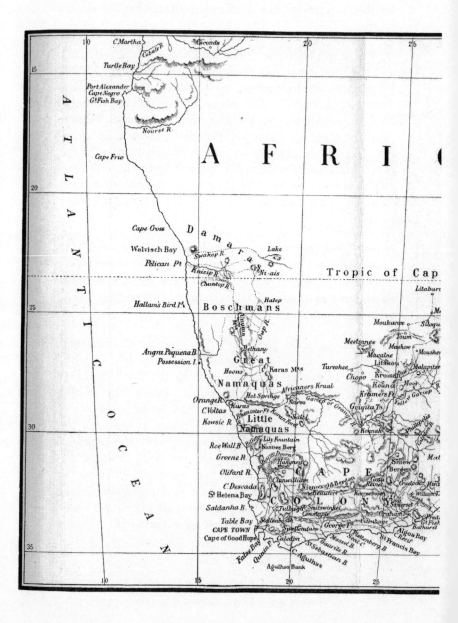

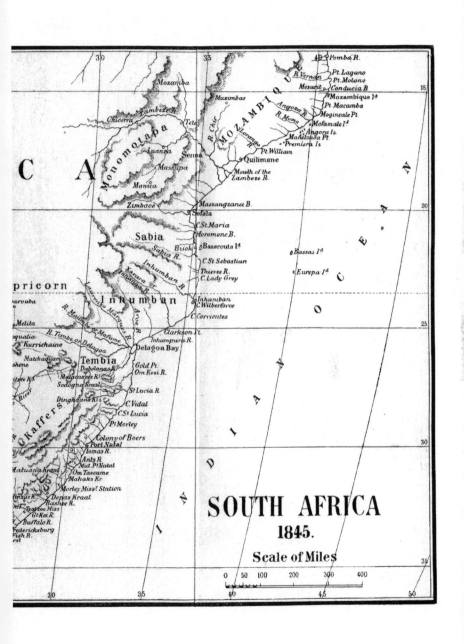

SOUTH AFRICA
1845.
Scale of Miles

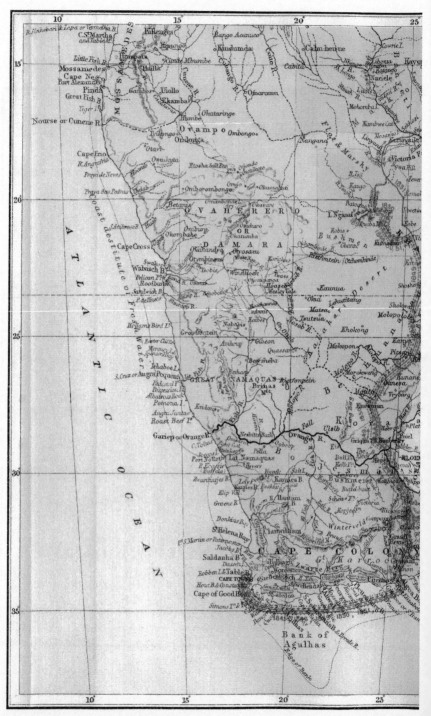

15

Sitama
Inyonko
Chirowe
Molilo
Kingene
Chefus
Quimtangona
R. Senevo
R. Tembo
Shalowe
Mesuri

Zepulia
L. Shirwa
Smwe
Chiwawa
Namirola
Mamuli
Anthony R.
Mafumale
Angozha I.
Caldera
Koendros I.
Kremeira P.

Banyai
Tete
M. Pirone
Hoshia

Salisbury
F. Charter
Batonga
Mtoko's
Senao
Pinda
Mts. of the Olinda Bar.
K. Zambesi
Kongone
Quillimane T. & R.
Hippopotamus P.

M A S H O N A
Umtali
Gouveia
Makaia de Sena
Chuabo

MATABELI
Inyati
R. Pungue
R. Posi
R. Mata

MAKALAKA
Bulawayo
GurandRana
Mapanda
Sabia R.
Sofala T. & Bay
Shiluane I.
C. S. Maria
Meromone B.

26

Zoupansberg
Albasim
Umbienga
Bazaruta or Punga R.
Bazaruta I.
Umharire
S. Sebastian
Thieves R.
C. Lady Grey

Marabata
Pilulca
Ehlat
Bassas da India
Europa I.

SOUTH AFRICAN
PRETORIA
Lydenburg
Inhambane T. & Port (F.)
C. Wilberforce
Corrientes
Maxixe

Rustenberg
Johannesburg
Heidelberg
Standerton
Barberton
Lagoa R.
Lorenzo Marquez
Delagoa Bay or Lorenzo Marquez
Inyack I. & C.
Cape Colato

25

Potchefstroom
Gold P.
Gold Downs R. or Um-koosie R.
Sirdwana R.
St. Lucia
L. Vidal
L. Lucia R. & Cape

FREE STATE
Ladysmith
P. Durnford

OEMFONTEIN
Besala R.
R. Umvoa
R. Tugeni
Durban, Port Natal

30

Aklwal
R. Umkomanzi
R. Umzimkulu
R. Umtavuni
R. Oase or Umsamvaba

East London & Buffalo R.
Umtamvuma
Umtata R.
Buntingville
Umzumvubo R.
Um-Bashee R.
Omabaka R.
Gt. Wei R.

45

Port Alfred
Coombie R.
Kowie R.
King William's Town
Gt. Kei R.
Keiskamma R.

Francis B.
St. Francis B.

35

SOUTH AFRICA
1899

Scale of Miles

0   50   100   200   300   400

M. Oswell's routes   — — — — 1845
          ———— 1846
          ·········· 1849
          ++++++ 1850
          1851

Stanford's Geog.l Estab.t London

Printed in Great Britain
by Amazon.co.uk, Ltd.,
Marston Gate.